The Politics
of Global
Economic Relations

The Politics of Global Economic Relations

DAVID H. BLAKE
ROBERT S. WALTERS

UNIVERSITY OF PITTSBURGH

PRENTICE-HALL, INC., Englewood Cliffs, New Jersey

Library of Congress Cataloging in Publication Data

BLAKE, DAVID H (date)
    The politics of global economic relations.

    Includes bibliographical references and index.
      1. International economic relations.
I. Walters, Robert S., (date)   joint author.
II. Title.
HF1007.B54   382.1   75–35856
ISBN 0–13–684712–9

© *1976 by Prentice-Hall, Inc.,*
Englewood Cliffs, New Jersey

PRINTED IN THE UNITED STATES OF AMERICA

10 9 8 7 6 5 4 3 2 1

PRENTICE-HALL INTERNATIONAL, INC., LONDON
PRENTICE-HALL OF AUSTRALIA PTY. LIMITED, SYDNEY
PRENTICE-HALL OF CANADA, LTD., TORONTO
PRENTICE-HALL OF INDIA PRIVATE LIMITED, NEW DELHI
PRENTICE-HALL OF JAPAN, INC., TOKYO
PRENTICE-HALL OF SOUTH-EAST ASIA PRIVATE LIMITED, SINGAPORE

To
David, Jennifer, Kimberly,
Scott, and Claire

Contents

4

The Multinational Corporation:
Challenge to the International System?   *76*

5

Aid Relations
Between Rich and Poor States   *127*

6

Technology, Ecology, and World Politics   *143*

7

Strategies for States
in the Periphery of the Global Political Economy   *168*

8

The Dominant State in the Global Economy:
The Policy Process in the United States   *197*

9

International Political Economy:
Current Problems and Future Needs   *223*

Index   *237*

Preface

This volume is intended as an introduction to the analysis of international political economy. It is an outgrowth of our inability in January, 1973, to find a book broad enough in scope and open enough to divergent viewpoints to serve as a text for a course on the politics of international economic relations. This is the book we were looking for then. Events are moving so rapidly in the global economy and in the discipline that one always risks producing a study that is obsolete upon its publication. In an effort to avoid this, we have organized the volume around the more permanent substantive and theoretical questions of international political economic relations, rather than around the hottest trade, monetary, or investment incident of the day. The material presented here has met with a good response from our students at all levels of undergraduate and graduate work. We hope this volume will stimulate others' interest in what we feel are the vital global challenges of the coming years.

In our efforts to keep the book within manageable bounds, we have not attempted to cover all the relevant dimensions of the global political economy. The most glaring casualty of our commitment to brevity is the omission of communist states from this analysis. It is admittedly an arbitrary decision. Communist states account for only 11 percent of world exports, provide less than 10 percent of total foreign aid to less-developed countries, and generally do not figure prominently in aggregate statistics of international economic relations. However, they clearly play a much larger role in international relations than data indicate, and with the rapid development of East-West ties they will become more integrated into the global economy, which is now dominated by the West. Nevertheless, the bulk of transnational economic relations presently flow among Western states and between Western states and less-developed countries. This will be the focus of our study.

Finally, an attempt has been made to shed light on the problems inherent in the global political economy by examining it through the eyes of classical liberal economic thinkers and radical thinkers. We have not attempted to examine radical or liberal economic theory per se; rather, both are utilized as means to examine the global political economy. We recognize the danger of attempting to characterize the basic orientations and policy prescriptions of schools of thought as rich and as complex as these. But we feel that their dialogue goes to the heart of disputes among decision makers as well as scholars over international economic relations. The purposes and length of this study have made it necessary for us to simplify some of the arguments propounded by advocates of each analytical orientation. We believe we have managed to avoid distortion of the logic inherent in either liberal economic or radical thought in spite of this need to simplify. We also expect some liberal economic and radical analysts to disagree with us on this and other points. But if analysts from the two schools of thought begin talking with each other rather than past each other, one goal of this study will have been achieved.

We wish to express our thanks to the graduate and undergraduate students whose reactions to the material in this volume shaped it more than they realize. Readers of the book owe a substantial debt to Bill Keefe for his laborious, if only partially successful, efforts to clarify our writing style. We also want to acknowledge the superb secretarial assistance that Linda Perkins, Regina Fritz, and Patty O'Toole provided under the pressure of sometimes excessive demands we imposed upon them. Finally, we wish to thank our families for providing us with constant support and a happy environment—absolutely essential requirements for any analyst of the global political economy writing during the years 1973 to 1975.

The Politics
of Global
Economic Relations

1

Introduction:
Economic Transactions
and
World Politics

We are currently in the midst of a key transition in American foreign
policy that in some respects is even more profound than the dramatic
foreign policy moves made by the United States immediately following
World War II. The Bretton Woods system, membership in the United
Nations, the Truman Doctrine, Marshall aid, NATO, and the construction of a complex of alliance systems ringing the Communist world are
commonly viewed as evidence of that turning point in United States
history when we abandoned our tradition of isolationism (however
different its face in different parts of the globe). Through these instruments the United States was seen as having moved into a series of
multilateral commitments that saddled it with tremendous responsibilities
abroad and circumscribed American freedom of action in ways the
United States had found unacceptable in the past. But the United States
must, during the 1970s, formulate a new set of foreign policies that are
likely to result in even more constraints on America's freedom of action
than its agreements in the 1940s.

As an isolationist, the United States could maximize freedom of
action in its international relations (economic and political) by avoiding
formal commitments; this was a basic theme, for example, in opposition
to American membership in the League of Nations. Following World
War II, when the United States did bind itself by numerous multilateral
commitments in the economic and political spheres, it did so from a
clearly preeminent position and, thus, was able in substantial measure to
shape the various agreements to conform to American interests. The
postwar multilateral agreements were typically of a sort that committed

1

all member states to abide by specified global norms of behavior, which, while ensuring benefits for these countries, would also facilitate the perpetuation of American preeminence. These commitments had the net effect of ensuring America's freedom of action in the globe rather than circumscribing it.

Now, however, the United States is in the process of having to reformulate its foreign economic and political relations to take into account new global realities. Without underestimating the importance of a limited détente between the United States and the USSR, as well as the depth of the Sino-Soviet split, in producing alterations in contemporary American foreign policy, economic factors in the noncommunist world have become crucial. Among these economic factors are the persistent weakness of the United States balance-of-payments position, the emergence of Japan and an expanded European Economic Community as economic entities capable of competing effectively with the United States, lack of confidence in the dollar as an international reserve asset, and the transition of the United States to the status of a major petroleum and natural gas importer. These and other developments have combined to necessitate the construction of a new global economic and political order within which the United States will occupy a significantly less preeminent status. The United States is already committed to involvement in protracted multilateral negotiations over trade, monetary, and energy issues, which if successful will circumscribe American freedom of action in foreign policy in a way that was not true even of our multilateral commitments following World War II. In short, it is in the 1970s, not the 1940s, that the United States is of necessity engaging itself with the rest of the world, as opposed to maintaining its freedom of action by either avoiding formal multilateral commitments or shaping them unilaterally.

The political significance of global economic relations goes well beyond this contemporary transition in the international position of the United States. The increased sensitivity in economic interdependence among virtually all states compels us to assess the political implications of international economic transactions everywhere. Even if economic transactions between states have grown at a slower rate than economic transactions within them,[1] the volume and speed with which economic resources can now be transferred between states places tremendous economic and political strains upon them. For example, modern communications and the management capabilities of giant international banks and corpora-

---

[1] See K. Deutsch and A. Eckstein, "National Industrialization and the Declining Share of the International Economic Sector, 1890–1959," *World Politics*, XIII, No. 2 (January, 1961), 267–99; and K. Waltz, "The Myth of National Interdependence," in *The International Corporation*, ed. C. Kindleberger (Cambridge, Mass.: The M.I.T. Press, 1970), p. 208.

tions, which command assets greater than the gross national products of numerous states, allow massive capital transfers in response to even small disparities in the market conditions and the political milieus of various states.[2] Long-term investment by these economic actors and the movement of their liquid assets in international monetary markets can undermine domestic economic and political programs and produce severe conflicts between states. Indeed, some observers of these banks and corporations feel they may ultimately undermine the contemporary nation-state system itself.[3]

Though international economic relations among private and public actors necessitate profound alterations in contemporary American foreign policy and in political relations among states everywhere, American students of international politics have virtually ignored analysis of the interrelationships between economic transactions and international politics. This situation must be remedied if we are to understand contemporary global politics and the transition of the United States' role in the world. A major obstacle to our understanding of these problems, however, is the poverty of conceptual frameworks with which to address systematically the various interrelationships between international political behavior and international economic behavior. It is important to ask why this is the case and what can be done to increase our analytical capabilities for examining these problems.

Analysts of international politics develop conceptual frameworks in order that they may better address what they perceive to be substantive problems of overriding importance. Almost without exception, American specialists in international politics for two decades following World War II saw the cold war and the defense of the non-Communist world as the substantive focus of United States foreign relations. As a consequence, they relied heavily upon paradigms in which security and power relations among states were postulated as constituting the quintessence of world politics. The dominant paradigm (political realism) led to a focus upon states as sole or primary actors in world politics,[4] and except insofar as economic instruments (such as aid and trade) were directly employed in power struggles between states, the distribution of benefits from domestic and international economic relations were seen as lying outside the

---

2 For an elaboration of the sensitivity of international economic interdependence and its substantive implications, see Richard Cooper, "Economic Interdependence and Foreign Policy in the Seventies," *World Politics*, XXIV, No. 2 (January, 1972), 159–81. See also Chapter 7 of this book.

3 See Frank Tannenbaum, "The Survival of the Fittest," *Columbia Journal of World Business*, III, No. 2 (March-April, 1968), 13–20.

4 See Hans Morgenthau, *Politics Among Nations*, 4th ed. (New York: Alfred A. Knopf, 1967).

boundaries of international politics.[5] Within this analytical tradition, international economic transactions such as trade and monetary affairs were typically looked upon as essentially nonpolitical relationships. They were seen as being managed, in the non-Communist world at least, according to politically neutral, technical criteria and administered by functionally specific ("nonpolitical") international organizations such as the General Agreement on Tariffs and Trade and the International Monetary Fund. The study of such affairs was left to international economists, international lawyers, and students of international organizations—most of whom neglected to analyze the significance of such transactions (and of international economic organizations themselves) in world politics.

In short, until recently the conceptual frameworks most frequently used by American analysts tended to relegate economic relationships to the periphery of inquiry; the interrelationships between domestic and international politics were not systematically examined; and interests other than those of states (such as corporate, partisan, or class interests) received almost no attention in studies of international politics. Marxist analyses dealing explicitly with interests and relationships that were of little concern to scholars representing the dominant analytical tradition of American scholarship on international politics were virtually ignored. These are some important reasons accounting for the poverty of conceptual frameworks useful in studying the politics of international economic relations.

However, some recent developments have brought the economic dimension of world politics back into prominence. New conceptual orientations are fostering systematic analysis of the relationship between international economic and political behavior, in contrast with paradigms focusing exclusively on power and security aspects of world order. The dollar devaluations of 1971 and 1973, the activities of multinational corporations, resource scarcities, and the trade issues creating political conflict among the United States, Europe, and Japan are economic issues that emerged alongside the issues of security and power as top-priority foreign-policy problems for numerous states. These problem areas, as well as increased interest in revisionist interpretations of the cold war and the phenomenon of American imperialism, are exciting substantive and theoretical areas of inquiry that are now widely perceived as being of overriding importance in contemporary world politics and United States foreign policy. None of them can be handled well within the conceptual frameworks most frequently used in the past by American international-politics specialists. In response to these facts, and as a result of a logical evolution of focus, considerable progress has been made during recent

5 Ibid., pp. 25–26.

years in the field of international relations theory. Instead of theories that focus on states as sole or primary actors, we now have new conceptual schemes that admit to a much broader range of actors and processes integral to the study of international politics than was the case just a few years ago.[6] These new schemes constitute the precondition necessary for addressing systematically the relationships between international economic and political behavior.

As a consequence of this gradual evolution in substantive and conceptual focus, specialists in international politics are becoming fascinated with the economic dimensions of world politics. Nonetheless, no theory has emerged that adequately specifies the relationships existing among various actors and processes now viewed as integral to the study of world politics. No attempt will be made in this volume to provide such a general theory. Instead, our aim is to describe more richly and explain more adequately the political significance of various economic relationships by contrasting the assumptional bases that underlie alternative views of political and economic behavior. The chapters that follow examine the major substantive areas of trade, monetary relations, foreign investment, aid, technology transfers, global ecological problems, alternative bargaining strategies for poor states, and the formulation of foreign economic policy in the United States. Each of these areas, and the interdependencies among them, will be described in terms of how they affect political relations among rich states as well as how they affect relations between rich and poor states. In addition, we will examine how various conceptual frameworks lead to alternative conclusions about which policies are most appropriate for resolving conflicts of interest among states and other actors.

Without attempting to force all analyses of global economic relations into one or the other of the following schools of thought, the major clash in description, explanation, prediction, and policy prescription relating to these problems appears to be between those analysts and decision makers subscribing to the assumptions of classical liberal economic thought and those subscribing to the assumptions of what Americans refer to as radical thought. The classical liberal economic approach is evident in the various works of analysts such as Harry Johnson[7] and in

---

6 See particularly Robert Keohane and Joseph Nye, eds., *Transnational Relations and World Politics* (Cambridge, Mass.: Harvard University Press, 1971). See also Oran Young, "The Actors in World Politics," in *The Analysis of International Politics*, ed. James Rosenau, Kenneth Davis, and Maurice East (New York: The Free Press, 1972), pp. 125–44.

7 See, for example, his *Economic Policies Toward Less Developed Countries* (Washington, D.C.: The Brookings Institution, 1967); "The Link that Chains," *Foreign Policy*, No. 8 (Fall, 1972), 113–19; and "The Multinational Corporations as an Agency of Economic Development: Some Explanatory Observations," in *The Widening Gap*, ed. Barbara Ward (New York: Columbia University Press, 1971), pp. 242–52.

the basic contemporary foreign economic-policy orientations of the United States and other governments of advanced industrial societies in the West. They are evident as well in the policy orientations of key international economic institutions such as the General Agreement on Tariffs and Trade, the International Monetary Fund, and the International Bank for Reconstruction and Development. Examples of radical thought can be found in the works of cold war revisionists, analysts of contemporary American imperialism, and theorists of *dependencia* (American imperialism in the Latin American context) such as William Appleman Williams,[8] David Horowitz,[9] Gabriel Kolko,[10] Harry Magdoff,[11] Susanne Bodenheimer,[12] Andre Gunder-Frank,[13] and Johan Galtung.[14] Radical interpretations are also reflected among vocal political elements throughout the Third World.

Although there are many differences of opinion among the statesmen and scholars within each of these two general schools of thought, there are nevertheless certain basic assumptions that are shared widely by the adherents of each school; these assumptions clearly distinguish the two orientations. In particular, there are important differences between the two schools' basic assessments of the primary values underlying actions taken by decision makers on behalf of states, the distribution of benefits from international economic relations, the degree and patterns of conflict inherent in international economic relations, and the location of the major obstacles to the achievement of national economic aspirations. The central tenets of these two analytical traditions are summarized in Table 1-1.

Adherents of classical liberal economic thought tend to see the focus of states' economic policies as the maximization of economic growth and efficiency. The basic value determining policy choice in regard to economic issues before the state should be the optimal allocation of resources for national growth in the context of a global economy that operates in accordance with the norms of liberal economic principles. Success or failure is usually stated in terms of aggregate measures such as the level

---

8 *The Tragedy of American Diplomacy* (New York: Dell Publishing Co., 1959).

9 *The Free World Colossus* (New York: Hill and Wang, 1971).

10 *The Limits of Power* (New York: Harper & Row, 1972).

11 *The Age of Imperialism* (New York: Monthly Review Press, 1969).

12 "Dependency and Imperialism: The Root of Latin American Underdevelopment," in *Readings in U.S. Imperialism*, ed. K. T. Fann and D. C. Hodges (Boston: Porter Sargent Publisher, 1971), pp. 155–82.

13 "Sociology of Development and Underdevelopment of Sociology," in J. Cockcroft, A. G. Frank, and D. Johnson, *Dependence and Underdevelopment* (Garden City, N.Y.: Doubleday and Company, 1972), pp. 321–98.

14 "A Structural Theory of Imperialism," *Journal of Peace Research*, VIII, No. 2 (1971), 81–117.

TABLE 1-1. Central Tenets of Liberal Economic and Radical Thought

Basic Premise	Liberal Economic Thought	Radical Thought
1. Primary value being pursued by states.	Maximum aggregate economic growth in national and global economies.	Maximum national economic growth consistent with capacity for national self-determination and with equitable distribution of income within and between states.
2. Distribution of benefits from global economic relations conducted according to liberal principles.	Mutual benefit if not symmetrical distribution.	Clearly asymmetrical distribution in favor of rich states.
3. Degree of conflict *inherent* in global economic relations conducted according to liberal principles.	Minimal.	Very great.
4. Persistent cleavages *inherent* in global economic relations conducted in accordance with liberal principles.	None.	Cleavages between rich states and poor states.
5. Major obstacle to achievement of national economic aspirations.	Irrational state policies.	Rules of behavior governing international economic relations.
6. Overall result of activities of international economic institutions.	Provision of infrastructure advantageous to all states in conduct of international economic relations.	Provision of infrastructure for perpetuating dominance by rich, Western states.

and growth of GNP, trade, investment, per capita income, and so forth.

In this context, global as well as national economic growth and efficiency dictate that all states open themselves to foreign goods and capital and that they specialize in the production of those goods in which they possess a comparative advantage. Existing international economic relationships are viewed as mutually beneficial, even if the distribution of benefits among states is not completely symmetrical.

To the extent that existing international relationships do not enhance growth and the efficient allocation of resources, this view blames the unwillingness of decision makers within states to pursue rational liberal economic policies. In other words, to the extent that the global economy as a whole, and individual states' policies, conform to classical liberal economic principles, *all* states' growth and economic efficiency will be maximized. Of course, world production will be maximized also.

Inherent in this positive-sum view of international economic relationships is minimal conflict of interest between states. For the adherents of classical liberal economic thought, policy prescription is universalist: no basic differentiation is made among policy prescriptions appropriate for different types of national actors (large or small, rich or poor). The formal rules of behavior in international economic relations, and the policies of international economic institutions enforcing these rules, are seen as politically neutral among all states.

The assumptional bases of radical thought are vastly different from those underlying the liberals' world view. Although growth and economic efficiency are seen as priority goals of states, national self-determination and equitable income distribution are just as crucial. Indeed, these last two goals would be ranked above economic growth by most radicals if, in the short run, the choice had to be made. The radical analyst tends to see income equality and the capacity for economic and political self-determination among poor states, at least, as incompatible with integration into the existing global economy, which operates in accordance with the norms of classical liberal economic thought. A poor state's open acceptance of foreign goods and capital, along with its specialization in the production of those goods in which it enjoys a comparative advantage, is felt to generate a form of international economic relations in which unequal economic units are afforded equal access to, and compete for, markets and resources around the globe.

The benefits of such international economic relations between rich and poor states are distributed asymmetrically, in favor of the rich. This continued asymmetry in the distribution of benefits forms a basically exploitative relationship between dominant and dependent states that is seen by adherents of radical thought as the explanation for the existence and the widening of the gap between rich and poor countries. Hence, in a fundamental sense the major obstacle to the achievement of the national aspirations of poor states (most states in the world) is seen to be the nature of the international economic system itself, rather than the policies of individual poor states. Even if a poor state does formulate economic policy in accordance with classical liberal economic thought, the asymmetrical distribution of benefits in its international economic relations will condemn it to perpetual poverty, foreign penetration, and continued dependence upon rich states.

Clearly great conflicts of interest between states are inherent in this basically zero-sum view of international economic relations. Policy prescription is not universalist. Policies appropriate for rich states in the center of the global economy are not appropriate for poor states in the periphery. Classical liberal economic thought is viewed by radical thinkers as compatible with the interests of rich states but not with those of poor states. The existing international economic system is not politically neutral, as the classical liberal economists argue. The policies of all the key international economic institutions and the distribution of benefits from most public and private economic transactions inherently favor rich states, insuring their dominance in global economic and political relations.

Quite obviously, the analysts and decision makers who employ these alternative sets of primary assumptions will differ greatly in their assessment of, say, multinational corporations and in their prescriptions for the treatment of multinationals by nations, acting individually and in concert. The profound cleavage in their basic premises leads adherents of the two schools of thought to talk past each other in analyzing specific economic issues, such as multinational corporations. To the classical liberal, for example, foreign investment appears mutually beneficial; to the radical it is exploitative. Analysts from both schools seldom examine the appropriateness of the different assumptional bases from which their perceptions and policy prescriptions flow. In the absence of this examination, political conflict over economic issues is exacerbated. The typical analyst or decision maker within each school of thought simply sees no necessity to question seriously the assumptions underlying his own stance on the issue and continues to propose policies that are seen as harmful in their incidence or intent by adherents of the other analytical tradition.

The clash between these two schools of thought not only has important substantive implications for international relations, it also affords an opportunity to analyze the political implications of various dimensions of global economic relations. In the following chapters, we will refer frequently to these alternative perspectives and we will develop them more fully in specific contexts.

We will utilize other conceptual frameworks as the subject matter requires. For example, the theory of collective goods[15] tells us that severe conflicts of interest will emerge even among actors that maintain congruent assumptions about the nature of international economic relations and that see the desirability of achieving a common goal from which all actors will benefit. Thus, however useful the juxtaposition of liberal

---

[15] See Mancur Olson Jr., *The Logic of Collective Action* (New York: Schocken Books, 1968).

economic and radical thought may be as a means to examine political implications of global economic relations, it would be misleading to assert that this "dialogue" is itself sufficient to address all aspects of these complex problems.

Our essential objective in this volume is to clarify major political problems associated with international economic relations, rather than to offer specific solutions to them; the latter can be done intelligently only after the problems themselves are better understood. There is really a great deal at stake in the success of this enterprise, toward which this volume is only a beginning. We are entering an era in international relations during which political conflicts are widely perceived to be centered in economic relations. Yet, as political scientists we are presently ill equipped substantively and conceptually to analyze behavior in such an era. By the same token, if economists are to be in a position to prescribe policies appropriate in an era of highly politicized international economic relations, they must begin to examine systematically the political efficacy of their various economic "solutions."

2

World Trade Dilemmas

There is no area of international economic activity that demonstrates more clearly than trade relations the general thrust of the remarks in Chapter 1. During the past decade, trade issues have figured prominently in political controversies between less developed countries and rich states, between East and West, and among the United States, Europe, and Japan. At a time when America's trade is becoming increasingly important to its overall economic well being, its loss of economic preeminence relative to that during the immediate postwar period makes it increasingly more difficult for the United States to shape international trade in conformity with its particular economic and political interests. But before examining trade issues of contemporary political importance, we need to look at certain basic characteristics of the global trade order as it has evolved since World War II.

THE POSTWAR ECONOMIC ORDER

Following the war the Western states, under vigorous American leadership, were most anxious to construct an international economic order within which trade would flourish. In particular, efforts were devoted to avoiding the explicitly competitive "beggar thy neighbor" foreign economic policies that characterized international commerce during the 1930s.

> Intensive economic nationalism marked the . . . decade. Exports were forced; imports were curtailed. All the weapons of commercial warfare were brought into play; currencies were depreciated, exports were sub-

11

sidized, tariffs raised, exchanges controlled, quotas imposed, and discrimination practiced through preferential systems and barter deals. Each nation sought to sell much and buy little. A vicious spiral of restrictionism produced a further deterioration in world trade.[1]

These policies contributed not only to a deterioration of world trade, but also to global economic depression. Trade and monetary policies emerged as primary instruments used by major states to reinforce a division of the world into tightly knit political-economic regions, which in turn helped contribute to the outbreak of World War II. In light of the consequences of the foreign economic policies characteristic of the 1930s, the need to encourage relatively free international movement of goods and capital was widely felt to be essential for world peace as well as for global prosperity.

It was toward the ends of peace and prosperity that the major Western states created the General Agreement on Tariffs and Trade (GATT) in 1947. GATT is a legally binding codification of rules for the conduct of trade among its member states. This tiny institution, located in Geneva, Switzerland, has also provided the international infrastructure and the locus for all the major multilateral tariff-reduction negotiations since World War II. Its general goal is to maximize growth in world trade and the global economy through a reduction in trade barriers pursued on a nondiscriminatory basis.

GATT seeks to promote trade in ways that avoid "beggar thy neighbor" policies or the creation of highly competitive regional economic blocs of the sort characterizing the 1930s. Protection of domestic industry is to be carried out exclusively through tariff duties (as opposed to other trade barriers such as quotas, controls on the use of foreign exchange, and so forth), and the general level of tariff protection is in turn to be reduced through successive multilateral negotiations. The progressive lowering of tariffs under these circumstances is expected to stimulate international trade. Tariff reductions are to be implemented in a nondiscriminatory fashion in accordance with the "most-favored-nation" (MFN) principle. Accordingly, any state in GATT is assured that its goods will enter the markets of all GATT members at rates of duty no less favorable than those applied to similar products of any other country. The MFN principle is designed to accelerate the pace of tariff reductions and trade growth throughout the world as well as to avoid the creation of new preferential trade blocs protected by discriminatory tariff barriers, except under conditions specified in the General Agreement.[2]

[1] Clair Wilcox, *A Charter for World Trade* (New York: The Macmillan Co., 1949), pp. 8–9.
[2] See *The General Agreement on Tariffs and Trade*, Article XXIV.

The last point reflects the most significant contribution of GATT to the promotion of international economic order. The General Agreement establishes international norms of responsible trade policy against which the national trade policies of its member states can be evaluated. In cases where a national policy is found to be inconsistent with GATT principles, there are established procedures to settle grievances in a manner designed to minimize further restrictions of international trade. During the 1930s the absence of a permanent international institution with these functions undoubtedly contributed to the escalation of discriminatory trade policies during that period and to the more general deterioration in economic and political relations among states. Thus, GATT's primary utility has been to introduce a form of permanent international oversight and accountability for commercial policies that, prior to its existence, were viewed as exclusively national prerogatives.

GATT was complemented by the creation in 1944 of the International Monetary Fund (IMF), which was designed to promote the stability and liberalization of international monetary transactions.[3] The goals of GATT would have been impossible to achieve without both an adequate global supply of foreign exchange and provisions for capital mobility to finance trade flows. Through the IMF, states became to some extent internationally accountable for their monetary policies. These two institutions, along with the International Bank for Reconstruction and Development (IBRD),[4] became the foundation for multilateral efforts to prevent the political and economic consequences of economic nationalism that preceded World War II.

The United States provided the driving force for the construction of this postwar international economic order. It did so not only for the reasons discussed above, but also because the United States was in a peculiarly advantageous position to benefit from international economic transactions conducted in accordance with the norms established by GATT and the IMF. Immediately following the war, with the economies of most countries in a state of devastation and disarray, the United States was in a commanding position as a source of global credit and exports. An international economic order based on the principles of free movement of goods and capital served perfectly America's domestic and foreign economic interests and capabilities. Such an economic order was an effective means of allowing the United States to penetrate the trade preference systems, especially Britain's sterling area, from which it had

---

[3] The IMF and the political implications of international monetary transactions will be examined in Chapter 3.

[4] The IBRD is the dominant multilateral aid agency. Multilateral aid is discussed in Chapter 5.

been excluded prior to the war.[5] The economic and political preeminence of the United States during the 1940s and 1950s assured the creation of an international economic order that was tailor-made to American interests, however sensible such an economic order might also be, from the perspective of liberal thought, for maximizing world trade flows, global prosperity, and peace.

The framers of GATT would look with considerable pride upon the evolution of world trade and production within the context of the economic order established following World War II. The original GATT membership of twenty-three states has climbed to eighty. Tariffs on dutiable manufactured and semimanufactured goods have been reduced through six rounds of GATT negotiations to an average level in 1971 of 8.3 percent for the United States, 8.4 percent for the European Economic Community (EEC) of the Six, 10.2 percent for Britain, and 10.9 percent for Japan. In the case of the United States, for example, this represents a substantial reduction of its level of tariff protection, which averaged 60 percent in 1934 and 25 percent in 1945. Partly as a consequence of these tariff reductions, world exports increased from $60 billion in 1950 to $310 billion in 1970. Over the same period, the real GNP of advanced industrial states grew from $836 billion to $2,012 billion. On the basis of these aggregate indicators, it would appear that the lessons of the 1930s have been learned: international oversight of national foreign economic policies has been successful in curtailing the excesses of economic nationalism and its negative economic and political consequences.

As remarkable as these developments in world trade may be, they nevertheless present a false picture of the extent to which trade issues have been defused as a source of tension in international relations. International institutional arrangements in trade and monetary policy have facilitated rapid growth in world trade, but the benefits have not been distributed symmetrically across products and geographical regions. Trade problems are reemerging as questions of high politics among all variety of states. That is, trade issues are once again occupying the attention of presidents and prime ministers as priority problems of foreign and domestic politics. These issues contribute significantly to the overall tone of states' foreign relations, and as such they are too important to be treated as essentially technical problems to be handled by nonpolitical experts. We will examine trade policy as foreign policy in two contexts: (1) relations among advanced industrial states and (2) relations between these states and poor countries.

---

[5] For an elaboration of this point, see Robert Gilpin, "The Politics of Transnational Economic Relations," in *Transnational Relations and World Politics,* ed. Robert Keohane and Joseph Nye (Cambridge, Mass.: Harvard University Press, 1971) , pp. 57–59.

TRADE ISSUES AMONG ADVANCED
INDUSTRIAL STATES

Trade issues have played a central role in the political dialogue between less developed countries and rich states throughout the period since World War II. However, only recently have trade issues among noncommunist advanced industrial states reemerged as important political problems. Several factors have contributed to this turn of events after a period of some fifteen or twenty years following the creation of GATT, a period during which trade issues among these states were effectively depoliticized—that is, "discussed and resolved in their own realm . . . without intruding into high policy."[6]

As long as the United States had no economic peer in the noncommunist world and as long as the cold war was perceived as the most salient problem in international politics, economic relations among Western states were not a predominant source of political tension. A shared perception of threat from the Communist world made advanced industrial states in the West relatively content to defer to Washington for security policy. The primacy of security concerns and the obvious dependence of Western states upon the United States in this area inhibited them from adopting trade, investment, and monetary policies wholly at odds with American interests. In any event, as long as other Western states were critically in need of American capital and production to reestablish their economic health, there was little incentive to challenge directly the postwar economic order that provided both. For its part, the United States was quite willing to tolerate departures by Western European states and Japan from GATT and IMF norms in national trade and monetary policies as long as these states remained crucial cold war allies and as long as they were unable to pose a serious threat to American economic interests at home and abroad. These conditions prevailed in substantial measure until the late 1950s. They were conducive to an essentially constructive, though not always harmonious, approach to trade, investment, and monetary relations among advanced industrial states outside the Communist world.

As limited détente between the superpowers gradually superseded their intense cold war postures, intra-Western conflicts of interest previously subordinated to the dictates of alliance cohesion began to emerge. Conflicts arose over appropriate security policy and the desirability of

---

[6] Richard Cooper, "Trade Policy is Foreign Policy," *Foreign Policy*, No. 9 (Winter, 1972–73), 19.

continued dependence upon the United States in this domain. Also, during the 1960s Japan and Western Europe became economically strong enough to act in accordance with new political and economic interests that they defined apart from the United States. A substantial reduction in the perception of threat from the Communist world made advanced industrial states in the West less prone to subordinate their particular interests to those of the United States in an effort to preserve Western unity. Whereas earlier all these states were desperately in need of American capital and exports, by the 1960s they were large exporters in their own right and had accumulated excess dollars as foreign exchange reserves. Thus, they were less dependent upon the United States and, indeed, were able to compete effectively against an increasing number of American goods in markets at home and around the world. This new economic strength enabled European states and Japan to adopt certain policies, such as regional trade ties and trade and investment restrictions, that were at odds with the spirit of postwar economic agreements and American interests. Moreover, now that they were strong enough to pose a serious threat to American economic interests, less competitive American industries and organized labor mounted increased pressure for protection. As a result of these changes in the domestic and international environment, the United States became much less willing than it was previously to tolerate departures by European states and Japan from GATT and IMF norms for national trade and monetary policies. For their part, the advanced industrial states in the West pointed to protectionist American policies such as demands for "voluntary" export controls on the part of others and to persistent U.S. balance-of-payments deficits as evidence of American departures from GATT and IMF principles.

In short, the cold war détente and the economic resurgence of Western Europe and Japan have combined to place a severe strain on cohesion among major Western states. As the data on shares of world production, exports, and foreign exchange indicate (Figures 2-1, 2-2, 2-3), the United States finds itself in a much less commanding position relative to its major economic partners than was the case during the creation and formative years of GATT and the IMF. The present international political and economic problems among Western states are in a fundamental sense a result of this profound structural alteration in the international economy. These new economic realities will make it much more difficult for the United States to place its formative stamp on new global political-economic relations.

Rather than attempting to survey all the major trade issues confronting advanced industrial states, let us examine a number of behavioral traits and political and institutional characteristics that are likely to

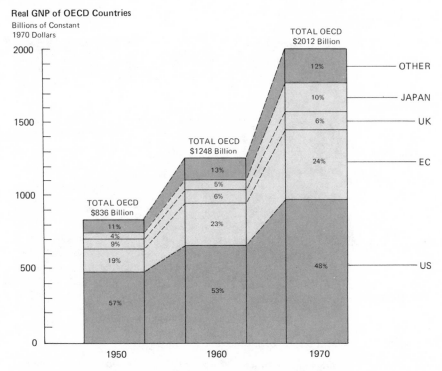

FIGURE 2-1.   Western States' Production (Billions of U.S. $)

Source: *United States International Economic Policy in an Interdependent World,* Report to the President submitted by the Commission on International Trade and Investment Policy, July, 1971, p. 344.

persist and, thus, to condition efforts to expand trade in the 1970s. Monetary and investment relations have so much importance in their own right that they will be examined separately in subsequent chapters, but it is important to remember in any discussion of trade issues that all of these phenomena are inextricably intertwined.

Neomercantilism

One characteristic feature of the advanced industrial states' trade policies throughout the postwar period, notwithstanding GATT, has been the persistence of a neomercantilist orientation. This orientation manifests itself in numerous ways and is the source of some major trade conflicts of contemporary importance. Neomercantilism is a policy whereby a state seeks to maintain a balance-of-trade surplus by reducing

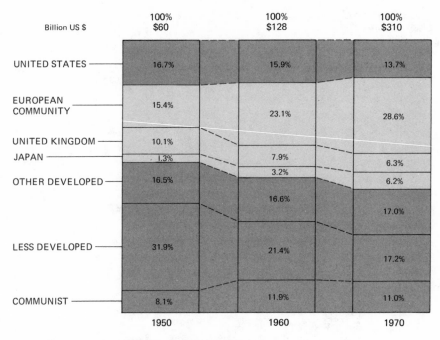

FIGURE 2-2.   World Exports (Billions of U.S. $)

Source: *United States International Economic Policy in an Interdependent World,*
Report to the President submitted by the Commission on International Trade
and Investment Policy, July, 1971, p. 351.

imports, stimulating home production, and promoting exports.[7] The
attractions of this policy for any single state are obvious. But by the very
nature of trade balances, a state can gain a trade surplus only when other
states run a trade deficit. It is evident, therefore, that all states cannot
successfully implement neomercantilist policies simultaneously. Nonetheless, the United States and its major economic partners are all pursuing
policies and making demands upon one another in international trade
negotiations of a neomercantilist variety.

Neomercantilist policies have been an integral part of Japan's remarkable economic resurgence during the 1960s and early 1970s. Japan's
share of world exports almost doubled (3.2 percent to 6.2 percent)[8]
between 1960 and 1970 by virtue of a very aggressive business-government partnership in export promotion. By 1970 Japanese exports were
expanding at a rate of 20 percent per year. During this period Japan was

[7] Harold Malmgren, "Coming Trade Wars?" *Foreign Policy,* No. 1 (Winter,
1970–71) , 120.

[8] See Figure 2-2.

Billion US $

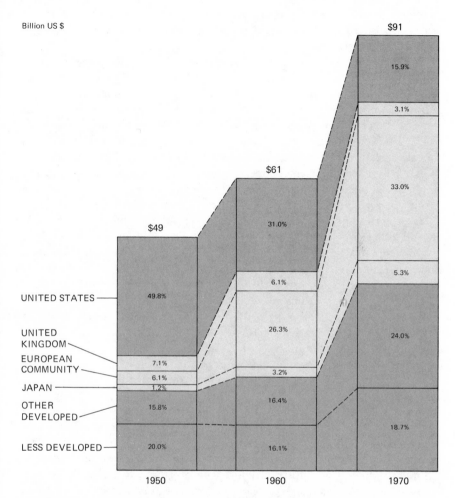

FIGURE 2-3.   International Reserves (Billions of U.S. $)

Source: *United States International Economic Policy in an Interdependent World*, Report to the President submitted by the Commission on International Trade and Investment Policy, July, 1971, p. 384.

able to generate a trade surplus and to protect domestic production by maintaining an undervalued yen and a large variety of import and foreign investment restrictions designed to make it extremely difficult for American and European firms to penetrate the expanding Japanese market. By the early 1970s these aspects of Japan's foreign economic policy were all contributing to a severe strain in political relations between Japan and other advanced industrial states of the West. These economic measures were particularly resented in the United States, which had contributed substantially to Japan's economic reconstruction following World War II.

The EEC, like Japan, has adopted a neomercantilist trade stance, particularly in its Common Agricultural Policy (CAP). The CAP has been described as "the ultimate in mercantilism: decrease in imports, stimulation of home production to substitute for imports, and increase in exports."[9] The CAP protects and stimulates high-cost domestic agricultural production within the Common Market by placing variable duties on all agricultural imports. In the absence of production controls, the policy has generated agricultural surpluses in Europe that are priced too high to compete in world agricultural markets. The revenues derived from the agricultural import duties are thus used to subsidize Common Market agricultural exports to international markets that the Europeans would otherwise be unable to penetrate. The CAP has emerged as a major issue of dispute between the EEC and the United States, which is anxious to maximize its export potential in agricultural products.[10]

In spite of its posture as the world's leading proponent of free trade, the United States, too, has adopted neomercantilist trade policies. When foreign imports of steel and textiles began to pose a serious challenge to domestic producers in the 1960s, the American response was to reduce these imports and stimulate relatively inefficient national production by applying vigorous pressure on foreign states and their industrial producers to impose "voluntary" export controls on their sale of these products in the American market. When in 1971 the value of American imports exceeded its exports for the first time during the twentieth century, the United States imposed a temporary 10 percent import surcharge and ultimately negotiated a devaluation of the dollar at the expense of its major trading partners. These moves were designed to stimulate domestic industry, reduce imports, and increase American exports—another classic example of neomercantilist trade policy. The United States insisted that these policies were necessitated by the mercantilist policies of Europe and Japan—in particular, the CAP, which produced a dramatic decline in certain American agricultural exports to the EEC during the late 1960s; Europe's barriers to Japanese exports, which made the United States bear the brunt of the rapid growth of Japanese exports; the EEC's construction of regional preference arrangements that discriminated in favor of trade with numerous Mediterranean and African states; and Japanese barriers to American imports and investment.

---

[9] Malmgren, "Coming Trade Wars?" p. 121.

[10] As in the case of Japan, the memory of Marshall aid to Europe produces added American resentment of contemporary protectionism by Europe.

Even if this is true, however, such a response by the world's leading spokesman for free trade is symptomatic of the pervasive appeal of mercantilist policies.

The leading trade powers alone account for over half of world trade. They all employ neomercantilist policies to some degree, and each justifies its own departures from GATT norms in this regard by pointing to the similar policies conducted by the others. This approach to trade policy could easily lead to trade wars and severe political cleavages among the leading economies, particularly during a period of stagnation or decline in the global economy.[11] Even in the context of a buoyant global economy, negotiations over the growth of Japanese steel and textile exports to the United States, for example, have been bitter and protracted affairs that have soured overall political and security relations between these allies.

Inflation

Neomercantilism is a trade policy designed primarily to protect national producers and maintain domestic employment to the detriment of competitive foreign producers and laborers. It also contributes to inflation by suppressing imports and, hence, reducing the supply of goods in domestic markets. The severe inflation confronting all major industrial states in the 1970s has increased interest in using trade policy to protect domestic consumers from price rises. This use of trade policy leads to measures that are quite the opposite of mercantilism, but if carried to extremes these measures can be just as threatening to growth in world trade and production. In particular, trade policy can be used to combat inflation by *lowering* import barriers to make available greater supplies of goods to consumers. If the process stopped at this point, trade policy designed primarily to maximize consumer interests might provide a constructive antidote to mercantilist policies. However, the process has not stopped there. Advanced industrial states are also experimenting with export controls for the purpose of cutting off foreign demand on nationally produced products and thus increasing supplies available for domestic consumption. In 1973 the United States invoked temporary controls on its major agricultural exports, wheat and soybeans, toward this end. Its major trading partners, particularly Japan, are heavily dependent on the United States for these vital food needs. Indeed, shortly after the imposition of export controls on soybeans U.S. Treasury

---

[11] The implications of economic growth for the resolution of political conflict are examined more fully in Chapter 6.

Secretary Shultz visited Japan. While there, he was a guest at a seventeen-course Japanese dinner in which every dish contained some soybean ingredient. "I got the message," he said.[12] Such trade policies carry with them great potential for global trade disruptions and political conflict.

Only a few years ago, the prospect that all the major industrial states of the West would simultaneously find themselves confronting economic stagnation and chronic inflation was generally felt to be quite remote. Yet, following 1972 this was the case. Thus, structural conditions are present in the global economy that are conducive to the development by the major economic powers of national trade policies employing *both* import barriers to protect jobs and export controls to lower prices. Increased political hostility is the likely result of either policy.

Protectionist Domestic Political Forces

These structural conditions give rise to strong domestic political pressures on the part of producers, organized labor, and consumers for their governments to erect various trade barriers. Domestic political considerations make constructive trade alternatives difficult to achieve, no matter how enlightened statesmen might wish to be in their attempts to avoid a resurgence of economic nationalism. Whereas the economies of advanced industrial states may in the aggregate be better off in the absence of protectionist trade policies, those particular interests (such as textile and steel manufacturers in the United States) hurt by liberal trade policies bring extraordinary protectionist pressure to bear on their governments. For example, during the presidential campaign of 1968, Nixon's Southern strategy dictated a firm pledge to protect the Southern textile industry from strong Japanese import competition. This campaign commitment was honored by President Nixon and lay behind his administration's hard and bitter negotiations with Japan to sharply curtail Japanese exports of textile goods to the United States.

Since the late 1960s, there has been a notable resurgence of protectionist sentiment in the United States Congress for the reasons already discussed more generally in connection with the politicization of trade issues among Western States. At the same time, organized labor has moved from its keystone position among domestic interests supporting liberal trade policies to a highly protectionist position. American labor is particularly interested in arresting the increasing practice by American-based multinational firms of exporting American-made parts for assembly

---

12 Mary Locke and Hans Binnedijk, "GATT Talks Begin," *European Community*, No. 170 (November, 1973), 16.

by cheaper labor and then reimporting the finished products to serve the American market. As the leading spokesman for organized labor in the United States, the AFL–CIO put its full weight behind a neomercantilist bill introduced by Representative James Burke and Senator Vance Hartke that would eliminate these "runaway shops" and otherwise inhibit the free flow of goods, technology, and capital between states. It seems plain that domestic political pressures will make it considerably more difficult for the United States to pursue liberal trade policies in this decade than at any time since World War II.

It is also important to realize there are strong internal political pressures that make it difficult for America's major trading partners to move toward more liberal trade policies. For example, a goal of the United States in its trade relations with the European Common Market is to secure Europe's abandonment of the Common Agricultural Policy in favor of reliance upon cheaper American agricultural supplies.[13] But such a move by the EEC would fly in the face of strong domestic pressure by European farmers for protection, and it would go to the heart of a political agreement holding the Common Market together. The CAP was the quid pro quo that France, as the Common Market's leading agricultural producer, secured for its willingness to open itself up to more efficient industrial producers within the EEC, such as West Germany. Many observers feel there could be no Common Market without the CAP. This is a prime example of how political pressures *within* the EEC are likely to frustrate the growth of trade and development of smoother political relations *between* Europe and the United States.

The Crisis in Multilateral Institutions

The internal and external forces prompting protectionist trade policies in the major industrial states indicate the need for strong multilateral action to prevent further deterioration in contemporary global trade relations. Yet here too the world faces a major challenge in the 1970s. The General Agreement on Tariffs and Trade is unable to contribute much more to world trade growth merely by performing the tasks it has repeatedly done so well in the past. It succeeded admirably in reducing the level of tariff protection of industrial trade among its member states. These tariffs are now down to the point where nontariff barriers such as government procurement regulations, quantitative restrictions, and health and environmental control standards are relatively

---

13 Ironically, by initiating its embargo on grain exports in 1973, the United States gave the EEC its strongest argument against relying upon cheaper American agricultural imports for its food needs.

more important than tariffs as barriers to trade. Hence, advanced industrial states are entering a period of diminishing returns from mutual tariff reductions on industrial goods. Domestic pressures for protectionism stimulated by any further tariff cuts are likely to be intense, yet, because tariff levels are already low for most industrial goods, the growth in world trade from further tariff cuts on these products is likely to be less dramatic than in the past. Major efforts to stimulate trade among Western states must now be focused on the complex issues of agricultural trade and nontariff barriers to trade. In short, the outstanding trade issues among the major economic powers in the West are concentrated in precisely those areas in which states have been least willing to agree upon international oversight by GATT.

What seems to be required, therefore, is the negotiation of a widely accepted, enforceable system of new rules, somewhat like those already developed by GATT for trade in industrial goods; such a system would be designed to encourage nondiscriminatory trade expansion through international supervision of national policies on nontariff barriers and agricultural and commodity trade. The seventh (Tokyo) round of GATT negotiations, begun in 1973, will have to confront this challenge. As an indication of the basically different character of these negotiations, compared with earlier ones, the legislation giving the American president authority to participate in the talks is titled the Trade *Reform* Act of 1973; the United States negotiated during the preceding Kennedy round of GATT talks under authority of the Trade *Expansion* Act of 1962.

Several considerations make rapid progress on significant international trade reform particularly difficult at the present time. First, at the same time that existing GATT arrangements for the regulation of trade are recognized as being inadequate to cope with current trade problems, international mechanisms for handling monetary relations among states have also proved inadequate. The dollar devaluations of 1971 and 1973 marked the end of the Bretton Woods System. Thus, during the 1970s the world faces not only the need for trade reform, but also the construction of a new international monetary order. These two problems are so closely related that both sets of complex negotiations must proceed simultaneously for either to be truly successful. This situation has not faced the world since the 1940s, and it leads directly to a second major obstacle to the resolution of current trade problems.

The present situation is not unique. In their early postwar negotiations on trade and monetary relations, advanced industrial states had serious conflicts of interests. But the United States was in such a commanding economic and political position relative to its negotiation partners that it was able to secure agreements on trade (GATT) and monetary affairs (IMF) that were substantially in accord with American preferences. The present negotiations find Europe and Japan as major economic powers alongside the United States, even if the United States is still the strongest single economic power in the world. Thus, the United States cannot expect to emerge from contemporary and future trade and monetary negotiations with agreements that conform perfectly with American preferences. But more important, this current distribution of economic and political power among advanced industrial states is likely to make a truly significant final agreement very difficult to achieve at all. The Europeans and the Japanese are now strong enough to challenge American leadership in the construction of a new economic order, but at the same time they are too weak and divided to replace United States leadership in the global political economy. This situation in the 1970s in some ways makes the challenge of constructing a new trade and monetary order even more formidable to the United States and the world than the challenge of the 1940s.

The existence of these various pressures for the reemergence of economic nationalism among advanced industrial states has led to the fear that the future may bring an international trade order characterized by highly competitive regional trade blocs led by the United States, the EEC, and Japan.[14] The prospects for such a development are enhanced by the fact that the multinational institutions that are guardians of the principle of nondiscrimination in international economic exchange are themselves in a state of disarray.

The harmonization of trade policies among advanced industrial states will be a formidable task indeed. These states must cope simultaneously with neomercantilism, global inflation, domestic pressures for protectionism, alterations in the relative economic strength of states, and the emergence of new problems in international economic relations with which existing international economic institutions are ill equipped to deal. These factors constitute general parameters that condition any efforts to construct a new global trade order. Their existence need not prevent progress toward that goal, however. These forces are clearly evident to decision makers within all advanced industrial states. At least in a general way, all recognize the danger that excessive economic nationalism poses for the maintenance, much less the growth, of their national prosperities. The acute oil crisis of 1973 and 1974 reinforced the fact that their national economies are increasingly interdependent. It amply demonstrated that even the largest powers are incapable of exter-

---

14 For empirical evidence of the existence of such trends already, see D. Calleo and B. Rowland, *America and the World Political Economy* (Bloomington, Ind.: Indiana University Press, 1973), pp. 123–24. See also Ernest H. Preeg, *Economic Blocs and U.S. Foreign Policy*, National Planning Association Report No. 135, Washington, D.C., 1974).

nalizing their economic problems by means of unilateral actions harmful to others. Thus, the salience of the threats to global economic prosperity posed by trade issues may provide the momentum necessary for constructive multilateral efforts to establish a new, more resilient framework for the promotion of orderly trade and monetary relations.

Economic prosperity is of course at stake in the settlement of trade problems. But more than that, in the absence of widely accepted multilateral norms of trade conduct, each trade conflict threatens to produce serious political confrontations among states. Moreover, the entire gamut of security and political issues among states becomes inordinately more difficult to manage in a global economy characterized by the stagnant or declining real income that is likely to be produced by "beggar thy neighbor" trade policies.[15]

TRADE AND LESS–DEVELOPED COUNTRIES

Export earnings account for 75 to 80 percent of less-developed countries' foreign exchange resources, clearly dwarfing foreign aid and private investment as alternative sources of foreign exchange. Thus, it is not surprising that trade issues have long figured prominently in the political dialogue between less-developed states and the advanced industrial states with which they conduct three fourths of their trade. In particular, less-developed countries share a profound sense of frustration with the international trade order developed after World War II. This frustration stems from a number of substantive trade practices and institutional characteristics of GATT that, in their view, combine to inhibit the development of their economies and relegate them to a secondary status in the global economy.

Less-developed countries are particularly sensitive to the tariff structures of most advanced industrial states. As we noted earlier, successive rounds of negotiations under GATT's auspices have reduced the *average* level of tariffs on dutiable manufactured and semimanufactured products to about 10 percent. But the manufactured and semimanufactured products of particular export interest to less-developed countries typically face tariff levels of two to four times this average, and tariffs on these items have frequently been ignored altogether in GATT negotiations. In addition, agricultural commodities, which account for the bulk of less-developed countries' exports, face a variety of trade barriers—quantitative restrictions; tariff, health, and environmental regulations; and so

---

[15] The political implications of a zero-growth global economy are developed more fully in Chapter 6.

forth—that are designed to protect the agricultural sector in many advanced industrial states, such as the EEC and the United States.

These explicit barriers to less-developed countries' exports are supplemented by more subtle aspects of tariff structures in advanced industrial states. For example, tariff protection typically increases by stages of production, thereby presenting greater barriers, say, to processed mineral resources than to raw materials in their unprocessed state. Accordingly, effective tariff protection is actually at much higher levels than nominal tariff rates would indicate.[16] Tariff rates are also typically higher for the more easily produced consumer goods than for capital goods.

Tariff structures and the trade policies of advanced industrial states impose particularly severe barriers to goods that less-developed countries are most capable of producing for export—agricultural goods, semiprocessed commodities, and labor-intensive consumer goods.[17] Capital goods and industrial products that face the lowest tariff barriers in world trade are traditionally the exports of rich states.

Less-developed countries also complain that when they are capable of penetrating these barriers, advanced industrial states, responding to domestic political pressures, erect new ones to protect inefficient domestic producers. In this regard, less-developed countries frequently refer to the Cotton Textile Agreement, which governs trade between the United States and Japan but which also applies to textile exports of numerous less-developed countries, such as Taiwan, Malaysia, India, Pakistan, and Hong Kong. They are also embittered by the opposition of organized labor in rich states to the growing practice of assembling electronic goods in less-developed countries for sale in advanced industrial states.

Less-developed countries argue, further, that certain institutional characteristics of GATT contributed to the emergence of these trade practices and made it difficult for them to secure trade reforms commensurate with their needs. The most-favored-nation principle is one of the problems they see in GATT, notwithstanding the fact that its existence has meant that tariff reductions negotiated among advanced industrial states have lowered trade barriers to exports of less-developed countries as well. Their main objection to the MFN principle is that it prevented rich

[16] To illustrate this fact, let us assume that copper ore faces no tariff protection whereas refined copper faces a tariff of 10 percent. Let us also assume that refining a unit of copper ore raises its value from 75 cents to one dollar. The 10 percent tariff (10 cents) on the refined copper applies to the one-dollar price, not just to the 25 cents of value added by the refining process. Thus, the *effective protection* on refined copper is 40 percent (the 10-cent tariff ÷ the 25-cent value added by refining), not the 10 percent nominal tariff rate.

[17] For an excellent discussion of the obstacles to less-developed countries' exports, see Harry Johnson, *Economic Policies Toward Less Developed Countries* (Washington, D.C.: The Brookings Institution, 1967), Chap. III.

states from granting preferential treatment to less-developed countries' exports of manufactured goods as a spur to their development efforts.

> There are no industrial products of importance that are not produced for export by some developed country. Therefore, no country can now eliminate tariffs on manufactured goods for the benefit of the developing industries of poorer countries without simultaneously opening its markets to unrestrained competition from developed countries [because of the MFN principle]. It is this problem that has given rise to the demands of less-developed countries that the most-favored-nation clause [of GATT] be suspended in their behalf.[18]

The bargaining principle of reciprocity underlying all tariff reduction negotiations is another characteristic of GATT long criticized by less-developed countries. Poor states feel they are placed at a disadvantage by the necessity to offer rich states an equivalent tariff concession for every tariff reduction they receive from them. They argue that reciprocity is equitable when applied to negotiations among states at approximately the same stage of economic development, but in negotiations between industrialized and less-developed states, reciprocity (like the MFN principle and the whole philosophy of the existing world trade order, for that matter) is a call for equal competition among fundamentally unequal economic units. Spokesmen for less-developed countries argue that the reciprocity principle has made it difficult for them to participate actively in GATT negotiations, and this in turn helps account for the fact that tariffs remain high on industrial products of particular export interest to them:

> The developing countries of course had had no bargaining power, politically or economically. The rule of reciprocity has required them to give a matching concession, but clearly they are not in a position to give any. While over the past fifteen years, tariffs on industrial products of interest to industrial nations have been gradually brought down, those on products of interest to developing countries have remained at a high level.[19]

Less-developed countries' criticism of the MFN principle and reciprocity are symptomatic of a more general charge they level at the GATT. They view it as a club created by advanced industrial states and

---

[18] John W. Evans, "The General Agreement on Tariffs and Trade," in *The Global Partnership*, ed. R. Gardner and M. Millikan (New York: Frederick A. Praeger, 1968), pp. 92–93.

[19] Ambassador K. B. Lall of India, cited in John Evans, "The General Agreement on Tariffs and Trade," p. 76. Evans goes on to argue, however, that rich states have in fact extended tariff reductions to less-developed countries without demanding equivalent concessions.

managed in accordance with their primary interests. The norms guiding trade policy, the nature of trade negotiations, and the principal dimensions of progress in expanding world trade all reflect this fact. In the view of less-developed states, these characteristics of GATT account for the continued existence of major barriers they face in their exports of agricultural products, mineral resources, semimanufactures, and industrial goods they are capable of producing. In substantial measure it accounts, in their view, for the decline of the less-developed countries' share of world exports from 31.9 percent in 1950 to 17.2 percent in 1970.[20]

There is no shortage of either alternative conceptualizations of the basic trade challenges facing less-developed countries or of policy prescriptions purporting to deal with these challenges. Not surprisingly, the proponents of liberal economic thought and the representatives of radical thought suggest starkly different courses of action on the part of various states to meet the trade needs of less-developed countries. Let us examine these briefly, as well as the prescriptions of Raul Prebisch, the noted Argentinian economist and international politician, who more than any other person has provided coherence for the Third World's demands of rich states in trade and financial matters since World War II.

The Liberal Economic Explanation and Prescription

From the perspective of liberal economic thought, the basic problem facing less-developed countries is the extent to which national trade policies of rich and poor states continue to depart from the ideal of free trade. Policy prescriptions focus upon the need for all states to return to the underlying spirit of GATT. This requires that both rich and poor states abandon their policy of negotiating waivers from conformity with free-trade principles to protect relatively inefficient domestic production. Having created GATT and provided its leadership, advanced industrial states should bring their actual trade policies into line with their liberal trade rhetoric. They are called upon to remove the remaining barriers to trade among themselves and, especially, those particularly high barriers facing the goods less-developed countries produce for export. For their part, less-developed countries are called upon to liberalize their own national trade policies, which, based on the protection of infant industries, are often more protectionist than those of advanced industrial states. Liberal economists feel that less-developed countries can facilitate the modernization process by exposing their domestic producers to exter-

[20] See Figure 2-2.

nal competition through the encouragement of trade and foreign investment. If rich and poor states were to follow these policies, the argument runs, global production would be maximized and trade could make a maximum contribution to the development of poor states.[21]

There are substantial questions concerning the political efficacy of policy prescriptions for trade and development advanced by liberal economists. This is the case even for decision makers who are basically committed to the tenets of free trade, becaue (1) all organized interests within their societies do not embrace free trade as a concept, and (2) those who do tend to abandon the concept when, in the short run, it adversely affects their particular jobs or industry or nation. Inefficient producers that would be hurt by the removal of existing trade barriers, whether within rich or poor states, will mount strong political opposition to policy prescriptions for further trade liberalization; notwithstanding the impact their action will have on the national economy or the global economy. They will repeatedly marshal the argument that the national economy will benefit from continued protection of its relatively inefficient enterprises, since jobs are thereby preserved at home and the nation is able to enjoy the security of maintaining an indigenous productive capacity in the affected economic sector.

We have seen how the complexity of the issues and the nature of domestic opposition to free trade will make it difficult for advanced industrial states to make great strides toward further liberalization of trade policies during this decade. In addition, less-developed countries will find liberalization of national trade policies of the sort prescribed here very difficult to achieve. Less-developed countries typically feel unable to compete on an equal footing with producers of advanced industrial states within their own economies, much less in international markets. The apprehensions of the less-developed states must be overcome if they are to implement the policies prescribed by liberal economists. This is unlikely to occur on a broad scale since exposing one's economy to competition through trade and foreign investment is seen by important political elements within countries throughout the Third World as inevitably leading to foreign penetration and further loss of control over their economic and political destinies. Whatever the aggregate economic results, any leader of a less-developed country who today embraces liberal economic policy prescriptions does so at the risk of generating substantial domestic political opposition by economic and political nationalists who are acutely sensitive to past injustices stemming from various forms of control that advanced industrial states have exer-

---

21 For a discussion along these lines, see Harry Johnson, *Economic Policies Toward Less Developed Countries*, pp. 47, 130.

cised over less-developed countries. The existence of these attitudes and political pressures in both rich and poor states suggests that the world is unlikely to move more than a little way towards the implementation of liberal economic solutions to the trade and development problems of less-developed countries.

The Prebisch Explanation
and Prescription

In his writings as an economist and through his activities as head of the Economic Commission for Latin America and later the United Nations Conference on Trade and Development, Raul Prebisch has mobilized considerable political support from less-developed countries for an alternative conceptualization of these states' trade difficulties. Liberal economists attribute less-developed countries' trade problems to the unwillingness of rich and poor states to adopt national trade policies consistent with the principles of a liberal trade order embodied in the General Agreement on Tariffs and Trade. Prebisch agrees that less-developed states would be better off if barriers to their exports were removed, by rich states in particular; however, the actual implementation of free trade would not get to the heart of their trade and development problem. Prebisch argues that even in a world of free trade, the benefits will be reaped disproportionately by advanced industrial states as a consequence of structural differences between countries at different stages of development.

The structural problem of central importance to less-developed countries, according to Prebisch, is a long-term decline in the terms of trade for the exchange of commodities for industrial products; that is, the value of primary products has declined relative to the value of manufactured products in world trade. Since less-developed countries typically are large exporters of primary products (such products constitute roughly 75 percent of their exports) and must import most industrial goods, they find themselves having to export ever larger amounts of primary products in order to earn the foreign exchange necessary to purchase the same volume of manufactured imports from year to year (see Figure 2-4).

A number of factors are cited to account for the decline in the terms of trade between less-developed states and advanced industrial states. Crucial among them, according to Prebisch, is the fact that productivity advances in advanced industrial states lead to wage and other input cost increases that keep prices constant or rising. In contrast, in less-developed countries productivity advances do not lead to wage increases and/or constant prices because of disguised unemployment and weak labor orga-

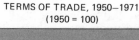

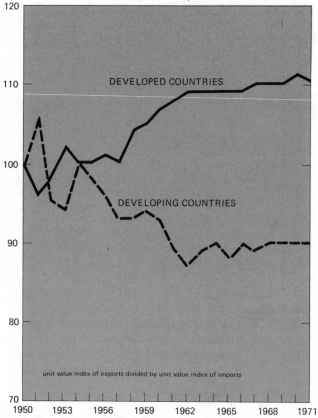

FIGURE 2-4.   Terms of Trade

Source: International Bank for Reconstruction and Development, *Finance and Development,* Vol. 11, No. 1 (March, 1974) , 14.

nizations. Instead, they lead to price declines that are passed on to the consumers—predominantly located in rich states.[22]

Additional factors involve the relatively lower income-elasticity of the demand for primary products, as compared with manufactures. This means, for example, that forces operate to dampen increases in demand for primary products as income increases: food expenditure as a percentage of income declines, and primary products as a percentage of total factor inputs needed to produce industrial goods decline. These forces,

[22] See Albert O. Hirshman, "Ideologies of Economic Development in Latin America," in *Latin American Issues* (New York: The Twentieth Century Fund, 1961) , pp. 14–15. Hirshman provides a concise overall summary of Prebisch's economic philosophy.

along with the development of synthetic substitutes, serve to depress demand and prices for primary products in world trade relative to manufactured goods, for which demand and expenditures increase as a proportion of income as income increases.

All of these factors are seen by Prebisch and most other spokesmen for less-developed countries as evidence of a structural bias in world trade that relegates producers of primary products to a permanent second-class status in the global economy, even if all barriers to free trade were to be removed.[23] Of course, numerous restrictions on trade continue to exist in fact, and as we have seen they make it particularly difficult for less-developed countries to transform themselves from exporters of primary products to exporters of manufactured and semiprocessed goods as a means of overcoming the problem posed by the terms of trade.

This conceptualization of the manner in which less-developed countries are denied their fair share of trade benefits is quite at odds with classical liberal economic theory. Not surprisingly, Prebisch and his followers find the liberal policy prescription for free trade a deficient solution to the trade and development problems of poor states. Instead, they call for a comprehensive program under which rich states compensate less-developed countries for the structural inequalities that produce disproportionate gains from trade for rich states. Such a program would include numerous commodity agreements covering primary-product exports of particular importance to less-developed countries. These agreements between major exporters and importers would be designed to insure access to the markets of rich states as well as to stabilize world market prices for specific commodities at levels assuring poor states both a larger income and smaller annual fluctuations in revenues. To the extent that such agreements fail to arrest the decline in the terms of trade between less-developed and industrial states, Prebisch insists that a compensatory finance scheme be established by which industrial states would return capital to less-developed countries in the form of grants or low-interest loans. This capital flow should be in amounts at least equal to the "excess" in revenues industrial states receive as a consequence of the decline in the terms of trade.

In addition, advanced industrial states should take action that

---

23 The dramatic price increases of commodities during the early 1970s raise considerable doubt about the persuasiveness of the terms of trade thesis. Nevertheless, adherents of the thesis would argue that in the same period inflation led to price increases in their imports of manufactured products as well. Moreover, with a recession in the Western states during the mid 1970s prices in international commodity markets can once again be expected to fall more than prices of industrial goods in world markets. In short, advocates of the terms of trade thesis are unlikely to see anything in the relative prices of commodities and industrial products during the 1970s that would convince them to alter their orientation or their demands.

would enable less-developed countries to expand their exports of manufactured and semimanufactured products. Prebisch argues that this cannot and should not be accomplished by reciprocal tariff cuts of the
GATT variety between rich and poor states. Rather, he summons the
rich states unilaterally to extend preferential treatment to less-developed
countries for their exports of manufactures and semimanufactures. Such a
move would help arrest the decline in the terms of trade between center
and periphery states while facilitating industrialization crucial to the
latter's rapid development.[24]

Quite obviously, Prebisch and his advocates do not want a return to
the spirit underlying GATT. Indeed, they want to create a new economic
order—one that recognizes the special needs of less-developed countries
and that affords them a greater share of the benefits from the conduct of
trade than could be expected even in a world of free trade. Trade in
accordance with GATT principles is viewed as a means of exploiting
poor states and denying them the opportunity of industrializing rather
than as a means of enhancing the welfare of all states. Consistent with
this orientation, less-developed countries pushed hard for the establishment of the United Nations Conference on Trade and Development
(UNCTAD) in 1964, with Raul Prebisch as its Secretary-General.
UNCTAD is the institutional expression of Prebisch's conceptualization
of the global economy and the less-developed states' role in it. It was
created to challenge GATT both philosophically and institutionally as
the central multilateral arena for world trade relations.[25]

As is the case with policy prescribed by liberal economists, the
Prebisch solutions for the trade problems of less-developed countries are
likely to be politically unobtainable. The policy prescriptions outlined
by Prebisch and his followers to benefit poor states place the burden of
international structural reform primarily on the shoulders of advanced
industrial states. In advanced industrial states relevant decision makers
typically think in terms of liberal economic principles. Liberal economists view the critical assumptions of Prebisch's economic theory (such as
the terms of trade arguments) with great skepticism. Thus, successful
implementation of the Prebisch program to meet the trade and development problems of poor states depends upon unilateral concessions by

24 For a complete account of Prebisch's economic analysis and policy prescription, see United Nations, *Towards a New Trade Policy for Development*, Report by the Secretary-General of the United Nations Conference on Trade
and Development [Raul Prebisch], E/CONF. 46/3, 1964.

25 For a comprehensive description and assessment of UNCTAD as an institution from an advocate's viewpoint, see Branislav Gosovic, *UNCTAD: Conflict
and Compromise* (Leiden: A. W. Sitjhoff-Leiden, 1972). See also R. S.
Walters, "International Organizations and Political Communication," *International Organization*, XXV, No. 4 (Autumn, 1971), 818–35.

advanced industrial states, whose decision makers are not predisposed to accept the philosophical underpinning that gives rise to demands for these concessions.

Differences in economic philosophy are only part of the problem. More important is the lack of a sense of community among center and periphery states that is strong enough to trigger a substantial redistribution of income through commodity agreements, aid programs, preference agreements, and the like, that are adequate to meet the development needs of poor states. At the heart of any effective income redistribution program is a prior sense of political and social community. Prebisch's program for structural reform in the global economy depends upon a sense of community *between* rich and poor states that is every bit as strong as that existing *within* advanced industrial states with a long tradition of national unity. This sense of community between rich and poor states simply does not exist at present.

Evidence of this fact, and still another obstacle to implementing Prebisch's policy, is the domestic opposition within the major advanced industrial states to unilateral concessions on the order of those demanded by Prebisch. For example, in the United States the proposal for extending preferential treatment to exports of manufactures and semimanufactures of less-developed states evoked strong protectionist pressures on Congress and the Executive. These pressures were so great that President Nixon waited two years after America's agreement to participate in a general preference scheme for less-developed countries before daring to submit it to Congress in 1973. In the meantime, the general preference schemes implemented by the European states and Japan in 1971 were carefully constructed to yield only a marginal increase in exports of manufactures by less-developed states. Protectionist forces within all advanced industrial states are likely to prevent a resource transfer to poor states from ever approaching the scale contemplated by Prebisch and less-developed countries in their demands for a general preference scheme.

The political obstacles to the implementation of Prebisch's proposals are not confined to advanced industrial states. Less-developed states, for example, must act together in pressing demands for structural reforms in the international economic order that are consistent with Prebisch's philosophy. Since commodity agreements, tariff preferences, aid programs, and other means of transferring resources to less-developed countries do not benefit each of them equally, there is increasing difficulty in maintaining political cohesion among periphery states in their negotiations with center states. In the absence of a united front by less-developed countries, it is unlikely that advanced industrial states will find it necessary to extend concessions along these lines.

Despite these political problems, some progress toward Prebisch's goals has been made. UNCTAD has emerged alongside GATT as a permanent source of multilateral pressure on rich states for a structural reform in the global economy that is advantageous to poor states. As of 1974, a general preference scheme has been offered by all Western states to less-developed countries in UNCTAD. Even though this scheme is more limited than less-developed countries desire, it does indicate their success in getting Western states to make explicit exceptions to the GATT tenets of most-favored-nation treatment and reciprocity as they relate to trade with poor states.

The Radical Explanation
and Prescription

The radical view of the trade and development problems faced by poor states has some things in common with Prebisch's orientation, but in other respects it differs sharply. Radical spokesmen in rich and poor states share with Prebisch the conviction that the free-trade prescription in the liberal economic tradition will not generate modernization and economic development in less-developed countries. They embrace Prebisch's argument about the decline in the terms of trade and view the conduct of trade between Western states and less-developed countries in accordance with GATT principles as an exploitative relationship.

In spite of these similarities with the Prebisch conceptualization of the global economy, the radical view goes well beyond Prebisch in its assessment of how profoundly the structural arrangements *among* and *within* states are at odds with the developmental possibilities and capacity for autonomy of poor states. Consequently, radicals differ greatly with Prebisch on what solutions are appropriate to achieve the basic political and economic interests of states in the periphery of the global economy.

Prebisch views inequities in international economic relations between rich and poor states as having evolved gradually out of certain structural characteristics of exchanges between states at different stages of economic development. As we have seen, his prescription to remove these inequities focuses upon comprehensive reform of the norms governing international economic relations. In essence, this means reliance upon policy changes by advanced industrial states designed to redistribute income to less-developed countries. Prebisch feels this can be accomplished through multilateral negotiations between less-developed countries and advanced industrial states if the former maintain a unified position in applying sustained political pressure for precisely defined alterations in the conduct of trade and other forms of international economic exchange. Since 1964, UNCTAD has been the locus of this effort.

Radicals see the poverty of poor states as a consequence of a capitalist (imperialist) international political economy in which periphery states are held politically and economically subordinate to Western states. The global political economy based on the norms of liberal economic philosophy is very effective in assuring center states access to cheap raw materials and cheap labor as well as new markets for capital investments and exports. These characteristics of the international political economy are the key to understanding both the poverty of the Third World and the prosperity of Western countries, the United States in particular. The development of center states and the underdevelopment of periphery states are both "outcomes of the same historical process: the global expansion of capitalism."[26]

Western states are able to continue this exploitative relationship with less-developed countries because of their control of the key international institutions that establish norms for international transfers of goods and capital. In addition, these governments buttress the leadership position of a small economic and political elite (client class), present in most poor states, whose source of domestic power derives from the maintenance of close external ties with the political and economic elites of advanced industrial (capitalist) states. This client class is viewed by radicals as a junior partner to elites in center states. Such a class benefits handsomely from its position in the international capitalist system.

Given these perceptions, it is easy to understand the radicals' criticism of both the liberal economists' and Prebisch's prescriptions for dealing with the trade and development problems of poor states. The liberal prescription of free movement of goods and capital among states is to the radicals merely a blatant effort by advanced industrial states to penetrate and further denationalize the political and economic systems of less-developed countries. Prebisch's prescriptions appear very naive to radical thinkers. Western states are not going to redistribute income to poor states to remedy inequalities in the benefits derived in international economic exchange. To do so would mean an end to the exploitative relationships that they created (consciously or unconsciously) and upon which their continued prosperity depends. In radical thought, multilateral negotiations of the sort Prebisch suggests hold no promise. The international economic institutions that define the post–World War II economic order (GATT, IMF, IBRD) are firmly controlled by Western (capitalist) states. Indeed, these agencies constitute the machinery through which rich states exploit less-developed countries. Radicals also see little progress resulting from negotiations in an international institu-

---

26 Suzanne Bodenheimer, "Dependency and Imperialism: The Roots of Latin American Underdevelopment," in *Readings in U.S. Imperialism*, ed. K. T. Fann and D. Hodges (Boston: Porter Sargent Publisher, 1971), p. 160.

tion such as UNCTAD, even though it ostensibly represents the interests of poor states. Not only will Western states refuse to agree to any critical reforms demanded by less-developed countries in such a forum, but also, since the leaders of most less-developed countries depend so thoroughly on Western ties for their economic and political survival, they will not even pose demands that would threaten the dominant position of advanced industrial states in the global economy.

In order for poor states to secure autonomy of economic and political action or to escape from the economic exploitation that has condemned them to poverty, they must interrupt the existing linkages between center and periphery states. Among the radicals there is general agreement that this can be accomplished only by replacing capitalism with a socialist political-economic order. New left spokesmen in the United States tend to focus their attention on the need for the emergence of socialism in the United States and in other center states. Only then will the rich states be predisposed toward a redistribution of income to less-developed countries and the erection of a new, nonexploitative global economic order based on socialist principles of exchange. Moreover, the external support critical for continued control by present-day political and economic elites in less-developed countries would be withdrawn by socialist governments in rich states. Hence, from this perspective the emergence of socialism in Western states would be necessary and sufficient to remove the primary local and international obstacles to the development of poor states. *Dependencia* theorists in Latin America, on the other hand, tend to focus their attention on socialist revolutions in periphery states, revolutions that would remove present domestic political-economic elites and clear the way for an interruption of the existing ties between poor states and the capitalist global economy that produces their poverty. Hence, the radical solution to the trade and development problems of poor states is revolution in the center states and/or in the periphery states of the global economy. It is dramatically different from the classic liberal or Prebisch approaches, which, though different from each other, are alike in that they call upon rich states merely to alter their foreign economic policies and to implement relatively modest reforms in trade and the larger economic order.[27]

A number of questions arise regarding the political efficacy of the radicals' policy prescriptions. The program of the new left in the United States depends essentially on the transformation of the United States and other Western states from capitalist to socialist systems. There is very

[27] For examples of the radical perspective on trade, see Arghiri Emmanuel, *Unequal Exchange: A Study of the Imperialism of Trade* (New York: Monthly Review Press, 1972) ; and Harry Magdoff, *The Age of Imperialism* (New York: Monthly Review Press, 1969) .

little evidence to suggest that such a transformation is likely to occur, at least in the near future. But even if it were likely to occur, careful scrutiny would have to be given to the categorical assertion that less-developed countries will be incomparably better off in dealing with a socialist West and a socialist United States than with the same states under capitalist systems. Whether Western states are socialist or capitalist, less-developed countries will be engaged in economic exchanges with economic and military giants. Throughout history, the largest economic and military powers have defined their relationships with lesser powers in a manner that lesser powers typically view as exploitative. This situation is likely to repeat itself even in a world of socialist states.[28]

The emphasis of the *dependencia* theorists upon socialist revolutions in the periphery states raises another basic problem. In most instances, if a state, or states, in the periphery of the global economy achieves a socialist revolution, its need for foreign capital, technology, and markets will still exist. Unless the advanced industrial states also abandon capitalism, the new socialist state, or states, in the periphery will still have to operate within a capitalist global economy. Even if the character of its linkages with the international economy is drastically altered by a socialist revolution at home, the state in the periphery will in all probability find that the alternative to dependency is not autonomy; rather, at best it will be a new form of interdependence, one that still sets severe constraints on domestic economic and political programs.

CONCLUSION

We have attempted to outline briefly how prescriptions for reforms in trade between states in the center and states in the periphery of the global economy follow logically from the assumptions that liberals, Prebisch, and radicals make about the nature of international economic exchange. Serious questions arise concerning the prospects for conducting trade completely in accord with the desires of advocates of each school of thought. The questions raised about each approach need not be seen as a cause of despair. No serious analyst truly expects global economic and political relations as complex as trade to lend themselves to solutions that are totally consistent with a single school of thought, particularly in an era when even the most powerful state in the world finds it increasingly

---

28 This discussion of the radical interpretation of global economic relations between rich and poor states has purposefully been couched in terms larger than the trade issue. The basic dynamics described here can be applied to other forms of economic exchange besides trade, such as aid, private investment, and monetary relations.

difficult to mobilize international and domestic support for policies consistent with the school of thought it has long championed. Rather, the questions we have raised point to the need for decision makers and analysts of the various persuasions discussed above to recognize the political, attitudinal, and structural realities that make their policy proposals difficult to implement. More fundamentally, these questions point to the need for decision makers and analysts to reexamine the basic assumptions that generate logically compelling, yet often unworkable, policy prescriptions.

To the extent that this reexamination of assumptions occurs, particularly within governments, workable solutions to the trade and development problems facing less-developed countries may be generated. If it does not occur, political discourse among states at different levels of economic development will continue to produce conflicts as to which is the most appropriate, if unattainable, utopia within which to conduct economic exchange.

In spite of these considerable obstacles to the trade prospects of less-developed countries, certain contemporary developments afford these states an opportunity to enhance their bargaining position in the global economy. First, the trade and monetary issues dividing advanced industrial states are so profound that, quite aside from the problems of less-developed countries, intensive negotiations are underway to construct a new trade and monetary order. Spokesmen for less-developed countries have pointed out that through unified action they could be in a position to take advantage of divisions among rich states to assure that some of their own demands in monetary, trade, and aid affairs be met.

> The process of monetary reform . . . will require near unanimity if it is to succeed in reestablishing stability and flexibility. It is an issue on which the rich countries are deeply divided; but the poor countries stand in broad agreement. It is therefore a situation in which the poor, very unusually, should be able to act in concert to ensure their reasonable demands are met.
>
> Those demands are not limited to the field of monetary reforms in general. . . . They include in rough order of magnitude, a new deal on agricultural exports, the adoption of GSP (the General System of Preferences for less-developed countries) by Canada and the United States, a revision by the EEC and Japan of their schemes of GSP, and a more rapid approach to the Second Development Decade aid targets.[29]

Earlier in the post–World War II era, the negotiating strength of the United States and the unity of advanced industrial states on trade, monetary issues, and other political issues precluded serious consideration of this type of bargaining by less-developed countries.

[29] Charles Elliot, *Fair Chance for All* (New York: United Nations, 1973), p. 63.

A second development that should enhance the bargaining position of poor states is the recent appearance of resource shortages as a primary concern in global economic relations. Until this decade, the central focus of international trade deliberations had been the securing of access by producers to the markets of consuming nations.[30] The oil embargo imposed by Arab states, and acute global shortages of grain, fishmeal, soybeans, and fertilizer during 1973 and 1974 have made the issue of assured access by consumers to supplies of raw materials as important as the traditional focus of trade negotiations since World War II. Since less-developed countries are major sources of some raw materials that are in short supply, they hold an unprecedented bargaining position with advanced industrial states. Though not all less-developed countries stand to benefit directly from current shortages in raw materials, there is evidence that pivotal less-developed states may use their bargaining leverage to focus attention on the general economic grievances of less-developed states as a group. This certainly seems to have been the logic of the special United Nations General Assembly sessions in 1974 and 1975 on problems of raw materials, development, and economic cooperation. Here again, divisions among the Western states over access to raw materials and over other economic issues enhances the prospects for success by less-developed countries in securing some of their reasonable economic demands of long standing.[31]

To cite these two developments is not to suggest that states in the periphery of the global economy now occupy the decisive position in the construction of a new economic order. But it is true that alterations in the political and economic relations among rich states, combined with the emergence of new economic problems that cannot be managed within existing institutional arrangements, give less-developed countries opportunities not available to them in the past. The last comprehensive attempt to alter basic trade and monetary relations took place when the decolonization drive was in its infancy; at that time, the interests of newly emergent states received scant attention. Now, states in the Third World are at least in a position to make themselves heard.

---

[30] This line of reasoning is developed nicely by James P. Grant, "The Fuel, Food, and Fertilizer Crises and the New Political Economics of Resource Scarcities," statement before the Subcommittee of the House Foreign Affairs Committee on Foreign Economic Policy, May 8, 1974, p. 7.

[31] In Chapter 7 we will focus on various specific strategies by which less-developed countries might enhance their share of benefits from international economic exchange.

3

The Global Monetary Order: Interdependence and Dominance

Most international economic transactions, such as trade, investment, international loans, and travel involve the exchange of goods, services, land, and labor for some form of monetary compensation, such as gold, British sterling, or dollars. Bartering arrangements, the exchange of goods and services for goods and services, long ago proved to be far too unwieldy to allow extensive economic transactions within a society, much less between societies. Consequently, internationally acceptable currencies and the emerging global monetary order have stimulated international economic transactions by making payment for such transactions relatively easy. As such, they are of central importance to all transnational economic relations. Moreover, international monetary relations simultaneously condition and reflect international and national political and economic developments. This chapter examines, on the one hand, the link between international politics and the global monetary order and, on the other hand, the linkage between the domestic political and economic concerns of states and foreign economic and political policies as they relate to monetary affairs.

INTERNATIONAL MONETARY ORDER: FUNCTIONS AND ISSUES

International currencies are those currencies that are used by several or many states in their economic and political transactions. They perform three basic functions.[1] First, international currencies function as a unit

[1] The following discussion draws heavily upon Robert Z. Aliber, *The Future of the Dollar as an International Currency* (New York: Frederick A. Praeger, 1966).

of account—that is, a standard by which prices can be defined. Thus, in international transactions prices of goods and services are frequently quoted in terms of dollars, British pounds, Swiss francs, German marks, and Japanese yen. Of course, within specific states prices are denominated in their own currencies, but by and large where international transactions are involved the domestic currency price is usually translated and defined in terms of an international currency. Thus, the international currencies serve as a common denominator for the quotation of prices.

Second, international currencies serve as a medium of exchange. Payment for goods and services acquired in another country or the purchase of a foreign investment must be made in a currency that is acceptable to the provider of the product. A currency is thought to be acceptable when its value in terms of other international currencies or gold is relatively stable, thereby affording that currency a stable purchasing power. On the other hand, though, if a currency fluctuates widely, the holders of the currency have no assurance that the money they have today will buy the same amount of goods tomorrow. Speculators may be attracted to gamble on these fluctuations, but most of those engaged in international commerce prefer to use a stable and widely accepted currency in the business they conduct. National currencies that are not convertible into international currencies cannot serve as the basis for much international interaction. The holder of such currencies may have little or no purchasing power outside its own country, for others will not accept the currency in payment for goods provided. Given the vast amount of international economic and political transactions involving monetary transfers, it is critical to have international currencies by which these transactions can be conducted.

Third, international currencies can serve as a store of value or "wealth." Private parties or governments holding international currencies in reserve have potential purchasing power in many areas of the world. Conversely, holders of many strictly national currencies have a purchasing power limited largely to the state issuing the currency. Therefore, large reserves of international currencies will enhance a state's international buying power, whereas small or no reserves of this type will make it difficult for such a state to buy anything from other countries.

As a result of the critical functions performed by international currencies, the nature of these currencies and the structure of the global monetary order have a great impact on the global economy and on the relative economic and political position of states. The international monetary order provides the vehicle for the conduct of international economic relations. Consequently, the nature of a state's participation in the international monetary order may partially determine its role in the more general global economy as well as in international politics. Of course, the national and international political objectives of states also have an important influence on the structures and processes of international monetary relations.

Given the large volume of international transactions requiring the extensive use and interchange of international currencies, there are several problems that cause serious difficulties for individual states and the international monetary order as a whole. These issues evolve from the various functions performed by international currencies.

The first issue, one of great importance to all states and to global economic and political stability, is the question of deficits in a state's balance of payments. Any state, in its international dealings, both earns and spends international money (foreign exchange). Whenever a state or its citizens purchase something from other states—perfume, oil, foodstuffs, automobiles, computers, stocks, support for armies, and so on—the payments for these goods and services are usually made in an internationally acceptable currency. Similarly, whenever a state or its citizens sell something to foreign purchasers, payment is usually made in an international currency. A particular state experiences a balance-of-payments deficit when the state and its private interests spend more in other countries than other countries spend in it. Conversely, a balance-of-payments surplus exists when a state earns more from its international transactions than it spends. For most countries a persistent balance-of-payments deficit means not only that it is living beyond its means in its relations with other countries, but also that it is using up whatever foreign exchange holdings it may possess. Theoretically, when a state exhausts its reserves of internationally acceptable money, it can no longer purchase desired goods or services from other states, for sellers abroad will only accept money that has an international purchasing power. This condition raises some critical issues, which are addressed in this chapter. What policy options are available to particular states seeking to overcome a balance-of-payments deficit? In what ways should states with a surplus in their balance of payments assist deficit countries? Do surplus states have an obligation to assist deficit countries at all? From an international perspective, what kind of monetary institutions and procedures are best suited to facilitate adjustments of payments imbalances among states?

Besides balance-of-payments considerations, a second major problem that confronts the international monetary order is the need to assure an adequate volume of international reserve currency to service the global economy. Countries that run short of reserves must reduce their international economic transactions. This usually means severe damage to their domestic economic and political aspirations. If numerous countries experience such a shortage, there will be a reduction of global demand for the purchase of goods and services from other countries. The result of a shortage of international reserves is likely to be a severe jolt to the global economy, if not a serious worldwide depression. International trade will decline because of the reduced amount of international transactions, and production and employment are likely to fall off, even in states with balance-of-payments surpluses. Consequently, for the continued growth of the global economic system and the economic health of most states, it is necessary that there be sufficient international reserves to finance the expansion of international economic transactions. This is the problem of liquidity or adequacy of international reserves. If the supply of international currencies is insufficient to keep up with the demand for financing international transactions, this scarcity will seriously retard international activity, causing unemployment in all countires in those industries linked to the international economy.

Chronic balance-of-payments deficits and inadequate international reserves in turn contribute to a third critical issue: lack of confidence in a particular state's economic health, or concern about the stability of the international financial order itself. A state whose economic health is in question and that has persistent balance-of-payments deficits will find other countries increasingly unwilling to accept its currency or to extend it credits to enable it to purchase goods and services abroad. When this happens to a state with one of the few international currencies, serious disruptions will be caused throughout the global economy. Exchange rates among the most important currencies, the value of one currency in terms of another (for example, 2.5 Swiss francs equals one dollar), may fluctuate dramatically. This means that trade and other international economic transactions are conducted with currencies lacking a stable value. Variations in exchange rates may greatly alter the costs of sizable economic activities and, thus, make them too risky to implement.[2] Moreover, serious international monetary crises are likely to be caused by extensive buying or selling of the important currencies with the objective of exchanging weak currencies for strong ones. In some cases, even the intervention of central banking authorities may not be sufficient to maintain international monetary order.

At first, these issues may all appear to be technical questions of little

---

[2] The authors recall arriving in Switzerland in early May, 1971 with approximately $1000 to finance several months' research and travel in Europe. A few days after their arrival, a dollar crisis occurred in which holders of dollars internationally were trying to sell them for stronger currencies, such as the Swiss franc or the German mark. The immediate implications of the resulting lack of confidence in the American dollar were twofold. First, for several days traveler's checks written in dollar denominations could not be cashed anywhere. Second, when the banks finally became willing to accept and exchange American dollars for Swiss francs, the $1000 in traveler's checks were now worth only $900 in purchasing power.

interest to students of world politics. Yet, the way in which these issues are resolved vitally affects political and economic relations within and among states. The political and economic implications of these issues will be developed further in discussions of American balance-of-payments difficulties, the nature of the existing international monetary rules, and the roles different types of states play in the international monetary order.

THE BRETTON WOODS INTERNATIONAL MONETARY ORDER

International monetary relations, with their widespread impact on states, are too important to be left to the uncoordinated, unilateral actions of many different states and to the fears and convictions of private and governmental money manipulators. Consequently, states have developed formal and informal mechanisms at the international level to try to monitor, regulate, oversee, and generally make more orderly, international monetary relations. In addition, private parties—individuals, banks, and corporations—have helped establish international procedures designed to facilitate international transactions.

The International Monetary Fund (IMF) was established in 1944 at Bretton Woods, N.H., as a formal mechanism to ease the problems of disequilibrium in the balance of payments of states, to facilitate payments adjustments and exchange-rate stability, and, more generally, to insure international monetary cooperation and the expansion of trade. Since its beginnings its functions and actions have evolved considerably, in response to new problems and the demands of new members. To help individual member states restore their balance-of-payments equilibrium and resist the attacks of speculators on their currencies, the IMF allows members to draw upon the resources of reserve currencies of the Fund (which come from mandatory quotas provided by member states) to meet their international debts. As countries have sought to increase their borrowing from the Fund, the IMF has had the opportunity to insist, where appropriate, that certain domestic economic measures be introduced to alleviate what the IMF views to be structural causes of a state's persistent deficit condition. Time has shown, though, that the initial mechanisms established by the Fund were inadequate to resolve the problem of payments imbalances. "Stand-by arrangements" were established for the precautionary use of states that fear possible balance-of-payments problems. Also developed were special facilities available to developing countries facing payments difficulties as a result of short-term declines in earnings from the export sale of primary commodities. In order to aid key currency states, "General Agreements to Borrow" were arranged in the early 1960s that provided for the loaning of reserves to those major states suffering from short-term currency problems.

As a result of the shortage of international reserves to finance expanded international economic transactions, as well as the increased pressure on the balance of payments of some member states, the IMF in 1969 agreed to create Special Drawing Rights (SDRs). SDRs represent the creation of an international reserve currency by an international organization in pursuit of a more stable and smoothly running international monetary order. This newly created currency avoided the problem of shortages of gold as a reserve currency (there just is not enough gold mined to keep up with currency demand and private uses of gold). It also allowed the creation of a new international asset that serves the function formerly served by gold, but that is not at the same time a national currency, such as American dollars—thus avoiding a link between international liquidity and the political and economic health of a particular state.[3]

These and other provisions adopted by the IMF are conducted within a general framework of commitment to monetary cooperation among member states. Exchange rates were to be fixed largely under the aegis of the IMF, and a major unilateral devaluation of a state's currency could occur only where persistent and chronic balance-of-payments deficits seemed to exist for basic structural reasons, and even then only with IMF approval. This regulation both made trading conditions more certain and inhibited the use of exchange-rate fluctuation as a means to enhance a state's trading position. In addition, the IMF urged states to abandon various impediments to currency exchanges, which have the effect of hindering trade among countries.

Outside the IMF, cooperative efforts have been mounted within various regional groupings of states or on some other bilateral or multilateral basis. For example, the 1961 Basel Agreements and the "swap arrangements" concluded by the Federal Reserve Bank of New York have established mechanisms by which some of the advanced industrial states can come to the aid of the hard-pressed American dollar and the British pound in currency emergencies.

In 1975, in response to the need to recycle petrodollars—the massive earnings achieved by the oil-exporting states from the increased price of oil—a formal IMF plan was created, and an agreement between ten industrialized states was made to aid countries facing severe balance-of-

---

[3] Of course, SDRs by no means represent a panacea for all the monetary ills of the world. Indeed, there is substantial concern that SDRs may be used to finance further the balance-of-payments deficits of states, thereby postponing the need to correct the situation.

payments problems caused by the increased costs of importing oil. The IMF established a $6.2-billion fund available to all of its members having difficulties financing their purchases of oil; at the same time, the ten industrialized nations created a $25-billion "safety-net" fund for the use of members of the Organization for Economic Cooperation and Development (OECD). These developments illustrate the varied nature of the attempts to manage international monetary problems.

Other agreements have been made, but in this brief discussion we do not seek to examine the total array of devices designed to manage the international monetary system more effectively. Of course, the IMF is a far more complicated institution than we have suggested here. Moreover, the Fund has not always been successful in obtaining its objectives, nor has it always received full cooperation from its member states: many states jealously guard their control over their own monetary affairs. However, our brief consideration of the IMF shows that states have indeed joined together to try to impose order on their international monetary relations. The development of SDRs is an attempt by states to develop a specifically international mechanism to supplement (and eventually replace, some suggest) the national currencies that have served an international function.

However, the governmental efforts referred to above have not satisfactorily accommodated the needs of private parties actively engaged in international economic transactions. Consequently, a number of private, as opposed to governmental, arrangements have been established to facilitate their activities. As trade, and particularly production and sales, have expanded internationally, banks and other financial institutions have developed an international character in order to provide many of the financial services necessary to facilitate monetary transactions on an international level.

A nongovernmental development of particular interest is the emergence and expansion of Eurodollars and Eurobond markets. Essentially, Eurodollars are deposits of American dollars in foreign banks; these deposits have become the basis for short-term loans to individuals, corporations, banks, and even governments elsewhere in the world.[4] In other words, these deposits have become another form of international currency, in that they support extensive short-term lending and borrowing. The rapid expansion of the Eurodollar market during the 1960s indicated that there was real need for an international money market that was not supplied by the formal and official arrangements of states. The interesting point is that the Eurodollar market emerged out of a felt need

---

[4] The Eurobond market is quite similar, except that long-term securities are bought and sold.

in a rather ad hoc and private fashion. It was not created nor is it regulated by any single state nor by collections of finance ministers from the leading industrial states. It is instead an ad hoc, private, and workable response to the necessities of financing expanded international transactions by various private entities.

The preceding discussion constitutes a brief overview of some general characteristics of the international monetary order following World War II. Now, some of the political implications of global monetary relations can be examined. Of particular interest are the strains that have produced a collapse of the Bretton Woods system and that must be dealt with in the new monetary order now in the making.

THE CHANGING ROLE OF THE DOLLAR

The changing role of the American dollar in the post–World War II period is the key to the collapse of the Bretton Woods monetary order. It is also a logical place to begin an analysis of the linkage between economics and politics in monetary matters. The war devastated the economies of the European countries and also destroyed many of the prewar international and regional economic arrangements, which had been based on the economic and political strength of these states. In contrast, the economy of the United States, immune from the destruction of the war, was stimulated by the need to supply its allies during the war and by the pent-up economic demands of a country trying to catch up after a decade of depression and five years of sacrifice for war. Internationally, the United States emerged with the strongest economy—the only one with the capacity to contribute on a large scale to the massive reconstruction effort in Europe and Japan. American aid programs, such as the Marshall Plan, provided the financing that enabled the Europeans to purchase large amounts of goods that only the United States could produce in sufficient supply at that time. As a result, the American economy played a critical role in Europe's reconstruction, and the American dollar became the major medium of exchange for purchasing American products and for buying goods from other countries as well.

Thus, the dollar emerged as the key international currency in a world that did not have enough gold to finance the desired level of economic transactions. Moreover, most countries experienced a severe shortage of gold holdings as a reserve currency since the United States had an embarrassingly large percentage of the world's total gold currency supply—73 percent in 1940, 63 percent in 1945, and 68 percent in 1950. Because of this gold shortage, the dollar became not only a transaction currency but also a reserve currency. In other words, it became as good as gold in the international monetary order in that it could purchase goods and services around the world and could also serve as an asset to settle accounts among states. In addition, the United States, with European encouragement, was anxious to help finance the reconstruction of Europe by running persistent balance-of-payments deficits with European states. All of these developments, coupled with the obvious international political importance of the United States, fostered the emergence of the dollar as the dominant international currency.

A number of important political and economic advantages accrued to the United States as a result of the postwar role of the dollar. As the dollar was the major international currency, a seemingly limitless amount of dollars were accepted throughout the world as payment for goods, services, investments, and military support, for the dollar was as good as gold. American business interests could readily establish new investments in foreign countries or buy existing enterprises. Similarly, the international stature of the dollar enabled corporations and individuals to purchase large amounts of goods abroad. The acceptability and widespread use of the dollar made it easy for Americans to travel all over the world with few limits on the amount of dollars that could be spent for such pleasure or for profits. Thus, an extensive private American presence abroad was promoted by the international importance of the dollar.

The United States government was also able to engage in a massive number of costly international activities. The international role of the dollar facilitated sizable foreign aid efforts, extensive military grants to unstable or threatened countries, and support for a widespread and expensive American military presence in many areas of the world. Because of its medium-of-exchange role, the dollar was an acceptable way to finance such activities. Moreover, because of its reserve-currency role, foreign governments were at first delighted and then, in the 1950s and 1960s, willing to accept large amounts of dollars *without* demanding convertibility into gold. Since the dollar was acceptable as a reserve currency, substantial amounts of unexchanged dollars began to pile up in the central banks of various countries.

No other country had the luxury of being able to act essentially as the world's banker. All other states had to try to balance the inflow and outflow of currencies and had to operate their domestic and foreign economic and political policies within the constraints of limited finances. Essentially, the United States obtained the benefits of operating internationally without incurring the domestic and international monetary costs of doing so. Then too, the economic and political importance of the United States and the dollar in the world arena meant that developments within the United States, as well as conscious governmental policies, had significant implications for world monetary affairs and for monetary systems in other countries. Thus, through the pervasiveness of the dollar the United States was able to exert influence on the political and economic affairs of most other states.

The international system characterized by the almost unchallenged dominance of the United States dollar was not to last indefinitely. The dollar shortage ended in the late 1950s and became a dollar glut in the 1960s and early 1970s. As this occurred, acceptance of and reliance upon the dollar standard declined for a number of important reasons.

First, the United States continued to exhibit serious and growing balance-of-payments deficits long after such deficits were needed to help finance the reconstruction of Europe. Naturally, this caused some alarm among American officials, but it was equally disconcerting to the economic officials of other countries whose central banks held sizable amounts of dollars as reserves. If the dollar were to be devalued, a step often taken by countries with chronic balance-of-payments deficits, then these huge reserves of dollars held by other countries would be worth less.

Second, with the resurgence of an economically healthy Europe as well as a more united Europe in the form of the European Economic Community, the earlier need to accept the leadership of the United States in political and economic matters decreased. Charles de Gaulle, always a vigorous advocate of the independence of France and Europe from the United States, challenged the supremacy of the dollar. He was no longer willing to accept the United States as the political and security spokesman of the West, or as the world's banker with all the attendant advantages of that position. He also was unwilling to allow free and unfettered movement of American capital in search of foreign investment. Instead, he insisted that the United States act in a financially responsible fashion, as other countries had to do. Consequently, France would not hold American dollars as a reserve currency, demanding instead that dollars be exchanged for gold. De Gaulle perceived that the role of the dollar added greatly to the political and economic strength of the United States. To undermine that strength, he sought to reduce the international position of the dollar.

De Gaulle passed from the political scene before achieving his objectives, but the immense international economic and political costs of America's involvement in Vietnam, its continuing balance-of-payments deficit, the economic and political instabilities evident within the United States during the 1960s, and the new economic vitality of Europe all combined to raise fundamental questions about the strength of the dollar and the capacity of American leadership. Many European countries, disagreeing strongly with American policy in Southeast Asia and

America's approach to Western relations with the Soviet Union and China, no longer desired to finance the United States balance-of-payments deficit by holding dollars. To do so would in essence be to underwrite United States foreign policies of which they disapproved, as well as to support other American public and private international actions, some of which were well beyond America's capacity to pay for them. By refusing to hold dollars, these countries were forcing the United States to shoulder fully the costs associated with these extensive public and private actions. This erosion of America's international political and economic position led to repeated dollar crises in the early 1970s, which included massive speculation against the dollar. The pressures mounted; finally, the dollar was devalued twice in fifteen months (December, 1971 and February, 1973). The dollar's convertibility with gold was suspended. This signaled the end of the postwar monetary order that began at Bretton Woods. The nature of its replacement is unclear.

This description of the changing role of the dollar illustrates a number of important points regarding the linkage between politics and economics in international monetary affairs. The political and economic advantages enjoyed by the United States as a "Top Currency" state, in Susan Strange's terms, have already been discussed.[5] However, there are a number of disadvantages of being a state whose world economic ties and leadership extend beyond its direct political control and influence. These disadvantages are the result of the widespread claims upon the Top Currency—in this case, the dollar—as an international medium of exchange and as a reserve asset.

The United States, as a consequence of the dollar's role as the Top Currency, was particularly vulnerable to economic and financial shocks occurring elsewhere in the world. The expanding international economy that relied heavily upon the dollar as the transaction currency transmitted financial crises to the United States through the dollar. Thus, the domestic economy of the United States felt the effects of developments in other areas of the world more acutely than if the dollar were not a Top Currency, especially since so many dollars were in the hands of foreigners. Domestic political and economic pressures within the United States, as well as a general commitment to the management of the domestic economy, required the American government to try to protect and safeguard its economy from these shocks. This was a difficult task because the international role of the dollar and the vast dollar holdings

---

[5] The following discussion of the dollar as a Top Currency is based on the excellent work of Susan Strange. See her article, "The Politics of International Currencies," *World Politics*, XXIII, No. 2 (January, 1971), 215–31; and her book, *Sterling and British Policy: A Political Study of an International Currency in Decline* (London: Oxford University Press, 1971).

of other states prevented the United States from exercising options such as devaluation of the dollar, options that were available to other states.

Moreover, because of the reliance of other states on the dollar as a reserve currency, as a transaction medium, and as a mechanism for financing growth and development, the United States often found itself unable or unwilling to take financial actions that might injure its allies and dependents. Harming these states in the course of pursuing its national interests was for a long time not a politically acceptable alternative for the United States during the contentious period of the cold war. This partially explains the long-run reluctance of the United States to devalue the dollar. It also explains why, upon devaluation of the dollar as a last resort, President Nixon and Secretary of the Treasury Connally expressed feelings of betrayal and resentment toward the ingratitude of friends and allies who refused to aid the United States after she had been so generous for so long.

Strange also suggests that the Top Currency status of the dollar led inevitably to the expansion of United States foreign investment. Private corporations and individuals were easily able, and often welcome, to purchase existing enterprises or build new concerns in many other countries. However, with this expansion there exists a tendency for the United States, or any Top Currency state, to become concerned about the political stability of the countries in which these investments are located. Thus, in response to its foreign investment abroad a Top Currency state often becomes involved in the domestic economic, social, and political developments of host states and in their international relationships as well.[6] Official United States government involvement in promoting open and safe investment climates for its foreign investors and in exercising pressure on states that have nationalized American firms is evidence of the political implications of foreign investments. It may be that some form of imperialist posture is a concomitant of a Top Currency status for any state, regardless of its internal political and economic system.

Because a Top Currency state perceives a close link between the health of its domestic economy and that of the international economy, such a state is likely to view the promotion of its own welfare as a means to improve the international economy. Thus, its views of what is best for itself tend to be imposed upon other states as being best for the international system. Offense is taken when other states disagree with the policy prescriptions offered by the Top Currency state, and a feeling of self-righteousness and moral imperative is frequently characteristic of the Top Currency state's approach to international economic relations. The

---

[6] See Chapter 4 for a more exhaustive analysis of the political implications of multinational corporations.

political implications of such a posture are obvious, particularly when one recognizes that the geographical range of the Top Currency itself is much wider than that of the state's political influence or control.

The disadvantages encountered by Top Currency states illustrate a more general phenomenon regarding international monetary affairs that affects advanced industrial states. This phenomenon is interdependency, defined by Richard Cooper as "the *sensitivity* of economic transactions between two or more nations to economic developments within those nations."[7] Interdependency describes much more than just the level of international economic interactions between two states or within the international economic system. Indeed, some analysts have suggested that the amount of international economic interactions has actually been declining.[8] Instead, interdependency reflects a pervasive economic and political interpenetration among different societies. The impact of international economic transactions extends well beyond the official level of exchanges, for certain domestic groups perceive that their interests are fundamentally affected by the nature of these interactions. Thus, there are exhibited within portions of the society deep-seated concern about and an acute sense of vulnerability to developments in international economic relations. Just as the radicals suggest that developing countries are highly sensitive to global economic developments over which they have no control, the notion of interdependency implies that advanced states, too, are not immune from these problems, even if they are in a better position to cope with them.

INTERDEPENDENCE AND THE BALANCE OF PAYMENTS

The concept of interdependency and the problems interdependency raises for the United States as a Top Currency country are well illustrated by a more detailed analysis of the American balance of payments. A country's balance of payments is determined by comparing the sum of all payments a country and its residents make to foreigners with the total of all receipts received from foreigners. As has been mentioned, states seek to maintain a balance between the outflow of money and the inflow of money; a balance-of-payments surplus is more desirable than a deficit.

---

[7] "Economic Interdependence and Foreign Policy in the Seventies," *World Politics*, XXIV, No. 2 (January, 1972), 159.

[8] See K. W. Deutsch and A. Eckstein, "National Industrialization and the Declining Share of the International Economic Sector, 1890–1959," *World Politics*, XIII, No. 2 (January, 1961), 267–99; and Kenneth N. Waltz, "The Myth of National Interdependence," in *The International Corporation*, ed. C. P. Kindleberger (Cambridge, Mass.: M.I.T. Press, 1970), pp. 205–23.

To aid us in our discussion of this issue, let us examine a balance-of-payments account for the United States for the year 1970, just before the monetary crises of 1971 and Nixon's "New Economic Policy" in August 1971.[9] By understanding some of the more important entries in this account, we will be better able to highlight some of the domestic and international political and economic conflicts that make it so difficult for a state to overcome a chronic deficit situation. Before beginning, though, let us state once again the basic principle of balance-of-payments accounting: any economic transaction in which money flows from the United States (or any country) to other countries adds to a deficit and is counted as a minus figure; any transaction that involves an inflow of money from other countries contributes to a surplus and is counted as a plus figure.

The merchandise trade balance (the difference between imports and exports of goods) is one of the major components of the balance-of-payments account. Table 3-1 shows that in 1970 the United States exported to other countries goods and services worth $2.1 billion more than the goods and services it imported, continuing a positive trade balance that had been enjoyed by the United States for many years.[10] The next major entry is a net deficit in travel and transportation. In addition to the payment of shipping charges to foreign ocean carriers, the $1.9-billion deficit indicates the extensive travel abroad by Americans, in comparison with the far fewer number of foreigners traveling in the United States.[11]

The net income from foreign investments is a surplus of $6.2 billion. Income from United States direct foreign investment abroad, essentially multinational corporations, is nearly $8 billion, and income from portfolio investments is $3.5 billion. In comparison with the income foreigners receive from their investments in the United States, the American balance of payments is very well served by foreign investment.

---

[9] The year 1970 has been chosen because it is more or less representative of the balance-of-payments issues facing the United States. The year 1971 was disastrous for the American balance of payments and, thus, is not at all representative. The years 1972 and 1973 were unsettled, in that new American policies were being tried out and the actions of other states were uncertain. In 1974, the balance-of-payments position of the United States (and of many other countries too) worsened drastically because of the huge increases in the cost of importing petroleum. Thus, through 1974, 1970 seems to be the last normal and reasonable year to examine the American balance of payments.

[10] Depending upon the set of figures used, the last year in which the United States had a merchandise trade deficit was either 1935 or 1888. However, the situation changed dramatically in 1971 and 1972, when the United States merchandise trade deficits were $2.7 billion and $6.9 billion, respectively. In 1973 the United States enjoyed a $471 million surplus, but in 1974 it incurred a huge trade deficit of $5.8 billion.

[11] Note how the Top-Currency status of the dollar and its resulting widespread acceptability makes it much easier for Americans to travel abroad for pleasure or profit.

TABLE 3-1.   Elements of the United States Basic Balance of Payments, 1970 (Seasonally Adjusted, Millions of Dollars)

Merchandise trade balance	2,110	
Exports		41,980
Imports		−39,870
Other services, net	588	
Travel and transportation, net	−1,979	
Investment income, net	6,242	
U.S. direct investments abroad		7,906
Other U.S. investments abroad		3,503
Foreign investments in the U.S.		−5,167
Remittances, pensions, and other transfers	−1,410	
Military transactions, net	−3,371	
U.S. Government grants (excluding military)	−1,739	
U.S. Government capital flows (excluding nonscheduled repayments), net	−1,837	
Nonscheduled repayments, of U.S. Government assets	244	
U.S. Government nonliquid liabilities to other than foreign official reserve agencies	−436	
Long-term private capital flows, net	−1,453	
U.S. direct investments abroad		−4,445
Foreign direct investments in the U.S.		969
Foreign securities		−942
U.S. securities other than treasury issues		2,190
Other, reported by U.S. banks		199
Other, reported by U.S. nonbanking concerns		576
BALANCE ON CURRENT ACCOUNT AND LONG-TERM CAPITAL	−3,038	

Source: This table is reprinted with slight modifications from David P. Calleo and Benjamin M. Rowland, *America and the World Political Economy* (Bloomington, Ind.: Indiana University Press, 1973), p. 97. By permission of the publisher.

Remittances, pensions, and other transfers refer to monies paid to residents of foreign countries by the United States government, private organizations, and individuals. Retirement or disability pensions, insurance payments to beneficiaries, and gifts from United States residents or organizations all contribute to this deficit figure in the balance of payments.

The next several entries in the balance-of-payments account reflect the important role of the United States government in international economic transactions. The military transactions category reports the costs incurred by the United States in maintaining its extensive military presence abroad, including Vietnam and Europe, as well as military aid programs, *minus* the large purchases of American-made military materiel by other countries. As shown in Table 3-1, the net figure is a deficit of

$3.3 billion. Similarly, United States government grants to other countries, primarily in the form of foreign aid (but excluding military aid), produces a negative figure of $1.7 billion. The United States government capital-flow entry records essentially the costs of maintaining an extensive foreign diplomatic and cultural presence in other countries, including such things as embassies, commercial offices, libraries, and cultural programs. The two remaining governmental entries are too technical for us to consider here, but it should be noted that overall official United States government transactions add up to a deficit of more than $7.1 billion.

The final category to be considered is long-term private capital flows. The net figure is an outflow of $1.4 billion, the major component being the large expenditures of money ($4.4 billion) by American multinational corporations for the purpose of purchasing direct investments elsewhere in the world. Another negative figure is that resulting from the purchase of foreign stocks and securities by United States residents. It is important to note that in 1970, foreign interests bought $2.1 billion worth of stocks and securities in the United States and foreign corporations made direct investments of $.9 billion. These investments partially offset the long-term capital expenditures by United States residents and multinational corporations.

Although Table 3-1 is not the complete balance-of-payments account for 1970, it does present the major components of the balance on current account and long-term capital.[12] As you can see, in 1970 there was a deficit of $3.038 billion. Deficits in selected previous years were $1.188 billion (1960), $1.804 billion (1965), $1.411 billion (1968), and $3.046 billion in 1969. The deficit in 1971 was an astounding and disturbing $9.550 billion; in 1972 it was $9.843. The situation improved in 1973 (a deficit of $1.026 billion), but in 1974 the deficit climbed to $10.580 billion. (These figures should be viewed in the light of the official gold reserves of $10.206 billion held by the United States in 1971.) It is no wonder, then, that many officials in Europe, in the IMF, and in the United States viewed with alarm the huge and chronic American balance-of-payments deficits in the early 1970s. As the dollar is a major

---

12 There are many different ways of setting up a balance-of-payments account, but the decision to examine the balance on current account and long-term capital enables the reader to focus on the major factors contributing to a deficit without being encumbered by the more technical entries involving short-term flows of funds, errors and omissions, and others. The category of short-term flows reflects investment of short-term funds and tends to be highly responsive to slight differences in interest rates in different countries. For the most part, over the last decade or so the tendency has been for more funds to flow out of the United States than to come in. This, of course, contributes to a deficit. The errors and omissions category is essentially a catchall and has been primarily a negative figure; in 1970 it contributed $1.1 billion to the deficit.

transaction currency and an important reserve currency, these deficits have not inspired confidence in the dollar or in the ability of the United States to manage this critical international currency.

Of course, many other states have had serious balance-of-payments deficit situations, and the dramatically higher costs of oil have created problems for countries such as Japan, which in the past have had payments surpluses. To reduce or reverse a chronic deficit, a state must choose among several different strategies, each of which involves significant domestic or international political and economic costs. Moreover, we must remember that reducing or eliminating one state's deficit can occur only as a result of increasing the deficit or reducing the surplus of some other country or countries. Consequently, the zero-sum game characteristic of balance-of-payments accounting means that one state's gain is another state's or other states' loss. Therefore, correcting a deficit is acceptable to other states as long as such efforts do not have a seriously adverse effect on their balance-of-payments situation. This fear of an increase in neo-mercantilist policies, as discussed in Chapter 2, in response to the increased costs of purchasing oil has led the IMF and smaller groups of states to develop measures designed to obviate the necessity of "beggar thy neighbor" policies.

Internal Measures to Correct
Balance-of-Payments Deficits

Surplus countries most often recommend that chronic deficit countries undertake domestic reforms to curtail the imbalance, implying that the deficit country is primarily at fault and that surplus states have no responsibility for the condition or for the cure. Internal measures, though, are effective only at the sacrifice of some other set of values and objectives important to large elements of society or to the state as a whole. Some of these internal mechanisms to reduce a balance-of-payments deficit, and their political implications, will be examined in the context of the situation faced by the United States in 1970.

One means of correcting a deficit situation is to increase exports and reduce imports. An internal mechanism for doing this involves deflating the economy. A deflationary policy generally results in a slowdown in growth, greater unemployment, and a stabilization or reduction in wages and prices. This has the effect of lowering the demand for imports; at the same time, exports become cheaper and more attractive to foreigners as the cost of labor and of other domestic factors of production are reduced. In the United States and in most other advanced industrial states with strong commitments to economic growth, an increasing standard of living, and full employment, deflationary policies for balance-of-payments purposes are not at all popular politically. By enacting such measures, a government risks severe opposition from trade unions whose members are out of work and from businesses who find it difficult to operate in a stagnant or declining economy. Consequently, a deflationary policy, which attempts to increase exports and reduce imports, has severe impacts on the entire economy and on other aspects of the balance of payments as well. As a result powerful political pressure groups, representing many types of interests that suffer generally from the effects of a slower economy, will seek to prohibit the adoption of deflationary measures.

Alternatively, the United States could seek to reduce its citizens' foreign travel by imposing limits on the amount of dollars that can be exchanged for foreign currencies. This strategy has frequently been adopted by other deficit countries, but such an action by the American government would run counter to the strongly held belief that a truly democratic system must not abridge the right to travel. Students, academic researchers, executives of multinational corporations, and the many individuals who have saved for trips abroad would undoubtedly raise a political fuss over such an effort. Moreover, other countries, such as Canada, Mexico, and a number of European countries that are quite dependent upon the American tourist dollar, would be seriously harmed by, and would therefore protest, such a policy.

We have noted the sizable role of the United States government in international transactions that have led to a deficit in the American balance of payments. Here also, efforts to drastically reduce American expenditures will provoke protests, both within the United States and abroad. The net outflow of dollars for military expenditures incorporates many programs whose worth depends very much upon one's objectives and values. However, there is widespread belief at home and abroad that these expenditures are justified by the need to maintain the national security of the United States and its allies. The erosion of American presence abroad necessitated by a reduction of foreign military expenditures would be criticized strongly by many Americans and by many allies. In addition, allies purchase many supplies from the United States as a result of military commitments, thereby providing jobs for thousands of Americans.

American military forces stationed in Europe and elsewhere not only act as a first line of defense for the United States but also afford protection for its allies. It has often been argued that if the United States reneges on its commitments to an ally anywhere, not only will that state be unwilling to trust the United States, but also other commitments will lose credibility in the eyes of our other allies and adversaries. Although

European countries were very much against American participation in the Vietnam war, they have strongly resisted suggestions by various American senators that American troop strength in Europe be halved or otherwise largely reduced. Yet, in Southeast Asia and Europe the presence of American troops has substantially drained American international reserves.

In sum, attempts to reduce American military expenditures abroad will bring protests from many countries, may reduce American security, may hearten America's adversaries and encourage adventuresomeness by them, and will generally leave the United States a less potent force in the international political arena. In addition, and not to be overlooked, are the many interest groups in the United States and their political representatives, who would object strongly to such reductions. Workers, unions, corporations, and whole geographic regions in this country that are associated with the defense industry would seek to prevent such a policy. The vast military organization and their many well-placed allies would look in dismay at reduced budgets. Many very able political analysts would fear that such reductions for balance-of-payments reasons would be extremely detrimental to American security and to world peace and freedom. None of these groups and their arguments can be dismissed easily, and they do represent important political forces within the United States.

Proponents of radical thought have very different views about the reasons for American military expenditures abroad. Essentially, they argue that the American presence in other countries is designed to protect existing opportunities for investments and exports by American corporations and to create new ones. The question of American national security is rejected by radical critics, whose main emphasis is on the self-aggrandizement of the United States and its business interests. Accepting this view or its variations results even more strongly in the conclusion that there will be exceptionally powerful interests within the United States resisting a reduction in the American military presence abroad.

Foreign economic aid could be reduced, but the proponents of such aid argue that it is a politically necessary expenditure designed to help countries develop themselves and thereby resist the forces of communism. Other advocates of foreign aid talk about the moral obligation to extend such aid to countries far less fortunate than the United States. These groups are greatly disturbed by any decline in American foreign aid. Moreover, much American aid is tied; that is, large amounts of the money granted is returned to the United States in order to purchase goods made in the United States. Thus, aid generates American exports, jobs, and profits. Also, since much of the aid is in the form of loans, the money is ultimately repaid to the United States with interest. In short, the overall economic impact of foreign aid on the American economy is favorable, and the program is an expression of American interest in the development and friendship of poor states.

The United States government capital-flows item in the balance of payments is incurred largely because of the status of the United States as a global power with embassies and consulates all over the world. Elimination of these outflows would imply a retreat into isolationism that many feel would be bad not only for the United States but also for the world. It would be exceptionally difficult for an economic and political power like the United States to withdraw from the world.

Long-term private investment abroad could be restricted in an attempt to reduce the drain on the balance of payments. Indeed, first voluntary and then mandatory restraints were enacted in the last half of the 1960s, but these were eliminated in 1974. However, restricting investments today may reduce the inflow of funds from income earned on these investments in the future. Table 3-1 shows $4.4 billion flowing out to finance direct investments in 1970, but existing investment returned $7.9 billion to the United States during that year. Thus, the figures argue against a policy of restricting direct foreign investment for balance-of-payments purposes. Also, many of the largest and most powerful corporations in the United States are international in scope; certainly, they would, and have, struggled to prevent the adoption of more restrictive investment constraints. Moreover, if the United States sought to reduce its balance-of-payments deficit by having these firms repatriate all profits rather than reinvesting some of them abroad, strong objections would be registered by most host states as well as by the companies.[13]

This discussion by no means exhausts the many internal mechanisms available to the United States as a deficit country to correct a chronic balance-of-payments situation. Additionally, the policies mentioned and the issues raised are far more complex than we have been able to indicate in this chapter. However, the object of the discussion has been to show that any and all of these measures can be adopted only at severe costs to various internal and global interests of the United States. In the United States and other deficit countries, interests that are adversely affected by the imposition of these policies will seek to redress their grievances through intense political activity focused on the administration. In sum, there are no painless internal measures that can be adopted to alleviate a chronic balance-of-payments deficit. Similarly, many internal actions will have unfavorable consequences for other countries and for the international posture of the deficit country. The linkages between international monetary matters, domestic economic groups and therefore

13 See Chapter 4, pp. 110–11.

domestic politics, and international political concerns are illustrated by this brief analysis of the problems associated with internal measures to correct a chronic balance-of-payments deficit.

External Measures to Correct
a Balance-of-Payments Deficit

Unlike internal measures, external methods for adjusting balance-of-payments difficulties place the major economic and political burden on other countries. Again referring to Table 3-1, one area in which external methods are often imposed is the merchandise trade balance of imports and exports. The objective of such efforts is to increase exports and reduce imports, thereby contributing to a surplus through means other than deflation of the deficit state's economy. More specifically, tariffs on goods entering the deficit country, quotas on the amount of various items that may be imported, health, safety, and pollution standards designed to prohibit entry of some goods, and import surcharges—all have the effect of making it more difficult for other countries to sell products to a deficit country. Internally, the cost of such measures may be higher prices for some products that no longer have to compete with less expensive foreign-made goods, a shortage of these goods if domestic manufacturers cannot meet demand, and some unemployment in industries associated with the imported goods. However, the major costs are borne by the countries and firms abroad that find it more difficult to sell in the deficit state. The United States has resorted to another external measure to reduce its imports: prevailing upon other states to adopt "voluntary" export quotas. These quotas are voluntary only in the sense that the United States has not unilaterally restricted these countries' exports. However, the distinction is for political and symbolic purposes; the effect is the same as it would be if the quotas were imposed by the United States. The most notable voluntary export quotas have been in the area of textiles, but other products, such as mushrooms and steel, have also been subject to them. Some states, such as Japan, usually accede to American demands because of the intense political and economic pressure applied by both the executive and legislative branches of the United States government. The implied threat is that if the voluntary quotas are not undertaken, the United States might have to act in a more drastic fashion to bring about desired changes.

A state with a balance-of-payments deficit also seeks to increase exports. Direct subsidies to exporters and relief from various tax payments on exported goods are two measures frequently used by states to make their products more competitive in the international market, and thereby to increase their exports. Many European states waive taxes on goods that are exported, and the United States has urged companies to establish domestic international-sales corporations, which are designed to provide tax advantages to exporters. In addition, many countries offer government financing and credit programs for the purpose of making their exports more easily obtainable. The United States has even resorted to direct political leverage to force West Germany, Japan, and other countries to purchase specified amounts of military hardware, agricultural products, or manufactured goods in order to offset a United States balance-of-payments deficit with them. In all of these cases, the costs of correcting the deficit are passed on to other countries.

Another external measure that may be pursued by a deficit country is to vary the exchange rates of either the deficit country or the surplus countries. More specifically, the devaluation of the dollar, as was done by the United States in 1971 and 1973, meant that the dollar was worth less in all international transactions. Therefore, imports from other countries were more expensive after the dollar was devalued; similarly, exports from the United States were less expensive for foreigners to purchase. A devaluation of the currency of a deficit country will make that country more competitive in the international economy, but at the expense of the competitiveness of other states. If the damage to the position of other countries is too great, some of them may also devalue their currencies, thereby removing the advantage gained by the initiating state. Indeed, many analysts and policy makers fear the widespread use of exchange-rate devaluations by states to gain competitive advantages in international trade because such devaluations can disrupt the international monetary order and the global economy. States frequently try to avoid a currency devaluation since it implies economic weakness and a loss of international prestige. As we pointed out earlier, the IMF is specifically charged with preventing the outbreak of currency warfare of this sort. For example, as a result of the damage done to the balance of payments of states by the greatly increased costs of importing oil, the IMF has sought to develop measures to obviate the necessity of currency warfare.

Surplus countries may aid deficit countries by revaluing their currencies upward. Where it is felt that a currency is undervalued relative to other currencies, it may make some sense to raise the value of the currency, thereby also making the state somewhat less competitive. Generally, surplus states are reluctant to take this step, for in doing so they become less competitive for the sake of those countries that, for a variety of internal and external reasons, are not able to control their payments deficits. As a deficit country, the United States pressured Germany and Japan as surplus countries to revalue the mark and yen and thereby ease the American deficit. To Germany and Japan, it looked as though the

United States was seeking to have these states bear the burden of its domestic and international economic mismanagement. From the United States point of view, it was only "right" that these countries help the United States because they had both benefited from the costly military defense posture of the United States in Europe and Japan. Also, the Japanese economy had recovered primarily because of the privileged access to American markets enjoyed by Japanese goods. The point is that official currency fluctuation benefits one set of states, but always at the expense of some others. The potential for disagreement and political conflict is apparent. Moreover, disagreement over whether devaluation or revaluation should occur is fostered by the different impact of such measures on various states. Only a minor portion of American economic activity is involved in international commerce—less than 10 percent— but Japan and many European countries depend heavily upon imports and exports. Consequently, exchange-rate changes will have a much greater effect on them than on the United States.

External measures, then, characteristically place the major political and economic burden on states other than the deficit country employing them. To the extent that such activities seriously injure a target state of these actions, the political relations between the states are likely to be strained. The many efforts of the United States to pass the costs of correcting its chronic deficit to other countries has raised a number of disputes with Europe and Japan. The United States has mounted political and economic threats and pressure to convince these states to accept the costs of correcting the American deficit. American threats to reduce or pull out its troops in Europe have been used to extract concessions from European allies regarding American balance-of-payments problems. At the same time, Japan and the European countries frequently urged the United States to reduce its expenditures abroad (selectively, it might be added) and to dampen its economy in order to achieve a balance-of-payments surplus. Of course, it is important to remember that behind these international disputes are numerous domestic economic groups in each country that are, to varying degrees, harmed or helped by the particular set of measures adopted. Thus, they seek to advance their particular interests by attempting to influence the political decision makers to adopt favorable policies.

The Use of Reserves to Finance a Balance-of-Payments Deficit

A third way of responding to chronic balance-of-payments deficits is to finance the deficit (not all transactions) by paying to claimant countries and their central banks gold or other foreign exchange reserves that are acceptable for such payments. This method may be appropriate if a state has very large reserves relative to its import requirements and if it is experiencing only a temporary deficit. But gold or other reserves may be reduced to a dangerous low point if the deficit is chronic. For example, the dramatic increase in the costs of importing oil for Japan resulted in a decline of its official reserves of gold and foreign currencies from $19 billion in February, 1973 to $12 billion in March, 1974. Since Japan's oil bill is $9 billion higher than it was prior to the new-found strength of the Organization of Petroleum Exporting Countries (OPEC), Japan will be unable to continue to finance its oil imports with its reserves. This explains why the IMF and its member countries have sought to establish procedures to provide emergency reserves to deficit countries through SDRs, swap agreements, and other measures mentioned earlier. However, the financing of deficits will bring relief only if the problems are temporary.

Conclusion

A state attempting to correct its balance-of-payments deficit will probably adopt some mixture of the three types of strategies discussed above. Relying solely upon internal measures will place the cost primarily on the domestic economy and thus stimulate political reactions among domestic groups. Conversely, adopting a strategy of only external measures will require other countries to assume the costs, and their response is likely to be retaliatory to some extent. Financing measures can be pursued only at the cost of draining precious reserves or relying upon international financing, which may not be available or may be granted only with the acceptance of some domestic modifications required by the lending agency. Recognizing the costs associated with each set of policies, many states attempt to develop a mix of measures, which, by spreading the costs between internal groups and other countries, will forestall or prevent severe reactions from any quarter. Regardless of the alternative selected, however, it is apparent that corrections of a state's balance-of-payments position do not entail merely technical questions. They inevitably raise profound political questions involving the role of government in society, the pocketbooks of all citizens, and the role of that state in the international political economy.

Balance-of-payments matters dramatically reveal the links between domestic economic and political interests and international economic and political relations. Complicating the problem and reducing the autonomy of the state to control its own affairs is the great number of private international transactions that are largely beyond the control of the individual state. The sizable liquid assets in the hands of banks, multinational corporations, and wealthy individuals such as the oil sheiks can be moved with relative ease across borders and through private channels, thereby escaping the jurisdiction of states and playing havoc with domestic and international economic policies. These private economic transactions reduce the autonomy of a state to achieve desired objectives. The state enjoys economic sovereignty in being able to pursue various policies, but its ability to insure the effectiveness of these policies is compromised by the existence and size of the private transactions.

The autonomy of the individual state is also reduced by the expansion of interdependence, referred to earlier in this chapter. Interdependence among states, particularly advanced industrial states, has meant that state policy makers have had to cope with an increasing number of disturbances originating in other states or in the international economic system, disturbances that affect domestic economic concerns. For example, West German efforts to reduce rising inflation in the early 1970s were obstructed by the strong demand for German products in other countries and by the actions of currency speculators who found the German mark to be a very attractive currency. Thus, the state and its domestic economy is no longer isolated from events that occur elsewhere. Moreover, a state's efforts to manage its economy will be hindered or at least slowed if other states adopt counter-policies to protect their own interests. Interdependence also means that competitive struggles by two states in the economic realm may well have the effect of spilling over into the broader international arena, causing widespread harm to many states and, more generally, to the international order.

DEVELOPING STATES AND MONETARY RELATIONS

Thus far, we have examined the nature of international monetary problems and their relationships to domestic and international politics by focusing on advanced industrial states, particularly the United States. Developing countries encounter a number of particularly severe difficulties in their attempts to interact with and adapt to the international monetary order. Before examining these issues, though, we need to consider briefly how the monetary problems of the advanced industrial states adversely affect the developing countries. Center-state concerns about balance-of-payments deficits frequently result in policies that are detrimental to the interests of developing countries. To reduce a deficit, advanced industrial states may seek to erect any of the barriers against the import of goods from other countries discussed above. The burden of such an action falls heavily on the developing countries since they often depend upon the export of a few products. The 10 percent American surcharge referred to earlier was particularly harmful to less-developed countries that relied upon exports to the United States for much of their foreign currency needs. Moreover, as we examined in Chapter 2, tariffs or quotas on semimanufactured goods, which often compete with economically marginal but politically powerful industries in advanced states, inhibit less-developed countries' diversification and industrialization efforts. Both the textile and the shoe industries in the United States have actively sought and received some protection from foreign competition.

Other center-state policies might involve the establishment of restrictions on capital outflows for investment purposes. To the extent that a less-developed country desires such capital to further industrialization, to tap natural resources, or to obtain needed capital and technology, it will perceive these restrictions as harmful. Similarly, balance-of-payments problems in center states may lead these states to reduce foreign aid expenditures or to require that such funds be used to purchase goods from the donor country; either strategy is at the expense of the needs of the developing countries. As we will discuss in Chapter 5, the United States foreign aid program has declined steadily in recent years for a variety of reasons, including balance-of-payments deficits. Thus, in trying to correct balance-of-payments deficits advanced industrial states may adopt policies that are detrimental to the interests of the developing countries. There are few remedies for these states, since they are often innocent bystanders to conflicts among and within the advanced industrial states. Moreover, the developing countries, singly and as a whole, seldom have the opportunity or the ability to influence the policies of the rich states.

Balance-of-payments adjustment problems and liquidity concerns are as important to the developing countries as they are to center states. However, the less-developed countries are confronted with a number of special problems. Less-developed states attempting to industrialize have a great need for imports of capital and consumer goods that their domestic economies are unable to produce in sufficient quantity. Consequently, in order to satisfy this persistent demand, developing countries must have sufficient amounts of international currency to pay the large import bill. Few of the developing countries, though, have enough reserves to finance these purchases. Moreover, most of these countries have chronic balance-of-payments deficits that are caused largely by their excess of imports over exports.

This problem has been greatly exacerbated by the phenomenal rise in the cost of importing petroleum and by the more modest increases in the prices of other critical natural resources. Some less-developed countries—the oil-producing states, for example—derive great benefit from

TABLE 3-2.   Oil Price Rise Impact for Selected Developing Countries
(In Millions of American Dollars)

		India	Pakistan	Korea	Morocco	Uruguay	Brazil
Estimated oil import bill	1973	415	85	327	80	60	540
	1974	1350	260	1075	215	160	1425
Increased costs of oil imports over the period 1973–74		935	175	748	135	100	885
Total reserves estimated for 1974		1320	458	1094	315	219	6505

Source: *Business International,* March 22, 1974, p. 90.

these developments, but a large number of other developing countries are
faced with huge increases in their oil import bill and with no obvious
way to pay for it. Table 3-2 indicates that the estimated oil import bill
for some developing countries in 1974 is nearly as large or larger than
their holdings of reserve currencies. Few developing countries are as
fortunate as Brazil in this regard; furthermore, not many enjoy the
export successes that Brazil has achieved to offset the higher oil costs.

The range of options to correct the balance-of-payments problems
of the developing countries is limited for a number of reasons. Many of
these countries have undertaken several different types of internal
mechanisms to control their outflow of funds. Deflationary policies to
reduce imports are not at all popular, particularly because of the tendency toward widespread underemployment and unemployment in many
less-developed countries. Exchange controls that restrict foreign travel
and some imports from other countries have been initiated, yet modernization and development require sizable imports of capital and consumer
goods. Moreover, developing countries' efforts to restrict the repatriation
of profits from foreign affiliates to parent firms will certainly be protested
by the foreign investors, and in some cases by their parent governments.[14]
Such an action might also cause foreign investors to hesitate investing
under such conditions; an important source of capital is thereby dried
up. Thus, many less-developed countries have already enacted internal
mechanisms to reduce the size of their payments deficits, and the options
they have not attempted tend to be very unpopular politically. The
policies they have undertaken have rarely been sufficient to cure the
problem.

External measures, including efforts to increase exports in order to

14 See Chapter 4, pp. 110–11.

cover the high import requirements, encounter a number of structural problems. As we discussed in the previous chapter, dependence upon the export of primary products has resulted in a basic decline in the terms of trade for developing countries. The costs of capital goods and other industrial imports have risen more rapidly than the income earned by these countries from the export of most primary commodities. Moreover, dependence upon such exports increases the susceptibility to wide fluctuations in foreign exchange earnings, since slight variations in the world market price for a commodity will have very large effects on the amount of international currency earned through its export.

In addition, as we discussed in Chapter 2, the advanced industrial states have erected a number of trade barriers designed to protect domestic industries and employment and to maintain a favorable balance of payments by discriminating against semimanufactured and semiprocessed goods from the developing countries. Such policies tend to reinforce the less-developed countries' dependence on the production and export of primary commodities and to discourage their attempts to develop an export-oriented manufacturing industry.

Currency devaluation is often an inappropriate mechanism too, for its effect is to reduce the income received from exports and greatly increase the costs of imports. Since imports are crucial for development, a poor state that devalues its currency is as likely to produce a higher import bill as to reduce imports. Also, most primary commodities (the chief exports of poor states) exhibit a demand inelasticity; that is, lower prices made available to foreign consumers by means of devaluation will not lead to an increased volume of purchases. For example, the demand for coffee is not likely to increase much if the price drops. As a result, currency devaluation often is not a useful strategy for a less-developed state to adopt for the purpose of correcting a balance-of-payments deficit.

With the path to increased exports essentially blocked by their own developing status as well as by the actions of advanced states and by insufficient reserves of international currency, the fundamental question is how developing countries can obtain the money to purchase needed imports and to finance the resulting balance-of-payments deficit. Some form of borrowing from international or regional lending institutions, whether private or governmental, must frequently be resorted to in order to provide the necessary international financing. However, there are some critical problems regarding developing countries' access to international financial help that need to be examined.

The International Monetary Fund is the most important international lending agency for the purpose of financing balance-of-payments deficits. From the less-developed countries' point of view, though, the IMF (like GATT) is an organization that responds primarily to the interests of advanced industrial states. The advanced capitalist countries have about three fourths of the quotas (the basis upon which loans can be made) and about two thirds of the votes. In addition, many of the IMF procedures and arrangements are concerned primarily with the problems of advanced industrial states. For example, the SDRs, which are designed to increase world liquidity, are allocated according to a formula based on the quotas of member states—an arrangement that places most new liquidity in the hands of rich states.

In addition, the Group of Ten—operating under the auspices of the Organization for Economic Cooperation and Development and including only the most advanced industrial states—performed a kind of executive function for the entire international monetary order, including the IMF. International monetary policy and discussions for monetary reform were debated and formulated by this group of highly unrepresentative states. Since the less-developed countries were excluded from this small group, and because they felt that their concerns were largely ignored, they sought to achieve some representation in the directing of international monetary relations. As a result of this pressure, combined with a conflict among the advanced states over monetary relations following the dollar devaluation, the Group of Ten was disbanded in 1972 in favor of the creation of a Group of Twenty under IMF auspices with important participation by less-developed countries. However, there is evidence that ad hoc consultation and cooperation regarding international monetary affairs still takes place in the absence of participation by the developing countries. For example, in November, 1973 the finance ministers of Japan, Germany, France, Great Britain, and the United States met secretly to discuss the implications of the Arab oil embargo for the reform of the international monetary system. No representative from developing countries was invited to participate in these sessions. Also, many of the ad hoc arrangements as mentioned on page 48 were created as the result of cooperation among advanced states; little or no input was obtained from the developing countries.

Like any lending institution, the IMF has the right to refuse to help a borrowing country if it determines that the applicant is not a good risk. Moreover, it can require changes in domestic economic policies as a condition for granting loans. As a result of these two factors, the IMF is in a position to shape domestic economic policies of potential borrowing countries. This power is more effective in the case of developing countries than it is with wealthy, powerful, and more independent advanced industrial states. The Chiles and Bolivias are subject to such requirements, but the United States is much less vulnerable to such international meddling.

In addition, it is important to recognize that the IMF is essentially a conservative and capitalist-oriented institution. The board of governors, composed of representatives of all the member states, the executive directors, and the staff primarily embrace a finance minister's approach to monetary issues. Thus, the nature of advice offered by the IMF, as well as the requirements for loans, reflect the conservative market approach of the institution as a whole. The IMF frowns upon perceived "radical" social or economic policies, and it frequently seeks to impose fiscal responsibility upon borrowing states by insisting upon stabilization programs that include domestic anti-inflationary policies, such as reduced government expenditures, devaluation of currency, elimination of exchange controls, and the encouragement of foreign investment. Obviously, a revolutionary regime such as Salvador Allende's Chile found such demands to be contrary to its strongly held ideological beliefs and objectives. Yet to obtain the needed loans of reserve currency, the borrowing state has to accept the requirements of the IMF. Some regimes, like Allende's, refused to accept loans under these terms; they see serious economic collapse as a price worth paying to assert national autonomy and pride.

The willingness of the IMF to impose capitalist policies of fiscal conservativism on borrowing states has led some radical critics to denounce the Fund as a mechanism for imposing capitalism on borrowing countries, thereby insuring the dominance of the advanced market-economy states over the developing countries. The IMF's reliance upon traditional financial advice, its rejection of "radical" or different policies, and its attempt to more closely bind borrowing states to the current system through loans and interest rates are offered as evidence of its complicity with the center states. Harry Magdoff charges that "the very conditions which produce the necessity to borrow money are continuously reimposed by the pressures to pay back the loan and to pay the interest on these loans."[15] Another radical critic of the IMF writes that "IMF missions descend like vultures in the wake of right-wing coups in countries such as Ghana, Indonesia, and Brazil."[16] Moreover, "The discipline imposed by the IMF has often eliminated the need for direct military intervention in order to preserve a climate friendly towards foreign investment."[17]

The influence of the IMF is not limited to its ability to impose conservative policies on developing countries that seek to borrow from the Fund. Equally important, according to radical thought, is the central

---

[15] *The Age of Imperialism* (New York: Monthly Review Press, 1966), p. 98.

[16] Cheryl Payer, "The Perpetuation of Dependence: The IMF and the Third World," *Monthly Review*, XXIII, No. 4 (September, 1971) 37.

[17] Ibid., p. 38.

role the IMF occupies in the entire public and private credit system at the international level. If a deficit developing country seeks to obtain funds from the IMF but refuses the latter's advice or is otherwise denied a loan, then most of the other major sources of credit—including multinational institutions such as the World Bank, regional development organizations, bilateral government-to-government loans, and private sources of credit—also refuse to loan money to that country. The IMF acts somewhat as a central credit agency, then, setting the standard by which other sources of funds may be obtained. The radicals claim that it is no coincidence that President Allende of Chile was unable to find many loans after the IMF rejected his request for funds because of his unwillingness to accept the conditions that the IMF sought to impose. Note, though (the argument continues), that in the wake of the military coup in September, 1973 the IMF did indeed provide funds to a now more pliable Chile, and this was followed by loans from other sources, both public and private. In sum, the IMF is perceived by some to be the linchpin of the entire international monetary and economic order, which is designed to perpetuate capitalism and the subservience of developing states to the advanced industrial states.

Regardless of the veracity of charges made by radical critics of the IMF, it is true that the developing countries have found it difficult to politicize international monetary relations. As we indicated earlier, monetary matters at both the national and international levels have traditionally been placed in the control of ministers of finance, central bankers, and other technical specialists familiar with the complexities of the international monetary order. In the advanced *and* the developing countries, the more politically sensitive officials usually did not have the technical expertise necessary to have much impact on the deliberations of the IMF. For this reason, the less-developed countries have attempted to bring monetary issues to the attention of more responsive and more political institutions, such as the United Nations Conference on Trade and Development (UNCTAD).

One result of this attempt is that UNCTAD has consistently urged the IMF to implement an SDR link proposal. This plan would distribute SDRs primarily to the developing countries so that these countries could increase their monetary assets. Because of the less-developed countries' great need for imports, the newly granted reserves would finance increased purchases from the advanced states; these purchases would in turn contribute to the development objectives of the developing countries. Greater liquidity would be provided in the world monetary system, but instead of SDR reserves sitting more or less idle in rich countries with balance-of-payments surpluses, they would be working to provide needed goods and services in the poor countries, goods and services that would be obtained largely from the rich states.

Notwithstanding this procedure and others, from the perspective of the developing countries, it seems that the international monetary order and its various institutional components are not primarily concerned with or responsive to the problems of the less-developed countries. The great preponderance of international economic transactions involve advanced industrial states; consequently, the difficulties of these states tend to monopolize the efforts of international cooperation and management. As in the area of trade, the less-developed countries appear to be almost peripheral to the large majority of transactions: they are just not deemed to be important unless they control a critical commodity or natural resource, as the oil producers do. If we are correct in this assessment, then the very critical problems faced by most of the developing countries will continue to be neglected by the international monetary order and the advanced industrial states that are attempting to manage it.

ALTERNATIVE SCENARIOS

As we discussed in the beginning of this chapter, three critical issues confront current international monetary relations: balance-of-payments adjustment problems, the adequacy of international reserves to facilitate the increased economic transactions among states, and the establishment and maintenance of confidence in the international monetary order. The seriousness of these problems are heightened by the importance of the dollar in the current monetary system and the present weakened state of the dollar. With the dollar serving as the major transaction currency as well as a major reserve currency, its importance is obvious. However, the United States' difficulties in managing its own balance-of-payments problems, the general instability and vulnerability of exchange rates among advanced industrial states, the greatly increased costs of certain natural resources and commodities, the vast amount of international reserves flowing to the oil-exporting countries, and the increasingly vocal concerns of the less-developed countries have destroyed the postwar international monetary order established at Bretton Woods.

As a result, a number of proposals have been presented to develop an international monetary order that will be responsive to the liquidity needs of an expanding international economy but that is not as vulnerable as the monetary order that preceded it. One recommendation made in a number of different forums is to create an international currency. This currency, possibly SDRs, would become the medium of exchange for international transactions and in addition would serve as a common standard for the definition of prices. More important, a created currency of this sort would be subject to monitoring and management by an international monetary body such as the IMF. In 1974, a less sweeping but similar proposal was accepted by the IMF. This proposal based the value of SDRs not on the official gold price but on a basket of sixteen different national currencies. According to this proposal, international management would still be required, but perhaps to a somewhat lesser degree than that implied in the first suggestion. This act indicates a universal unwillingness to have the dollar remain in the position it occupied as Top Currency under the Bretton Woods system.

Other observers have felt that either of these types of multilateral cooperation would be difficult to organize and maintain in the face of different interests and periodic crises. Instead, they foresee the emergence of a number of regional monetary and/or economic blocs, which would be more manageable and also more responsive to the interests of particular states. Common international policies would be pursued, but with some degree of monetary and trade discrimination against countries outside the bloc. The number of potential blocs vary: some observers foresee a bipolar arrangement focusing on the United States on the one hand and the EEC on the other. Others feel that Japan might serve as the center of a Pacific Basin bloc, and a few others see the eventual possibility of a bloc centered in the Soviet Union.[18] Although a regional bloc system may be more manageable, there is also the possibility that inter-bloc relations will at times involve conflict over economic and therefore political issues. The relationship of the developing countries to these blocs is also unclear, but there is a reasonable likelihood that dominance would still be perpetuated, albeit within a system of regional blocs.

The path to the formation of a regional currency bloc is not an easy one. The great difficulties encountered by the EEC in 1973 and 1974 in trying to develop a common policy regarding exchange rates indicate that many countries prefer to respond to their own conceptions of national interest rather than to the more distant and ambiguous regional interest. The political demands of certain powerful domestic interests are difficult to counteract by appeals to the greater good of a region.

Of course, in the long run the international monetary order may continue to limp along with some degree of international cooperation, but with countries maintaining a basic commitment to sustaining if not maximizing the welfare of their own citizens. This implies the continuation of periodic crises, cooperation only on narrow and limited issues,

18 See Ernest H. Preeg, *Economic Blocs and U.S. Foreign Policy*, National Planning Association Report No. 135 (Washington, 1974).

and antagonism whenever influential domestic economic interests feel harmed by international monetary relationships. Moreover, neglect of the needs of developing countries might persist, as would the predominance of the economic superpowers. Which of these scenarios will emerge is difficult to predict, but much depends upon the willingness of the advanced states to accept a reduced amount of autonomy in exchange for greater international cooperation.

4

The Multinational Corporation: Challenge to the International System?

The multinational corporation is probably the most visible vehicle for the internationalization of the world economic system. As the economies of different nations have become increasingly linked and functionally integrated, the multinational corporation seems to have been the institution most able to adapt to a transnational style of operation. Indeed, multinational corporations are a major result of and a prime stimulus for furthering in number and complexity transnational interactions and relationships.

A number of recent developments have focused attention on the multinational corporation as an international actor having important consequences for international politics and economics and for domestic political and economic systems. For example, multinational corporations have been charged with the prime responsibility for the run on the dollar that resulted in its February, 1973 devaluation. Moreover, the activities of multinational corporations have led to extensive investigations and studies by such diverse groups as the United States Senate, the United Nations, the International Labor Organization, and a large number of other governmental and nongovernmental agencies at national, regional, and international levels. Labor unions in the United States, Sweden, and the United Kingdom have charged their own multinationals with exporting jobs and have attempted to obtain government action to restrict the ease with which these corporations can invest abroad. In various host states, both United States and non-American multinational firms have been accused of economic imperialism, the fostering of inter-country competition, and the promulgation of insensitive and unsavory business practices. In sum, multinational corporations have become the most visible and the most attacked agents in the global economic system.

CHANGING PATTERNS OF DIRECT FOREIGN INVESTMENT

Multinational corporations or their predecessors have existed for a long time. For instance, in the fifteenth century the Fuggers, headquartered in Augsburg, created and managed financial houses, trading concerns, mining operations, and processing plants in many parts of Europe.[1] Companies such as Singer, Heinz, Unilever, Nestlé, and a number of others have been active direct foreign investors for most of this century. However, it is the rapid expansion of direct foreign investment during the last two decades that has focused attention on these firms as constituting one of the major mechanisms by which the world's economy has become increasingly internationalized.

The total value of all direct foreign investment in 1970 has been estimated to be at least $250 billion,[2] with the book value expanding annually at a rate between 10 and 20 percent.[3] Of the total amount of direct foreign investment in 1970, United States–based multinational corporations accounted for 55.6 percent; European firms, 37.5 percent; Japan, 2.6 percent; Canada, 3.9 percent; and Australia, .4 percent.[4] However, it is likely that the predominance of American multinationals will decline somewhat as the Europeans, Japanese, and oil-producing states increase their international activity as a result both of their new economic and political stature in the world and of the devaluations of the American dollar during the 1970s.

The general and seemingly inexorable expansion of multinational corporations has caused some analysts and commentators to express concern that these firms are challenging and circumventing the authority of states—both host states and parent states. Book titles such as *Invisible Empires, Sovereignty at Bay,* and *The Coming Clash* suggest that these international enterprises are locked in a struggle with states for economic and even political hegemony in the world.[5] Other analysts are concerned

---

[1] A. W. Clausen, "The Internationalized Corporation: An Executive's View," *The Annals,* vol. 403 (September, 1972), 21.

[2] Stefan H. Robock and Kenneth Simmonds, *International Business and Multinational Enterprises* (Homewood, Ill.: Richard D. Irwin, Inc., 1973), p. 44.

[3] Ibid., p. 37.

[4] Ibid., p. 45.

[5] Louis Turner, *Invisible Empires* (New York: Harcourt, Brace, Jovanovich, 1971); Raymond Vernon, *Sovereignty at Bay* (New York: Basic Books, Inc., 1971); Hugh Stephenson, *The Coming Clash* (New York: Saturday Review Press, 1973).

TABLE 4-1. Comparison of American Exports with American Direct Foreign Investment (In Billions of Dollars)

	1950	1960	1970	1973
U.S. Exports	10.3	20.6	43.2	70.3
U.S. Direct Foreign Investment (book value)	11.8	32.0	78.1	107.3

Source: U.S. Congress, Senate Committee on Finance, *Implications of Multinational Firms for World Trade and Investment and for U.S. Trade and Labor*, 93rd Cong., 1st sess., 1973, p. 95. The figures for 1973 are from the U.S. Department of Commerce, *Survey of Current Business*, August, 1974, Part II, p. 18; and *Survey of Current Business*, December, 1974, p. S-3.

more specifically with the spectacular growth of American multinational firms, which threatens to overrun many countries.[6] (In parts of Asia this view is directed at the extensive Japanese investments.) These fears are reflected in book titles such as *The American Challenge, The Americanization of Europe,* and *Silent Surrender.*[7]

All analysts agree that American multinational firms have a profound impact on the ways in which the United States is linked to the world economy. Data in Table 4-1 indicate the large size and rapid growth of American direct investment abroad since 1950. Moreover, they emphasize the fact that the foreign assets of American multinational corporations now dwarf American trade, and thus constitute the largest dimension of United States participation in the global economy.

The direction and composition of American direct foreign investment have changed dramatically. As Table 4-2 shows, by 1970 Europe had become the most important area for the operations of American multinational corporations; Latin America and the developing countries in general have become relatively less important. Just as foreign investment was stimulated by the emergence of an integrated and prosperous market in Europe, it is possible that a rapid expansion of American investment in Japan will take place as Japan reduces barriers to foreign investment. At the same time, the devalued dollar, the extensive amounts of petrodollars, and the more aggressive posture of non-American enter-

---

6 Another reason for the focus on American multinational enterprises is that more information and data are available about American firms than about those based in other countries. The federal government and private researchers have gathered vast amounts of data about the operations of these American corporations; comparable data on multinational enterprises originating in other countries do not exist.

7 Jean-Jacques Servan-Schreiber, *The American Challenge* (New York: Atheneum House, Inc., 1968); Edward A. McCreary, *The Americanization of Europe* (Garden City, N.Y.: Doubleday & Co., 1964); Kari Levitt, *Silent Surrender: The American Economic Empire in Canada* (New York: Liveright, 1971).

TABLE 4-2. Geographic Breakdown of American Direct Investment Abroad
(In Billions of Dollars)

	1929		1950		1960		1970		1973	
	$	%	$	%	$	%	$	%	$	%
Total developed areas	3.7	49	5.7	48	19.6	61	53.2	68	74.1	69
Canada	2.0	26	3.6	31	11.2	35	22.8	29	28.1	26
Europe	1.4	19	1.7	14	6.7	21	24.5	31	37.2	35
Others	.3	4	.4	3	1.7	5	5.9	8	8.8	8
Total less-developed areas	3.5	47	4.4	37	10.9	34	21.3	27	27.9	26
Unallocated	.3	4	1.7	14	1.5	5	3.6	5	5.3	5
Total	7.5	100	11.8	99	32.0	100	78.1	100	107.3	100

Source: U.S. Congress, Senate Committee on Finance, *Implications of Multinational Firms for World Trade and Investment and for U.S. Trade and Labor*, 93rd Cong., 1st sess., 1973, p. 72. The figures for 1973 were obtained from the U.S. Department of Commerce, *Survey of Current Business*, August, 1974, Part II, pp. 18-19.

prises are likely to lead to a rapid inflow of foreign investment in the United States. Already, there is more direct foreign investment in the United States, approximately $17.7 billion, than in any other country except Canada. Given the much larger market offered by the United States, it is not unreasonable to suggest that eventually the United States may be host to more foreign investment than any other state.

The composition of American investment abroad has also changed. During the 1960s American firms invested much more heavily in manufacturing facilities than in extractive operations. By 1973, 42 percent of American direct foreign investment was in manufacturing industries, compared with 35 percent in 1960. From 1960 to 1970 the share of investment in extractive industries decreased from 43 percent to 34 percent, even though absolute investment in these activities doubled during this period. Investment in other sorts of economic activity, such as service industries and financial institutions, accounted for 24 percent of all American direct foreign investment.[8]

These figures convey several important points. First American and non-American direct foreign investment and multinational corporations have expanded so rapidly within the last two decades that they now account for a major part of international economic activity. Furthermore,

[8] U.S. Congress, Senate Committee on Finance, *Implications of Multinational Firms for World Trade and Investment and for U.S. Trade and Labor*, 93rd Cong., 1st sess., 1973, p. 105.

although they do have predecessors, their size and growth make them an essentially new international economic institution. Third, the patterns of international business activity are changing. American foreign investment, at least, is much more likely to be a manufacturing or service industry located in other advanced industrial states than an extractive industry located in developing countries. Even within Latin America, a greater percentage of American direct investment is nonextractive in character.

THE NATURE OF MULTINATIONAL CORPORATIONS, AND DISTINCTIONS AMONG THEM

What is a multinational corporation? The definitions vary: some are broad ("all firms—industrial, service, and financial—doing international business of all types, within a myriad of organizational structures"[9]) ; others are much narrower, based on size, extensiveness of operation in foreign countries, type of business, and organizational structure and managerial orientation. The difficulty in arriving at a widely accepted definition is that various parties, such as government officials, international executives, and scholars, all have different interests and purposes in their analyses of multinational corporations. Consequently, their definitions vary. For instance, the Harvard Business School Multinational Enterprise Project is interested primarily in studying large international firms appearing in *Fortune*'s 500 with each firm having operations in six different countries.[10] However, government officials in a developing country may be faced with unemployment resulting from the closure of a subsidiary of a rather small foreign-owned firm with operating facilities in only two or three countries. In this case, the international character of the corporation is as real and as disconcerting as if the corporation were among the 100 largest manufacturing firms and had facilities in many areas of the world.

Our objective is to examine the political implications, both national and international, of these firms as increasingly important actors in the international arena. Consequently, a broad rather than a narrow definition seems more appropriate for our purposes, although finer distinctions will be drawn shortly. Multinational corporations are those economic enterprises—manufacturing, extractive, service, and financial— that are headquartered in one country and that pursue business activities

9 Ibid., p. 83.

10 James W. Vaupel and Joan P. Curhan, *The Making of Multinational Enterprise* (Cambridge, Mass.: Harvard University Press, 1969) .

in one or more foreign countries. We are concerned with direct, not portfolio, investment that is central to the business of the firm—not just tangential.

Although this definition is useful for incorporating the many variations found in this class of actors, it is too broad to allow more precise statements of relationship and analysis. For instance, questions regarding the impact of multinational corporations on host states or the importance of foreign operations to corporations cannot be answered in the general terms we used above. Instead, distinctions must be made among different types of multinational enterprises as they affect host states. To indicate the great diversity of multinational corporations, a number of important factors will be examined. The behavior, impact, and consequences of corporate activities will vary with the specific set of characteristics used to describe the enterprise.

Some multinational corporations are gigantic in size, but others are rather small. A United States Department of Commerce census in 1966 identified 3,400 American firms engaged in direct foreign investment and determined that these firms had a total of 23,000 foreign affiliates; however, a mere 298 of these firms accounted for 55 percent of the total assets and 66 percent of the sales of foreign affiliates of American companies.[11] These figures suggest that although there are many foreign subsidiaries that interact with host-state governments, society, and culture, no more than several hundred of them—large and well-known firms—dominate American foreign investment activity. The size and consequent visibility of these American firms make them particularly important domestic and international economic actors. On the other hand, the many smaller and often less sophisticated firms may themselves act in a fashion that poisons the atmosphere for all foreign investment. The 1973 struggle involving the attempted closure of a small Swiss-owned watch factory in France, and the subsequent occupation of the factory by its workers, harmed the cause of multinationals, big and small, throughout Europe.

The size of a corporation's international component relative to its overall operations is another important distinguishing characteristic. For some firms, such as Pfizer and IBM, international (non-American) activities may account for nearly 50 percent or more of their sales or profits, but for many other corporations international operations constitute a minor part of their business. Generally, it is likely that those firms whose international activities are quite large and critical will actively seek to secure a favorable environment for these activities in host states, parent states, and at the regional and international levels. Foreign investment is

---

[11] U.S. Department of Commerce, *Special Survey of U.S. Multinational Companies, 1970* (Springfield, Va.: National Technical Information Service, 1972), p. 3.

fundamental and important to their business success, but such investment may be of marginal concern to other, less internationally involved companies. However, the rapid expansion of direct foreign investment indicates that an increasing number of corporations are consciously attempting to broaden the scale and scope of, and thus their commitment to, their international operations.

A somewhat similar factor serving to differentiate types of firms is the number of countries in which a firm's subsidiaries are located. At the aggregate level, of course, multinational enterprises operate in every part of the world, including the socialist countries of Eastern Europe. A recent study by one of the authors of 56 of the 187 largest American multinationals in manufacturing revealed that on the average these corporations had subsidiaries in 17.7 different countries; one company had subsidiaries in 100 different countries.[12] The extent to which a firm's activities are located around the world may reflect its commitment to international business, and/or it may indicate a conscious effort to decentralize, and thus make its international activities less politically vulnerable. Firms with subsidiaries in only a few countries may just be beginning their international efforts; or they may have to do business where critical natural resources can be found; or the firms may have a highly centralized production function for their world business activities. Generalizations cannot be made regarding the meaning of the dispersion of a firm's activities throughout the world. Suffice it to say that there is great variation among the multinationals in this respect.

A fourth type of distinction that must be made among multinational corporations is based on the nature of the corporation's business. Figure 4-1 is a partial list of the different types of businesses conducted on an international scale. There is frequently a significant difference between the behavior and impact of an extractive type of multinational corporation and that of a capital-goods and consumer-product manufacturing concern. From the perspective of the host state, the costs and benefits of each type of firm are quite different. For example, host states tend to view direct foreign investment in extractive industries as more exploitative than investment in manufacturing. On issues such as employment, technological transfers, taxes and other revenues, and balance-of-payments matters, a host state's evaluation of a foreign firm varies with the specific character of the firm. Even within the category of extractive industries, for example, there are likely to be important differences in the relative bargaining strengths of firms in various industries, implying that

12 David H. Blake, "Cross-National Cooperative Strategies: Union Response to the MNCs," in *Multinational Corporations and Labour Unions,* ed. Kurt P. Tudyka (Nijmegen, Netherlands: Werkuitgave Sun, 1973), p. 226.

1. Extractive
   Petroleum (Exxon) [a]   ·
   Mining (Kennecott Copper)
   Lumbering (Weyerhaeuser Corporation)
2. Agriculture (Standard Brands)
3. Industrial
   Capital goods (Caterpillar Tractor Company)
   Intermediate goods (Ford)
   Consumer goods (Colgate-Palmolive)
4. Service
   Transportation (Greyhound Corporation)
   Public utilities (General Telephone and Electronics Corporation)
   Wholesaling and Retailing (Sears)
   Tourism (Holiday Inns, Inc.)
   Insurance (INA Corporation)
   Advertising (The Interpublic Group)
   Management Services (McKinsey and Co.)
5. Financial Institutions
   Banking (Bank of America)
   Investing (International Basic Economy Corporation)
6. Conglomerate (ITT)

FIGURE 4-1. Types of Business Activities Pursued by Multinational Corporations

[a] The companies in the parentheses are examples of the types of firms. However, many of these firms engage in numerous kinds of business activities and, thus, might be found in several of these categories.

there will be differences among the political and economic relations between host states and the multinationals.[13]

Another characteristic distinguishing multinational corporations is the pattern of ownership linking the parent firm with its subsidiaries. Multinational corporations may have wholly owned subsidiaries or they may share ownership, to varying degrees, with joint-venture partners of different types. Between 1961 and 1970, 56 percent of all new American foreign investment took the form of wholly owned subsidiaries or foreign branches.[14] Another 12 percent of new American investment involved a majority share for the American enterprise, and only 8 percent of the new investment was a minority investment. Unfortunately, information was not available for 24 percent of the new investment during these years. Japanese firms show a strikingly different pattern: only 29 percent of new

---

[13] Vernon, *Sovereignty at Bay*, Chap. 2.

[14] These figures were taken from a study by Booz, Allen, and Hamilton that was reported in "American Investment Abroad: Who's Going Where, How, and Why," *Business Abroad*, June, 1971, p. 9.

investment involved total ownership, 34 percent entailed majority ownership, and 37 percent involved minority ownership.[15] These data suggest
that American firms are less willing to accommodate the desires of host
countries for participation in the ownership and control of American
direct foreign investment. By such actions, American firms may stimulate
host-country regulations that require a certain amount of local participation.

Similarly, the host-country partner of a majority- or minority-owned
investment may vary widely. Three of the more likely partners are
private enterprises or entrepreneurs, individual stockholders, and host-
government or quasi-governmental agencies. There are a number of
other types of possible partners in joint-venture arrangements, but the
main point is that corporate practices and objectives as well as the
response of host-state government officials and other interested groups
may differ with the specific nature of the joint-venture relationship. For
example, some corporations may feel that a joint venture with a host-
state government agency may reduce the chances of nationalization, but
the price paid may be constant governmental meddling.

There are a number of other factors that are useful in attempting to
differentiate among types of multinational enterprises; two of the most
important are organizational structure and managerial orientation. A
number of schema have been developed by students of multinational
corporations to describe these aspects of international firms, and though
they differ in the terms they use, they are basically quite similar. Several
general types of organizational forms are examined below, but it must be
recognized that they are only archetypes; any specific firm is likely to
incorporate attributes from more than one of these models.

The parent-dominant/subsidiary-subservient type of enterprise is
organized in such a way as to insure that its international activities
enhance the efforts of the firm in its major market in the parent country.
Organizationally, the international operations are subordinate to the
objectives, standards, and actions of the domestic business of the headquarters. Similarly, management orientation is that of the parent company and parent country. As Howard Perlmutter has termed it,
management is ethnocentric regarding goals, frames of reference, perspectives, and nationality. The prevailing view in this type of organization is
that what is good and appropriate for the parent firm is paramount, and
the efforts of the foreign subsidiaries should support and supplement the
business in the parent country. Probably a majority of the multinational
corporations existing today resemble this parent-dominant type of enter-

15 Gregory Clark, "Japanese Direct Investment Overseas" (Unpublished manu-
script, 1971), Table II, as reported in Richard D. Robinson, "Beyond the
Multinational Corporation," mimeographed, p. 1.

prise. This is particularly true of the smaller and newer entries in the field of international business as well as some of the extractive industries. Also, this type of enterprise tends to emphasize the differences between the multinational corporation and the host state, for host-state objectives, practices, and standards are clearly secondary to those developed by the parent company.

A second type of multinational enterprise structure and orientation can be likened to an international holding company in which the various subsidiaries operate with a high degree of autonomy. In this, the subsidiary-independent form of organization, the parent company has very little to do with either the goal-setting or operational phases of the subsidiaries' business. Local managers, most likely citizens of the host country, determine their own objectives, standards, and ways of doing things with little interference from or reference to the headquarters. In this type of arrangement, clashes between host states and the international enterprise are less likely to occur, since the subsidiaries are very similar to local firms. The international nature of the subsidiary-independent type of corporation is primarily in the area of ownership, not in the area of control.

The third type of multinational organization, the integrated international enterprise, is quite different from the other two in that the parent-company operations as well as the subsidiaries' are incorporated into an overall managerial effort. The enterprise is organized in such a fashion as to advance regional or global objectives and activities; no particular nationality, whether parent or host country, prevails. Instead, corporate goals, corporate standards of performance, and corporate practices dominate. Decentralization of management occurs only within the framework of an integrated, centrally directed effort aimed at maximizing broad-scale corporate objectives. In this organizational structure and management orientation, the potential for clashes with host-state interests is great, but the source of such conflict comes from the international nature of the firm, not, as in the first archetype, from a foreign and rather ethnocentric nature.

Increasingly, multinational enterprises are tending to take on the characteristics of this third type of organization. The more progressive and successful United States multinationals are consciously attempting to develop a worldwide approach to business, in terms of organization, management orientation, and the substance of their business activity. W. J. Barnholdt, vice-president of Caterpillar Tractor Corporation, describes this type of enterprise:

> Caterpillar is owned by approximately 48,000 shareholders and our stock is traded on exchanges in the United States, France, England, Scotland,

West Germany, Switzerland, and Belgium. We have 65,000 employees, 22 percent of whom work abroad. We are a multinational company, treating foreign operators as co-equal with domestic, in both structure and policy, willing to allocate resources without regard to national frontiers.

We will one day become a transnational company—a multinational business managed and owned by people of different nationalities—through current programs aimed at developing more top managers of different national origins and greater ownership by investors outside the U.S. Thus, while we export from the U.S., our views as to transportation, markets, and product are worldwide. For example, there is no U.S.-made Caterpillar tractor. A Caterpillar product—wherever it is built—is just that—a Caterpillar product—graphic evidence that people of different national origins and political interests can achieve common objectives.[16]

What this means is that the activities of the enterprise are integrated on a regional or global scale. This type of firm is particularly sensitive to political and economic developments in various states and in the global economy, and through its worldwide orientation it seeks to capitalize on international economic interdependencies. Thus, for instance, capital needed for new investment or expansion is secured wherever the most favorable terms exist. Similarly, marketing strategies are integrated and coordinated in such a fashion as to take advantage of spillover advertising and similar markets. Of course, to the extent feasible, production is also integrated. Figure 4-2 reproduces a map prepared by the International Metalworkers' Federation to show production flows among subsidiaries of General Motors in Europe. As you can see, General Motors, and a number of other corporations, are pursuing business activities in a fashion that attempts to surmount the boundaries of specific states.

Although most multinational corporations are variants of one of the three archetypes discussed above, a number of other ideal types have been suggested. One proposes the existence of a supranational corporation that is truly nonnational in that its ownership, board of directors, management, and orientation are not dominated by one nationality. Furthermore, such an enterprise would be chartered by, and pay taxes to, an international body on the order of a GATT or an IMF established precisely for this purpose. This model, then, is based on the assumption that international firms should be subject to international rules and regulations, a procedure, it is claimed, that would protect both host states and multinational corporations.

Richard Robinson describes another type of organization, the trans-

---

[16] Quoted in *U.S. Multinationals: The Dimming of America*, a Report prepared for the AFL–CIO Maritime Trades Department, Executive Board Meeting, February 15–16, 1973, p. 12.

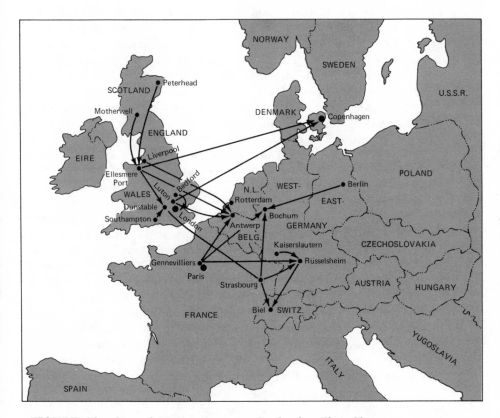

FIGURE 4-2. General Motors European Production Flow Chart

Source: International Metalworkers' Federation, World Automotive Councils, January, 1972.

national association, which a number of Japanese firms have adopted.[17] It is not like the forms of foreign investment already described, but it is a mechanism, he thinks, that might allow transnational business activity without severely threatening the sovereignty of states. Under this structure, the headquarters has little or no equity investment in the "subsidiaries" located in various countries. Instead, the "subsidiaries" are locally owned and managed, but they receive extensive managerial and technological assistance from the headquarters. In addition, most or all of the production of the "subsidiaries" is contractually sold to the headquarters, which then serves in some cases as the assembler and, most

[17] Richard Robinson, "Beyond the Multinational Corporation," in *International Business-Government Affairs*, ed. John Fayerweather (Cambridge, Mass.: Ballinger Publishing Company, 1973), pp. 17–26.

important, as the marketer and distributor for the association. The central headquarters still plays a dominant role in the integration of production and marketing, but its role as owner and as "subsidiary" manager is for the most part eliminated. Certainly, the implications for relations between the multinational corporation and the host state differ from those of other types of multinational firms.

The wide variation among multinational corporations has been demonstrated in this discussion. Differences in size, importance of international operations, type of business activity, ownership patterns, and organizational structure and managerial orientation result in different goals, actions, and responses from host states. Analysis of the nature or impact of multinational corporations requires a precise understanding of the type of enterprise involved.

A final caveat needs to be made. The characteristics of different types of multinational corporations may appear in combination in a single corporation. For instance, the same firm may contain an extractive subsidiary that is wholly owned and that is treated in an ethnocentric fashion, and a majority-owned subsidiary that is involved in the production of intermediate goods and that is linked closely with operations in other countries. Thus, it may be inappropriate to generalize from an overall pattern describing the enterprise as a whole to the specific cases of individual subsidiaries. As a result, assessments or predictions about the nature of the relationships between the host country and the multinational corporation depend very much on the specific characteristics of the subsidiaries as well as of the corporation as a whole.

MOTIVATIONS FOR CORPORATE INTERNATIONAL EXPANSION

Both corporate apologists and radical critics agree that corporations expand internationally for sound economic and business reasons from the capitalist's self-interested point of view. Certainly, as we will discuss later, these two groups differ as to the legitimacy of the capitalist perspective and, therefore, the impact of foreign investments. But in spite of this difference of opinion, both groups recognize a number of motivations for domestic firms to become international corporations. As we just indicated, though, distinctions need to be made among various types of multinational enterprises.

Extractive industries have traditionally been international in scope because they depend upon the location of fuel, mineral, or other raw material deposits. Consequently, even if domestic supplies exist, extractive firms must seek foreign sources of supply to supplement or substitute for domestic sites that are drying up or are too expensive to operate.

Moreover, control over numerous foreign resource supplies serves as a hedge against disruptions in supply or as a preemptive maneuver designed to deny competitors or potential competitors access to the same source.

Manufacturing corporations establish foreign subsidiaries for a number of different reasons. If the firm has obtained foreign markets through the export process, it is possible that increasing costs of production and transportation will lead the firm to serve these same markets more profitably through local manufacturing facilities. Establishing a local subsidiary also eases servicing problems and allows for greater adaptation of the product to local conditions and desires. The possibility of losing a market to either local or international competition also stimulates corporations to establish foreign subsidiaries. Furthermore, tariff and other trade barriers raise the cost of exporting to the protected market, and local subsidiaries constitute an effective mechanism to circumvent these barriers and maintain or increase market share.

A quite different stimulus to establish manufacturing subsidiaries abroad is the practice by many states of offering substantial investment incentives that are designed explicitly to attract foreign investment to depressed areas. Tax holidays, cash grants, the training of a local work force, and the provision of land and buildings are a few of the many ways by which host countries attempt to draw foreign investors. Often, actual cash grants are made to foreign investors. Canada, which is evolving a more restrictive policy toward foreign investment, provided IBM with a $6-million nonrepayable grant for the purpose of establishing a large computer facility in a depressed area of Quebec. Such efforts are duplicated many times over by most of the countries of the world, and they serve to emphasize the fact that multinational corporations are often pulled into specific foreign investments by the actions of host governments. This image is quite different from that of the corporation thrusting itself upon an unwilling host state.

Furthermore, parent-country policies may foster the development of foreign subsidiaries. For example, the tax credit and deferral policies of the United States government stimulated massive investment abroad by American firms. In response to fuel and natural resource shortages, the Japanese government has urged Japanese firms to find new sources of supplies in other countries.

Of course, some manufacturing concerns become international because of the existence of a substantial and growing overseas market, which offers excellent earnings prospects. The huge expansion of American investment in manufacturing in Europe during the 1960s reflected, among other things, the wealth, size, and stability of the market available in an economically healthy Europe. The attractiveness of the reduced trade barriers and the large market offered by the European Economic

Community were critical factors too. The establishment of the convertibility of European currencies further facilitated international economic
transactions, including investment. Additionally, the increasingly competitive and saturated market in the United States led dynamic American
firms to look to other countries as a place for new profit and growth
opportunities, for the effective utilization of restive managerial talent in
new and challenging areas, and for a method by which headquarters'
overhead costs could be shared over a larger base. Raymond Vernon and
his colleagues at Harvard summarize many of these motivations in the
concept of the product life cycle, wherein the firm facing a decline in its
technological advantage in the parent-country market essentially exports
this advantage to foreign countries through the vehicle of foreign subsidiaries.

These reasons for corporate international expansion do not suggest
a conspiracy among capitalists to dominate the world. Rather, they
suggest a rational response, from the capitalist perspective, to opportunities for the pursuit of business activities in other countries. Indeed,
business executives as well as most radical critics would agree that the
development of multinational corporations is a logical and rational step
in the evolution of capitalism.[18]

The growth and development of the more highly integrated and
managerially sophisticated multinational corporations are due to certain
motivations. Business operations with a regional or global orientation
can finance, produce, and market in a fashion that maximizes the ability
of the firm to take advantage of different costs and investment climates
around the world. New developments in communications and transportation systems and important improvements in management practices have
greatly facilitated the task of managing these complex international
enterprises. For example, some American-based multinational firms have
shifted production away from the well-organized labor and the high
production costs in the United States to the relatively docile labor and
the low production costs in developing countries. By integrating production, finance, and marketing, corporations are able to service American
and foreign markets without incurring the high costs of American production. Similar developments are starting to occur in European and
Japanese firms as they face rising labor and production costs in their
home countries.

Corporations, banks, and other firms involved in service activities
tend to expand overseas because of their need to provide services on an
international scale to their multinational clients. Banking, consulting,
and advertising firms became international because their customers in

18 We have not examined, and will only mention here, the traditional Leninist
   argument that the expansion of foreign investment is the result of the need
   to find an outlet for surplus investment capital.

the United States were multinational. Most assuredly, the reasoning goes, if one firm in a particular service sector failed to provide these necessary facilities and processes for its clients, competitors would do so on the international level and might, in that fashion, eventually capture the huge domestic business of serving such firms. Again, the logic and reasonableness of the growth of multinational enterprises is inescapable if the basic premises of capitalism are accepted.

Radical critics, while recognizing this logic, do not accept the premises of capitalism as an appropriate basis for organizing the economy and society, at either the national or international levels. Thus, although the growth of multinational corporations may logically follow from capitalism, radical critics focus on the disadvantages and evils of such firms, and of capitalism in general, for parent and host states as well as for the international system. They view the abolition of capitalism, either in parent states or in host states (according to *dependencia* theorists), as the only sure way to control multinational corporations. On the other hand, classical liberal theorists typically stress that the benefits of direct foreign investment outweigh some of its admittedly negative aspects. They feel that the problems associated with foreign investment can be alleviated or eliminated through more sensitive state and corporate policies.

THE IMPACT OF THE MULTINATIONAL CORPORATION: SOURCE OF CONFLICT OR AGENT OF GROWTH?

Various interest groups and policy makers within both parent and host states are likely to react differently to multinational corporations. Those with a particularly strong ideological commitment will see either great benefit or great harm resulting from the actions of these enterprises; most, however, will observe a mixture of effects, and policy debates and policy prescriptions will thereby reflect a mélange of promotion and restriction. Different postures that might be adopted by host and parent governments or by regional and international organizations will be examined below, but before doing so let us examine the complaints and praises stimulated by the existence of multinational enterprises.

Host States' Concerns

Corporations in extractive industries, which are more likely to be in developing countries than in advanced industrial states, are typically charged with exploiting the weakness of the host country by "stealing" its precious natural resources—the petroleum, copper, bauxite, or whatever is deemed to be a national resource. Yet significant profits are being obtained from this source of national wealth by multinational enterprises. Furthermore, such firms often exist in enclave-type surroundings and have no meaningful links to the local economy. The product is exported; the management is foreign; the benefits accrue primarily to the foreign firm and foreign societies. Moreover, because of the importance of the natural resource, the foreign firm and the parent government are often thought to collaborate and interfere in order to protect the investment from local political and social disturbances. In sum, the large and wealthy foreign firm—supported by a powerful, and probably imperialistic, parent government—is perceived to be exploiting a relatively weak, underdeveloped host state, which seeks to obtain a reasonable return on its natural resource while trying to maintain its national sovereignty and pride.

This somewhat exaggerated view of the negative aspects of international firms engaged in extractive operations is not nearly as appropriate for multinational manufacturing companies. Manufacturing firms, which are more extensive in advanced states than in developing countries, are much more integrated with host-state societies and economies. In many cases, the extractive operation seems to be almost a wholly foreign enterprise with the exception of some local workers and the location of the facility. Foreign-owned manufacturing subsidiaries, in contrast, become very much a part of the local scene. For example, they are likely to have local business supporters as well as domestic business enemies. Often, the products are consumed locally, a situation that is aided by massive advertising campaigns designed to increase consumer awareness of and predisposition towards the product. The plants tend to be located in the more heavily settled areas of the country, unlike the often isolated sites of extractive facilities. Generally speaking, manufacturing enterprises are more pervasive (though not necessarily more important) in the host-state environment than extractive operations. The charges leveled against such firms are particularly important because of the extent of international manufacturing, because of its rapid growth rate, and because acute concern has been expressed in advanced industrial states as well as in the developing countries.

Many host states fear that the size and wealth of multinational corporations, whether extractive or manufacturing, will dominate their economies. One frequently sees lists that rank states according to GNP and size of federal budget; the same lists include the sales figures of the largest multinational corporations.[19] Such lists show that the leading

---

[19] An example of such a list can be found in Turner, *Invisible Empires*, pp. 135–36.

firms have sales figures larger than the GNPs of most states, even some that are industrialized, and they are designed to indicate the huge power of multinational corporations. Aggregate data of this sort do support the fear that multinational corporations have the size and strength to dominate weaker states.

A more specific, and probably more realistic, concern is that within a particular state, foreign investment may dominate the most profitable, the most technologically advanced, the most growth-oriented, and the economic-trend-setting industries. Studies have shown that American multinationals tend to invest in the most profitable host-state industries and then to be even more profitable than their local competitors. As a result, host states perceive that important segments of their economy are increasingly subject to the control of multinational companies rather than national firms.

Host states at all levels of industrialization also fear that these circumstances will produce technological dependence upon the United States or other technologically active parent states, such as Japan. The charge is often made that the headquarters company and country will become technological innovators while the rest of the world becomes little more than technology consumers or technological colonies.[20] In the pharmaceutical, synthetic fiber, and chemical industries in Colombia, for example, Constantine Vaitsos found that a mere 10 percent of the patent holders (all of which are multinational enterprises) own 60 percent of all patents in these industries.[21] When this situation occurs, there is a realistic fear that host-state industry will be stunted and that the multinational corporation will be able to extract enormous profits. This process is advanced by the centralization of research and development activity in the parent state of most multinational enterprises and by the brain drain in terms either of the emigration of scientists to the United States or of their working for local subsidiaries of foreign firms.

All of these factors combine to produce fears that multinational enterprises will act in a fashion counter to what is perceived to be in the best interests of the host state. Failure to conform to national plans and the precedence of international or foreign business interests over national political, economic, and social interests are especially galling and are very noticeable when committed by foreign firms. For example, within a span of two weeks during 1962, French subsidiaries of General Motors and Remington Rand announced layoffs of 1,485 French employees without

---

[20] See Chapter 6 for a more comprehensive discussion of technological gaps in the international political economy.

[21] Constantine V. Vaitsos, "Patents Revisited," *The Journal of Development Studies,* IX (1973), 12.

apprising the French government of these actions. The layoffs occurred at a time when the government was attempting to establish a wage policy with employers and unions. Moreover, these moves contradicted the French belief that businesses—not labor—should shoulder the burden of market adjustments. More recently, the Dutch-German corporation AKZO sought to close a Dutch facility, only to incur the wrath of labor unions and government officials in the Netherlands. These instances show that multinational corporations act in ways that are considered inappropriate, clumsy, and alien by elements of the host state, including government officials.

Problems associated with controlling the activities of American multinational enterprises are heightened by the influence of the United States government (or any other parent state) over corporate policies. American antitrust policies may prevent a merger between the foreign subsidiary of an American firm and a host-country enterprise, even when the merger is expressly desired by the host government. Provisions concerning trade with the enemy, which are applicable to the foreign subsidiaries as well as the headquarters of American firms, have prohibited trade with some communist states. In 1968, for example, a Belgian subsidiary of an American multinational was not allowed by the United States Treasury Department to export farm equipment to Cuba. Host-state resentment of these extraterritorial extensions of parent-state policies are supplemented by fears that foreign subsidiaries may seek support from the government of the parent country in their disputes with the host state. The concerns of Latin America in this regard are well known.[22] In Asia, many countries have similar fears about Japanese foreign investments. Such fears have been realized: for example, France has come to the aid of French firms in trouble with Algeria.

Host governments are, of course, also interested in the impact of multinational corporations on their balance-of-payments position. Critics of these enterprises claim that they generally contribute to a deficit, in that they take more international currency out of the country than they bring in. Negative items (repatriated earnings, charges for royalties, licenses, and various management services, and expenses incurred by importing necessary equipment and component products) far outweigh positive items (the inflow of new capital, savings resulting from import substitution, and earnings gained through exports) in the balance-of-payments accounts. Analyses of the impact of multinational corporations need to be conducted on a case-by-case basis, but in the aggregate critics

[22] Many Latin American countries have incorporated variants of the Calvo doctrine in their investment laws. This doctrine suggests that foreign enterprises cannot legally turn to their parent governments for protection since they are subject to the laws and legal procedures of the host state.

can point to official United States government statistics showing that American multinational enterprises make a substantial positive contribution to the parent country's balance of payments. For example, Federal Reserve Board statistics for the 1972 United States balance of payments indicate that income from American direct investment abroad was $10.4 billion, whereas the outflow of capital funds was only $3.4 billion. This net positive contribution to the United States must, of course, be balanced by a negative effect on the payments position of some host states.[23]

Depending upon their nature and pervasiveness, multinational manufacturing enterprises may also be accused of undermining the culture and national identity of host states. Jean-Jacques Servan-Schreiber's best-seller, *The American Challenge,* was a plea for Europeans to counteract this challenge so that European economic, political, technological, and, most important, cultural independence could be preserved. To the extent that multinational firms threaten cultural identity, some host states will become quite concerned. Because of the many linkages between manufacturing subsidiaries and the host-state society, the foreign agent-of-change nature of the enterprise may be considered quite threatening. The same effect is somewhat less likely for extractive industries since they rarely are as closely integrated into the host-country environment.

Another factor that frightens host-state governments, and particularly labor officials, is the mobility and flexibility of the corporation, as opposed to the immobility of the state and its work force. In certain instances, multinational enterprises may be able to leave states in which the investment climate has become less satisfactory, for whatever reason. As a result, states compete with one another by offering more attractive incentives to foreign industry, and companies can play one state against another in pursuit of the more ideal opportunity. An interesting example of this, involving the work force, occurred in Europe when a European multinational firm told its employees in the Netherlands that they would have to operate on three shifts since that was the only way that the unprofitable facility could be kept open. Furthermore, the Dutch workers were told that the workers in the German subsidiary, which was also liable to being closed down, were willing to accede to management's request. The same story, but in reverse, was related to the German employees in an attempt by management to use its internationalism to coerce its employees. There are no statistics regarding the ease with which

23 For an interesting assessment of the negative balance of payments effects of multinational corporations in Latin America, see Ronald Müller, "Poverty Is the Product," *Foreign Policy,* No. 13 (Winter, 1973–74), 71–103. A more general critique of the impact of these firms can be found in Richard J. Barnet and Ronald E. Müller, *Global Reach* (New York: Simon and Schuster, 1974).

multinational enterprises can and do shut down operations in one state in favor of operations in others, but the concern about this alleged mobility is certainly real. Moreover, this mobility illustrates how private multinational corporations can take advantage of and indeed manipulate the sensitivity accompanying economic interdependency among states.

Many of the aforementioned causes for concern at the governmental level are shared by various economic, social, and political groups within the host state. Labor has been briefly mentioned, and its interest in these issues is obvious. In addition, segments of domestic business experience conflicts of interest with multinational enterprises. Multinational firms are fierce and often successful competitors with local firms for domestic and international markets. Their large size, huge managerial and financial resources, worldwide reputation, and product recognition often mean that multinational firms can literally overwhelm local corporations. Aside from marketing competition, domestic industries frequently face severe competition from multinational firms for skilled workers, research and development scientists, effective managers, and investment capital. The larger and more successful international enterprise can frequently offer higher wages and provide more attractive research facilities for scientists, and it generally sets the pattern that domestic firms must follow. In the financial arena, domestic business interests must compete with the international firms for local capital. Increasingly large amounts of local capital are being used to finance the acquisition and establishment of subsidiaries of multinational firms. Where investment capital is scarce, foreign firms may be using local sources of capital to the exclusion and disadvantage of local enterprises. As Servan-Schreiber plaintively cries, *"we pay them to buy us."*[24]

Bifurcation of the national economy and the society is one result of this ability of foreign firms to attract scarce factors of production in the host state, a result that is especially likely in the developing countries. The better paid and more skilled employees of the multinational corporations are linked to the global economic system through their employers. There is an increasingly wide gap between their life styles and orientations and those of their many countrymen who are essentially untouched by the international economy. Consequently, the state develops in an uneven fashion, for a small international-oriented elite coexists with a more backward and more parochial majority of the population.

Multinational corporations are also criticized for introducing and aggressively marketing products that are not necessary for the primary tasks involved in modernization and development. Such efforts draw money away from social, health, and educational necessities only to

[24] Servan-Schreiber, *The American Challenge,* p. 14.

contribute it to the coffers of wealthy corporations. For example, there is the feeling that it is wasteful, indeed immoral, for destitute people to be urged to purchase such things as Coca-Cola instead of purchasing education for their young.

The complaints discussed above apply to service industries as well as to manufacturing subsidiaries. Furthermore, they are voiced by elements of advanced industrial states as well as by the developing ones, whereas the fears associated with extractive firms seem more applicable to developing countries that are host states. Regardless, within this set of grievances there is ample substance and opportunity for the development of conflict between multinational corporations and host states over the objectives, policies, and even the existence of these firms. Tensions can be expected to rise as host states increasingly insist upon their right to exert more control over foreign investment.

Overall, there seem to be three major sources of conflict provoked by the existence and actions of multinational corporations in host states. First, the international corporation is a foreign entity that behaves in a fashion that is unusual, different, or wrong, from the point of view of the host state. Second, the corporation is often perceived as an enterprise that is closely associated with a foreign country—the parent state—which is able to exert its influence on the host state through the mechanism of the corporation. Third, the multinational enterprise is an international entity able to take advantage of economic interdependencies among states without itself being subject to the rules and regulations of a comparable international agency. Consequently, conflict continues between the host states, which seek to determine and control the nature of their relations with multinationals, and the corporations, which desire stability, predictability, and freedom to pursue their business in a relatively unfettered manner.

Host States' Benefits

Although host states hold substantial fears of multinational corporations, most countries of the world not only accept these foreign enterprises but also actively seek to attract them through a wide variety of incentives. This suggests strongly that the benefits of these corporations for most states are worth obtaining, particularly if the negative effect of their operation can be controlled.[25]

[25] For an excellent discussion of why host countries welcome multinational corporations, see Jack N. Behrman, *National Interests and the Multinational Enterprise* (Englewood Cliffs, N.J.: Prentice-Hall, Inc., 1970), Chap. 2. Much of the discussion that follows is based upon this chapter.

One of the more important benefits of multinational corporations for host countries is the mobilization and productive use of investment capital. The developing countries as well as certain regional and industrial sectors of the advanced industrial states often lack the capital to develop industries that tap natural resources, provide useful products, and generate employment and income. In such cases, the mobilization of investment capital, whether it involves a substantial amount of reinvested earnings of foreign subsidiaries or the actual transfer of funds from the parent country to the host country, accelerates industrialization that cannot take place without large infusions of capital.

A number of states have taken advantage of the flexibility of multinational corporations to entice them into establishing facilities in depressed areas of a country. One third of the United States investment in the United Kingdom is located in officially designated development areas and has created about 150,000 jobs.[26] Multinational firms are frequently more responsive to these incentives than indigenous corporations. For example, Behrman reports that from 1959 to 1966 Belgian incentives to locate companies in depressed regions attracted three foreign-owned firms for every Belgian firm.[27]

Furthermore, most countries are attracted by the employment foreign investors generate. In the United Kingdom, for instance, American subsidiaries directly employ 730,000 persons.[28] Herbert May estimates that the total employment of American subsidiaries in Latin America in 1966 was 1,230,000, compared with 830,000 persons in 1957.[29] In 1970, according to Tariff Commission extrapolations, the non-Americans employed by American-owned multinational corporations numbered approximately 5 million persons.[30] Furthermore, none of these figures include the secondary employment of those firms that supply these foreign-owned subsidiaries or service their employees. In addition, it is difficult to determine how much of this employment is new, created only by the foreign investment, and how much would have occurred in the absence of multinational corporations. Unfortunately, there are no estimates of the employment generated by multinational corporations headquartered in states other than the United States.

Host states are concerned about the effect of multinational corporations on balance-of-payments accounts, and as we have seen charges of

26 Economists Advisory Group, *United States Industry in Britain* (London: The Financial Times) , p. 4.

27 Behrman, *National Interests*, p. 20.

28 Economists Advisory Group, *United States Industry in Britain*, p. 5.

29 Herbert K. May, *The Contributions of U.S. Private Investment to Latin America's Growth* (New York: The Council for Latin America, 1970) , p. 19.

30 Senate Committee on Finance, *Implications of Multinational Firms*, p. 612.

decapitalization are frequently leveled as the result of the disparity between capital inflows to the host state and the outflow of funds for dividends, royalties, and various other services. However, Raymond Vernon suggests in a study for the United Nations that this argument is inappropriate since it fails to account for the changes that foreign investment can produce in domestic output, changes that in turn often have significant positive effects on a country's balance of payments.[31] Brazil is often cited as a country that has used foreign investment and export policies to achieve rapidly a satisfactory balance-of-payments position.

In addition, the manufacturing subsidiaries of multinational enterprises may provide significant benefits to the host country in terms of import substitution and export promotion. The former refers to products the host state once imported, therefore causing a drain on its balance of payments, but now produced domestically as a result of the foreign investment. Most available data seem to indicate that the subsidiaries of multinational corporations are more effective in exporting their products, especially manufactured products, than are domestic firms. In the United Kingdom, American subsidiaries in 1970–71 exported one fourth of their total output, a much larger share than that of British-owned firms. In fact, American subsidiaries accounted for one fifth of the United Kingdom's manufacturing exports during that two-year period.[32] Similar figures are available for Latin America, and they indicate that American subsidiaries accounted for 35 percent of all Latin American exports in 1966. With respect to manufactured products alone, in 1966 American affiliates exported 41 percent of all the Latin American exports of manufactured goods.[33] In both Latin America and Great Britain, the export efforts of American subsidiaries are growing at a much faster pace than those of domestic enterprises.

Although no generally accepted conclusion can be reached with regard to the ultimate effect of multinational corporations on a host country's balance-of-payments position, the studies by Vernon, May, and John Dunning all conclude that such enterprises probably contribute to a surplus rather than a deficit in the host country. It must be understood, however, that the impact varies according to the country and the specific type of investment.

States also actively court foreign investment because of the benefits received from the transfer of technology and managerial skills. Products

---

[31] Raymond Vernon, *Restrictive Business Practices* (New York: United Nations, 1972), p. 20.

[32] Economists Advisory Group, *United States Industry in Britain*, pp. 4–5. It is interesting to note that more than 50 percent of the exports of American subsidiaries are to other affiliates of the same multinational corporation.

[33] May, *Contributions*, p. 1.

and processes developed elsewhere in the multinational network of the corporation are rapidly dispersed throughout the firm, thereby benefiting those countries (both host and parent) that are the recipients of these innovations. Technological developments by multinational corporations have had a great impact on agricultural equipment and office machines in Great Britain, photography and movie production in France, and television throughout Europe, for example.[34] Although quantification of the benefits of technological transfer is nearly impossible, John Dunning reports that in 1970–71 American subsidiaries used both labor and capital more productively than British counterparts in 35 of 39 industries he examined. This advantage was greatest in the capital-intensive and technologically leading industries.[35] The flow of technology directly affects customers and users, and this, in conjunction with managerial innovations, stimulates domestic enterprises to improve and modernize their products and procedures in order to remain competitive. Thus, a side benefit of foreign investment may frequently be a general upgrading of the industrial efforts of the host country.

Host states also appreciate the fact that multinational corporations generate significant amounts of taxable income, which the state can use for its own objectives. It has been estimated that in 1966, the affiliates of American multinational corporations in Latin America paid $1.613 billion in taxes to the Latin American host governments. This represents 14.7 percent of the total fiscal revenues obtained by these governments.[36] Host countries have received massive income return from the major oil companies, and through the efforts of the Organization of Petroleum-Exporting Countries (OPEC) the host-state share is becoming larger all the time. It has been estimated that all the foreign subsidiaries of American multinational corporations paid $8.420 billion in income taxes to host governments in 1970.[37] Other tax payments, not of the income variety, amounted to approximately ten billion.

Although many journalistic, academic, and political commentaries emphasize the negative effects of multinational firms on host states, the actions of most host-state governments indicate clearly that important segments within host states perceive significant benefits from the operations of these firms. From this perspective, the most important challenge facing host states is how to increase the benefits and reduce the costs of foreign investments. If multinational firms were purely exploitative in their activities, they would be denied access to most countries.

---

34 Behrman, *National Interests,* p. 17.
35 Economists Advisory Group, *United States Industry in Britain,* p. 6.
36 May, *Contributions,* p. 5.
37 Senate Committee on Finance, *Implications of Multinational Firms,* p. 444.

Parent States' Concerns

Until quite recently, it was generally assumed that multinational corporations could only be an asset to their parent countries. However, beginning in 1971 American labor, led by the AFL–CIO, has mounted serious legislative challenges to the American-based multinationals, challenges that have brought to the fore a series of accusations regarding the harm caused by these firms in the parent country. Essentially, labor has charged that American international firms have profited from their internationalism to the detriment of the American economy and work force. The United States as a whole is not benefiting from this internationalization of production and marketing; only the corporations are.

Of paramount importance to labor, American jobs are being exported by multinational enterprises. This occurs in a number of ways, according to labor spokesmen. Foreign markets once served by exports from the United States are now supplied by the foreign subsidiaries of American corporations, with a consequent loss of jobs for Americans. Furthermore, some American multinationals, especially in the electrical and electronic appliance fields, have shut down operations in the United States and opened up new but similar facilities in low-wage areas of the world. The products of these foreign plants are then imported for sale in the United States market. This is another case where jobs seem to have been exported to take advantage of low wages and docile labor in other countries. Third, labor contends that multinational corporations telescope the technological transfer process so that technology, which is developed most likely with the help of federal government funds, becomes rapidly available to other countries by way of local subsidiaries or licensing agreements. Consequently, export markets are lost and so too are important numbers of American jobs. The figures vary, but one spokesman suggested that from 1965 to 1971 over 900,000 American jobs had been lost as a result of giving multinational corporations free run to operate wherever they chose.

Although American labor has been the labor group most concerned about the job export question, several European labor movements, specifically in Sweden and the United Kingdom, have expressed similar concerns. It is likely that other advanced industrial and high-wage countries will also be confronted with this issue in the future; particularly in the face of rising unemployment in 1974 and 1975. The series of revaluations of the German mark and the Japanese yen, along with rapidly rising wage rates in these and other industrialized states, suggest that the production of certain goods in those countries may be shifted to low-wage countries. This may be acceptable as long as appreciable unemployment does not exist in the parent country, but if employment falls, domestic labor will probably react as the AFL–CIO has done. Already, the British labor movement has expressed serious misgivings about the job export matter, and in Sweden a bill has been passed to review the effects of outward investment plans on domestic employment. In 1973 after the monetary changes, the average hourly compensation for Belgian manufacturing workers was $4.09, in France $3.13, in Italy $3.08, in the Netherlands $3.92, and in West Germany $4.45. In South Korea, the average hourly compensation was only $.30. The potential for production shifts and job exports is obvious.

American multinational corporations are also accused by the AFL–CIO of adversely affecting the American balance of payments. Markets once served by exports are now serviced by foreign subsidiaries, causing a decline in earnings from exports. Moreover, importing electrical appliances, textiles, cars, and other products from the foreign subsidiaries of American multinationals causes an actual outflow of American funds. In addition, the tax deferral provisions of the United States tax code enable corporations to retain earnings abroad and avoid any United States taxation until the profits are actually repatriated. Consequently, profits that could return to the United States and contribute to a balance-of-payments surplus are instead reinvested in other countries. Finally, the actual outflow of dollars in the form of private investment capital is of course a definite drain on the balance of payments.

Another result of the tax deferral provisions is that host countries are able to obtain tax revenue from the reinvested profits of the American multinationals; the United States government does not. This imbalance is supplemented by a tax credit provision that allows American firms to deduct directly from their United States tax bill all monies paid in taxes to host countries. Vernon estimates that in 1966, the foreign subsidiaries of American firms paid $10 billion in taxes to host countries, where the United States government received from the earnings of these subsidiaries less than $1 billion in tax revenues.[38]

American multinationals have also been attacked for the "ruthless" way in which their money managers brought about a series of monetary crises during the period 1971–73 by shifting large amounts of currency from a weak dollar to stronger currencies. There was in this action little consideration of what was good for the United States. National loyalty was subordinated to what was best for the corporation. American critics

---

[38] Raymond Vernon, "Does Society Also Profit?" *Foreign Policy*, No. 13 (Winter, 1973–74), 110. As a result of labor pressure, the Nixon administration in 1973 and 1974 sought to reduce the tax advantages accruing to firms that are multinational.

of multinational firms charge that their preoccupation with more efficient and profitable operations generally makes them prone to disregard national concerns about employment, balance of payments, monetary crises, and other matters. Their internationalism allows these firms to operate above and beyond the boundaries of specific states, including their parent country. Indeed, such firms are flexible enough even to dissolve themselves legally in countries such as the United States, Canada, and the United Kingdom in order to establish legal residence in tax havens such as the Netherlands Antilles.

The effect of American multinational corporations on United States foreign policy and foreign relations is another matter of great concern. It has been charged that because of the vast amount and wide scope of American investment abroad, the United States government is obliged to protect its multinationals around the globe. The American economy has become so dependent upon foreign investment in the aggregate and upon the critical raw materials obtained by its extractive firms in the developing countries, it is alleged, that United States foreign policy is designed to insure that host countries continue to be receptive to American investment. This relationship between United States foreign policy and American foreign investment is enhanced by the close links between executives of big business and the important political appointees in Washington. Both issues are discussed in subsequent chapters.[39]

Although new left critics typically focus upon these concerns, there is another aspect of the relationship between corporations and foreign policy that needs to be understood. The independent, insensitive, or perhaps even stupid actions of multinational corporations and their subsidiaries can seriously damage relations between the United States and host states. In such cases, the actions of the corporation are taken out of the private context in which they are often undertaken and transferred into the public domain by elements of the host state that fail to perceive, understand, or accept the distinction between official policies and those of private international firms. When official relations are harmed by private actions, it is the task of United States foreign policy to try to improve the relationship. Moreover, in some cases American multinational corporations appeal directly to the United States government for help in their conflicts with host countries. For example, they may call for the application of United States political power through diplomacy, aid reductions, or other mechanisms by which the American government can attempt to influence other states. In both situations the American government may be pulled into a situation not of its own doing, as a result

[39] The question of American dependence on foreign sources of raw materials is discussed in depth in Chapter 7. The relationship between American business executives and United States foreign policy is examined in Chapter 8.

of actions by a multinational firm. Again, the multinational corporation acts as an entity unto itself; it imposes few restraints upon itself in the form of feelings of national loyalty to any state.

There is also the danger that the parent government may attempt to use its multinational corporations as instruments of its foreign policy, thus causing conflict with the host country. For example, the United States government may enforce provisions of the Trading with the Enemy Act and parent states generally may pursue other, less formal actions through the multinational firm. This has already been discussed as a negative aspect of foreign investment for host states. The mere existence of American, French, or Japanese multinationals may tempt parent-state government officials to try to meddle in the internal affairs of host countries by means of these firms.

For the most part, parent-country concerns about multinational corporations are caused by the fear that these firms operate largely beyond the control of the parent state. Public officials in parent states fear that, contrary to the broader interests of their nation, their government will be pushed or pulled into situations by their own multinationals. Furthermore, to the extent that international businesses link the economies of the parent state and host states, these firms increase the interdependency of the parent state with other states, thereby reducing parent-state autonomy. Consequently, a parent state may be less able to manage either its domestic economy or its international trade and monetary policy. As a result of these concerns, particularly the feelings of helplessness, various groups in parent states are urging their governments to adopt more stringent regulations concerning the operations of their own multinationals. In many respects, these concerns of parent states are very similar to those of host states: both types of states feel that the internationalism of multinational corporations gives these firms an alien character and a flexibility that threaten national sovereignty.

Parent States' Benefits

Since the beneficial consequences of foreign investment for parent countries have been seriously questioned by the American labor movement and by other critics, supporters of these enterprises have had to develop a convincing rationale, with accompanying evidence, to counteract the charges. Several of the major arguments offered in support of multinational corporations, specifically those headquartered in America, will be examined here. These enterprises are said to contribute generally to an American balance-of-payments surplus; their international involvement keeps American enterprises competitive in both domestic and foreign markets; and their international nature fosters rather than retards employment in the United States.

A cautious and comprehensive Tariff Commission report finds that American multinational corporations do indeed contribute to an American balance-of-payments surplus, and their performance far surpasses that of the non-MNC sectors of the economy. The outflow of funds involved in American direct foreign investment was outweighed by the returns from export activity and the income from repatriated profits, royalties, interest payments, and other fees. Table 4-3 indicates in a rather general fashion the contribution of multinational enterprises to a balance-of-payments surplus.

The evidence gathered by the Tariff Commission suggests that multinational enterprises are particularly active exporters, especially to their own affiliates in other countries. For example, in 1970 26.7 percent of all United States exports involved the flow of goods from the American facilities of American-based multinationals to their foreign subsidiaries—

TABLE 4-3. United States Private Balance-of-Payments Summary: MNC-Generated and Non-MNC-Generated for 1966 and 1970 (In Millions of Dollars)

Item	1966		1970	
	MNC-Generated	Non–MNC-Generated	MNC-Generated	Non–MNC-Generated
Merchandise trade balance[a]	2,023	1,801	2,048	116
Balance on services[b]	4,473	−457	6,400	−1,947
Remittance and other transfers[c]	0	−613	0	−1,012
Balance on current account[d]	6,496	731	8,448	−2,843
Long-term capital net[e]	−3,252	246	−2,422	482
Basic balance[f]	3,244	977	6,026	−2,361

Source: U.S. Congress, Senate Committee on Finance, *Implications of Multinational Firms for World Trade and Investment and for U.S. Trade and Labor,* 93rd Cong., 1st sess., 1973, p. 173.

[a] Corporate exports minus corporate imports.

[b] Receipts of dividends, interest, fees, royalties, and travel expenses from abroad, minus payments for such services to other countries.

[c] Small remittances between American corporations and residents and residents or governments of foreign countries.

[d] The sum of the first three items, reflecting noncapital transactions.

[e] Long-term-investment capital flows overseas minus long-term capital from abroad.

[f] Current-account transactions minus long-term capital transactions.

in absolute figures, about $13 billion worth of goods.[40] Further analysis reveals the necessity of assessing the impact of multinational corporations on an industry-by-industry basis. Petroleum and smelting corporations contributed to a deficit, as opposed to the sizable surplus generated by manufacturing industries. However, there is wide variation even among the manufacturing industries: the larger and more visible industries have a more beneficial trade and balance-of-payments effect than the smaller, less technologically advanced industries.[41]

A corollary argument proposes that if American firms were not multinational in scope, the overseas markets that are now filled by foreign subsidiaries with significant exports from the United States would be captured by foreign companies. Thus, it is not a question of serving a particular foreign market by either a foreign subsidiary or by increased exports from the United States, for in most cases the latter alternative is not available. That is, non-American-based multinationals would move into the market and take away the export option, since local facilities are often less costly in terms of production, transportation, and service costs and more responsive to local conditions and sales opportunities. Thus the multinational corporate supporters claim that an either-or proposition does not exist in this case. Rather, the multinational enterprise must use foreign installations to service foreign markets; otherwise, the foreign market is lost entirely to American companies and their workers.

Employment is a third factor of great importance in this dialogue. American multinational corporations and their supporters point to the export figures mentioned above and conclude that American employment would decrease if American firms were not international in scope. Furthermore, not only do multinational enterprises export more than their strictly domestic counterparts, but in addition their domestic investment and employment increase at a rate more rapid than that of the purely domestic firms. The keystone of the argument is that international operations stimulate the domestic component of a business. International facilities are a substitute neither for domestic production for domestic markets nor for domestic production for foreign markets. Consequently, the international activity represents a net gain for the parent state that is over and above that produced by a strictly domestic firm.

Quite naturally, supporters of the multinational corporation reject the charge that the activities of these firms tend to draw the United States into conflicts with host countries. Although advocates admit to a few instances of such conflict, they believe it is more often the case that the efforts of a firm to increase the benefits to parent and host states are hindered by the policies and behavior of the United States government.

40 Senate Committee on Finance, *Implications of Multinational Firms*, p. 180.

41 Ibid. See pp. 321–52 of this report for an extensive analysis of the effects of multinational corporations on United States foreign trade.

Such policies—for example, the Vietnam war, the tilt towards Pakistan, the favoritism shown the Israelis rather than the Arabs, and the often assertive and unilateral actions regarding monetary and trade matters—have all tended to make life more difficult for the multinational corporations—not the reverse.

Moreover, American-based multinationals, along with their counterparts in France, Germany, the United Kingdom, and Japan, emphasize that their internationalism helps to find, mine, and then process raw materials critical to the health and welfare of the parent-state economy and society. Similarly, manufacturing industries develop important foreign markets for the products of American or other parent-state factories. Thus, the conclusion of this argument is that parent states should aid and foster their multinational enterprises because of the many positive effects of their activity. It is interesting to note, regarding this issue, that one of the conscious strategies adopted by a number of advanced industrial states to meet the challenge of foreign investment is the development of their own multinationals. Thus, multinationals must have some benefit to parent states.

THE MULTINATIONAL FIRM AND REGIONAL AND INTERNATIONAL ORGANIZATIONS

The impact of multinational enterprises on regional and international organizations has scarcely been considered, either by academics or by policy makers within these institutions. Multinational corporations have only recently had much impact on the United Nations. Various nations and other groups have successfully initiated formal studies of multinational corporations through the Economic and Social Council, through the UNCTAD machinery, and through the International Labor Organization. Indeed, the 1974 report of the Group of Eminent Persons of the United Nations recommended the formation of an information and research center in the United Nations to gather data about multinational corporations. The Group also suggested the creation of a permanent commission on multinational corporations to analyze trends in foreign direct investment and to suggest appropriate policies. However, in terms of the workings of the United Nations, multinational corporations have been quite unimportant.[42] This is also true with the IMF and GATT.

---

[42] This is not to say that these bodies have not had debates and commissioned studies on multinational corporations, for they have. Rather, the point is that except for these studies, the actions and impact of multinational enterprises seem to have little continuing importance for these institutions—at this time. This may change as the United Nations implements the proposals of the Group of Eminent Persons.

Although neither body has engaged in concerted discussions of the effect of such firms on their goals and operations, IMF efforts at promoting international monetary stability will be hindered to the extent that treasurers of multinational corporations are able to circumvent the policies of the IMF and its member states. GATT concerns with trade have largely ignored the impact of international firms on patterns of production and trade. Consequently, its efforts seem to leave out one of the more important actors in international trade. The point here is that international organizations such as the United Nations, the IMF, and GATT cannot carry out their mandates effectively without coming to grips with the multinational corporation as an important international actor. Policies developed in the absence of such a consideration are likely to be incomplete and ineffective.

At the regional level, the situation is a bit different. Within the European Economic Community, fears have been expressed that foreign enterprises (primarily from the United States and, more recently, Japan) initially adjusted most successfully to the advantages of the Common Market. Some critics felt, for instance, that the Common Market seemed to have been created for the American multinationals and not for European business concerns. Moreover, even within the EEC, the multinationals were able in a few instances to select the country most receptive to foreign investment and still serve the broader market. French pique at American investors, which focused on Ford, led that corporation to move its planned investment from France to Belgium. Belgium gained jobs and tax revenues; Ford obtained a site for its facility and still had access to France and other Common Market countries; France seemed to gain nothing except pride, since it did not have the newly created jobs and yet the French market was open to Ford cars. The EEC is beginning to establish rules and regulations designed to counteract these activities by multinational firms, but the Andean Common Market has progressed much further in the direction of common policies towards international enterprises. The important efforts of the Andean group to control multinational enterprises are discussed at greater length in the next-to-last section of this chapter.

With these few regional exceptions, there is little continuing interaction between multinational corporations and international organizations. Indeed, some of the firms are more international than the intergovernmental institutions in that they have an organized and centralized management that administers the operations of the firm almost anywhere, in spite of national boundaries. On the other hand, most of the more important international organizations are little more than federated organizations that are severely constrained by their components—the states. The coordinated worldwide view of the international firm with centralized managerial goals and practices stands in vivid contrast with the fragmented world view of the international organization, whose management has little authority and whose member states often disagree not only on the means to achieve objectives but also on the substance of the objectives themselves. As a result of these and other differences, it seems that multinational corporations are frequently more effective international structures than most international governmental organizations. Therefore, in conflict situations the unity and skill of the firm may prevail over the concerns of the disunified international organization, whose members are susceptible to inter-country competition and disagreements.

MULTINATIONAL CORPORATIONS AND CONFLICT IN INTERNATIONAL POLITICS

Thus far, we have focused on the impact of multinational corporations on several different types of political entities—host states, parent states, and international and regional organizations. Also important, but the subject of far less attention by both academics and policy makers, are the effects multinational firms may have on relations among these political institutions. It is important to examine the ways in which multinational corporations, by conscious policies or by unintended effects of their actions, may contribute to the worsening of relations among these other international actors.

Relationships between parent state and host state are particularly susceptible to strain as a result of the actions of multinational enterprises. Since both states seek to utilize the international firm for their own objectives, basic questions of sovereignty and jurisdiction arise, and the corporation may be caught in the middle. Antitrust provisions and the Trading with the Enemy Act have already been mentioned as sore points in the relationship between the United States as a parent government and other countries as host states. Questions of jurisdiction have on several occasions been raised in Canada and in other states regarding legal demands on American multinationals by the United States government or its courts. For example, in 1950 the provinces of Ontario and Quebec tried to prevent American subsidiaries from providing documents in compliance with United States court rulings, by passing laws prohibiting such actions. At times, tangled diplomatic negotiations are necessary to unravel the complications resulting from jurisdictional disputes. In all these cases, the existence of the transnational corporations brought into question the fundamental issue of which political entity had jurisdiction. Such problems are inherent in the multinational nature of the enterprise and will inevitably continue to plague relations between parent and host states.

The potential for conflict between host states and parent states is exacerbated by the fact that host states and parent states may have very different objectives for the same multinational enterprise and thus may clash in their attempts to achieve these objectives. Balance-of-payments policies constitute an excellent case in point. A parent state trying to correct a deficit might enact regulations designed to hasten and enlarge the repatriation of profits and management fees from the subsidiary; to hinder and restrict the outflow of new capital for investment, thereby provoking the use of local sources of funds within the host state; and to expand exports from the parent company and inhibit imports from the subsidiary. Of course, a host state troubled by a balance-of-payments deficit may institute regulations designed to produce results that are exactly the opposite of those desired by the parent state.

The parent and host states may also have different objectives regarding trade, domestic employment problems, currency stability and valuation, the impact of the location of research and development efforts, and foreign policy matters. It is possible to develop a conflict matrix, such as that in Table 4-4, to specify these and other differing objectives of host and parent states regarding the actions and effects of multinational corporations. A conflict matrix could also be constructed to illustrate the various policy actions that could be undertaken by parent or host states in pursuit of their essentially conflicting objectives. The purpose of such an exercise and of this discussion is to emphasize that the behavior and existence of multinational corporations may be the source of and vehicle for worsening relations between parent and host states, in that each attempts to harness such corporations to advance its own interests.

Parent states and host states may also clash as a result of specific actions taken by either host or parent state in the attempt to influence the behavior of multinational corporations. The efforts of Cuba, Peru, Bolivia, and Chile to nationalize American business enterprises within their jurisdiction had an obvious negative effect on official governmental relations between these countries and the United States. Somewhat similar problems have occurred involving French firms operating in Africa, and it is highly probable that difficulties will emerge with Japanese enterprises in Asia.

In addition to the fact that multinational corporations may be the object and source of conflict between parent and host states, these firms may also be the vehicle by which host and parent countries try to influence each other. There is a widespread fear, with some justifying examples, that multinational corporations may serve as a conduit for

TABLE 4-4. Parent State–Host State Conflict Matrix: MNC Effect on Balance of Payments

Issue	Host-State Desires	Parent-State Desires
Investment capital	Obtain from parent state	Obtain from host state and other foreign sources
Profits	Reinvest	Repatriate
Licenses, royalties, management fees	No payment for services rendered	Full payment for services rendered
Exports	From subsidiary to other subsidiaries and to parent-country headquarters	From parent-country plants to subsidiaries in host states

parent-state foreign policy actions. The United States government sought to hinder the development of a French nuclear force by prohibiting IBM from selling needed equipment. The ITT–CIA case regarding the Allende government in Chile is perhaps the most celebrated case that heightens fear and suspicion that multinationals are vehicles for United States foreign policy efforts.

The reverse is true also. Host states have attempted to influence parent states through multinational firms. In response to President Nixon's August, 1971, 10 percent import surcharge, many American firms with subsidiaries in Latin America loudly decried the measure and sought its rapid repeal since Latin America was already running a trade deficit with the United States. Whether out of enlightened self-interest or as a result of direct requests from host-state officials, these firms were seeking to influence United States policy on behalf of the Latin American host states. The Arab oil embargo of 1973 and 1974 was accompanied by Arab efforts to have multinational petroleum companies influence United States and Western policy towards the Middle East. Even prior to the embargo and the Arab-Israeli war, stockholders of Standard Oil of California were sent a letter urging "understanding on our [America's] part of the aspirations of the Arab people, and more positive support of their efforts toward peace in the Middle East." This behavior is a good example of a multinational's efforts to influence parent-state policy on the behalf of host states. As this pressure mounts and as the oil-producing countries and other countries that export natural resources begin to exercise their potential influence, one possible result is a deterioration in relations between the parent countries and host states. Whether this happens or not, it is clear that the multinationals will likely have an important effect on relations between parent and host states.[43]

The potential impact of multinational corporations on relations between a parent state and a host state is widely appreciated. Less obvious is the likelihood of increased competition among parent states on behalf of their own multinational firms. The expansion and success of American-based multinational corporations has led a number of European states to rationalize and consolidate their own companies with the objective of forming sizable multinationals of their own to compete with the foreign firms. Since these combined firms are often created as a result of government initiative and sometimes with government funds, it is reasonable to expect that the parent governments will in some cases seek to insure that their firms are successful in their efforts by actively supporting them, to the detriment of international enterprises of a different nationality. Some of the giant European multinationals, such as British Petroleum, Renault, and ENI, are even partially owned by their respective governments. Moreover, the concept of Japan Inc. suggests the very close relationship between the Japanese government and their multinational enterprises.

A further stimulus of conflict among parent states stemming from competition among multinational corporations is the current concern about raw material and energy shortages. For example, the lack of sufficient domestic supplies of petroleum, in conjunction with the current efforts of oil-producing states to control petroleum prices and supplies, prompted the Japanese government to help its firms explore for oil in other areas. An oil-hungry and dependent Europe is also seeking to establish new sources of supply for itself and its own firms, to the disadvantage of Japanese and American firms. Consequently, competi-

[43] From a more global perspective, it has been suggested that multinational corporations will widen the gap between developing countries, as the recipients for foreign investment, and those few advanced industrial states in which the headquarters of the multinational enterprises are located. Thus, a stratified international political and economic system will be created, with great amounts of power accruing to the few headquarters states. There also exists a second tier of regionally important states, which are likened by Stephen Hymer to middle-management levels of the corporation and which have influence only to the extent to which they serve the interests of the center states. Finally, there are the large number of passive and very dependent states who are the hewers of wood and haulers of water for the rich states and their multinational enterprises. Hymer and other radical critics predict that this stratification will provoke the seeds of its own destruction: the peripheral states will attempt to overturn the system by which they are dominated. See Stephen Hymer, "The Multinational Corporation and the Law of Uneven Development," in *Economics and World Order: From the 1970's to the 1990's*, ed. Jagdish N. Bhagwati (New York: The Macmillan Company, 1972), pp. 113–40.

tion among multinational corporations of different nationalities for what are thought to be vital, scarce resources may well lead to conflict among the parent governments of these firms.

The international airline industry, which is characterized by government support of private, quasi-governmental, or totally government-owned firms, may well be the forerunner of conflicts, which are likely to emerge as parent states seek to advance the interests of their international enterprises. The day may not be too distant when competition among multinational corporations from different countries will provoke political and economic involvement by the respective parent governments. Perhaps periodic formal negotiations involving both governmental and corporate representatives of competing parent states will be necessary to achieve "peace."

Conflict among host states is likely to occur as they compete to attract the benefits of foreign investment. Already, many host states compete with one another by offering various kinds of inducements to foreign investors. During a 1971 visit to the United Kingdom, Henry Ford made it clear to Prime Minister Heath and the British people that unsatisfactory labor relations in Great Britain might cause Ford of England to restrict new investment or even transfer some existing investment from Britain to other countries. The next day, a group of Dutch businessmen and government officials invited Ford to consider further investment in the Netherlands. Although this situation might not happen often, competition for foreign investment does exist among advanced industrial states and among the developing nations.

There are several possible effects of this competitive courtship of multinational corporations. If the competition is severe enough, one result may be an increase in the various states' incentive packages and/or a reduction in the investment risks and costs for the corporations. If states actively pursue foreign investment, they may undercut one another in offering inducements, thereby generally increasing the level of the returns or benefits accruing to multinational corporations and reducing the gains of the host states.

Moreover, the uneven pattern of foreign investment within a region may help to sour relations among potential host states. For example, within a particular region the combination of natural and human endowments, locational advantages, governmental policies, and other factors may mean that one or two states receive much of the foreign investment and other states very little at all. To the extent that multinational corporations are thought to bring more advantages than disadvantages, the less fortunate states in a region may seek to gain a greater share of the foreign investment through political efforts directed against the more successful host countries.

As a result of competition for investment and concern about the unequal distribution of such investment, some states in a particular region may seek to form a regional group to distribute foreign investment more equitably and purposefully, to harmonize the laws and incentives regarding these enterprises, and generally to reduce the possibility of intraregion conflict over these firms. Among other reasons, the desire to present a united front to foreign investors was a major stimulus for the formation of the Andean Common Market, which comprises Venezuela, Colombia, Ecuador, Peru, Bolivia, and Chile. Thus, in an almost dialectical fashion, competition among host states as a result of multinational enterprises may lead to the development of regional strategies designed to prevent this conflict. This may be thought by some to be a positive result of the activities of multinational corporations.

On the other hand, regional or international efforts to contain interstate conflict may be perceived by some host states as interfering with their ability to try to attract foreign investment or at least to determine their own policies on these issues. Colombia and Venezuela were reluctant to join the Andean pact because both countries have had relatively satisfactory experiences with a sizable foreign investment sector. In another example, Belgium was somewhat disturbed when the European Common Market Commission disallowed investment incentives for a certain region of Belgium, an action that the government felt was necessary for the promotion of industry and creation of employment. Host-state conflict with international or regional organizations emerges when a state feels that it will be able to obtain greater benefits from foreign investment by not subscribing to an international or regional agreement that establishes a common policy toward multinational corporations.

Conflict at the international or regional level may emerge when international organizations, in the form of producer cartels, align host states against a coalition of multinational firms and their parent states. Conflict of this sort threatened to develop between the major petroleum-consuming countries and the Organization of Petroleum Exporting Countries (OPEC). In the winter of 1974, the United States attempted to organize major petroleum-consuming countries as a counterweight to OPEC; leadership would supposedly be assumed by those states that had a number of multinational petroleum companies. The lack of immediate success in this endeavor by no means undermines the basic point that conflicts between organized groups of host states and an alignment of parent states are likely to be particularly severe where the dispute involves scarce natural resources or food products.

There are other potential conflicts between coalitions of states and international organizations that are centered in multinational corporations, but some of these seem far in the future. In general, though, the existence of multinational corporations may provoke disputes if certain groups of states attempt to increase their benefits and reduce their costs from these firms at the expense of other sets of states or international organizations.

POSITIVE IMPACTS OF MULTINATIONAL CORPORATIONS ON INTERNATIONAL POLITICS

Advocates of multinational corporations claim that these enterprises have had and will continue to have a beneficial impact on relations among states. In several different ways, multinational enterprises are thought to contribute to regional or functional integration and to other cooperative efforts. First, the threat posed by the existence of multinational corporations may prompt states to adopt common policies to counteract, adapt to, or get the most benefit from them. Concerns about the ability of multinational enterprises to exploit their common market led the Andean Common Market to adopt a set of stringent barriers and regulations to closely control multinational business activities. Similarly, OPEC has presented a united front to the giant multinational oil companies and the oil-consuming states. In these cases and others, the multinational enterprise has had a catalytic effect in the formation of coordinated efforts among states that were previously too much in conflict to cooperate.

Second, multinational corporations, as a result of their own integrated nature and their impact on other social units, may help provide an environment that is conducive to the promotion of integration among states, which is thought by some statesmen to be a desired goal. The ability of these enterprises to surmount national boundaries in the production and marketing of a product contributes to the establishment of a common regional culture and life style. Integrated production means that workers in a number of different states are closely linked to one another in terms of their work and, of course, their employer. In Europe particularly, regional unions are springing up to represent region-wide interests. Management personnel in Europe are beginning to develop a European perspective and to perceive themselves as having interests and opportunities that range beyond their own country.[44] Also, within Europe many products, brand names, and advertising efforts are common to several different states. In sum, the multinational corporation may help both to break down the barriers of separateness and to crystalize some of the common interests and culture that foster regional interest groups and regional orientations. Evidence seems to suggest that within

44 See Bernard Mennis and Karl P. Sauvant, "Multinational Corporations, Managers, and the Development of Regional Identifications in Western Europe," *The Annals,* Vol. 403 (September, 1972) , 22–33.

the EEC, multinational corporations have been useful in promoting integration rather than retarding it.

Some supporters of the multinational corporation claim that it is a force for peace among states since it represents an extremely successful form of internationalism, one that links states more closely. In spite of the political impediments of different national systems and national characteristics, the multinational corporation has succeeded in overcoming these barriers and making states more interdependent and thus less likely to engage in violent conflict. The president of the Bank of America expressed this thesis clearly:

> the idea that this kind of business enterprise can be a strong force toward world peace is not so far fetched. Beyond the human values involved, the multinational firm has a direct, measurable, and potent interest in helping prevent wars and other serious upheavals that cut off its resources, interrupt its communications, and kill its employees and customers.[45]

The previous section indicated many ways in which multinational corporations may adversely affect the patterns of relations between states and international or regional organizations, either as a matter of policy or merely because of competition for their benefits. In this section, we have offered arguments to show the beneficial impact of the multinational corporation on inter-state relations. Although serious conceptual and methodological problems make it difficult to precisely determine the net impact of these enterprises on international politics, it is important to be aware of the various implications of their existence for relations between states. Multinational corporations are crucial international actors, and any attempt to analyze international politics should incorporate an assessment of the impact of these firms, both individually and collectively.

MULTINATIONAL CORPORATIONS AND CHANGES IN THE INTERNATIONAL POLITICAL SYSTEM

To this point we have examined multinational corporations largely in terms of their relations with states. However, a different perspective is imperative, for not only do these firms have important consequences for states, they also have stimulated the development of international co-

---

[45] Reprinted from "The Internationalized Corporation: An Executive's View," by A. W. Clausen in vol. 403 of *The Annals* of The American Academy of Political and Social Science. © 1972 by The Academy of Political and Social Science.

operation among other nongovernmental actors. Within this relatively neglected area, some far-ranging and basic changes may be occurring. To oversimplify a bit, it appears that an international economic and political system may be emerging in which multinational corporations are the major institutions as well as the prime stimuli for the development of other structures. However, all this is occurring without a central political authority.

Because of the importance of the international economic system, various international groups organized around common interests are beginning to participate in the international system, as their domestic counterparts do in individual states. The reason for this activity is simply that international economic transactions have direct consequences upon the interests of these groups, and as a result the groups seek to exert control over these transactions. Nations have not been particularly responsive or effective in protecting these organized interests from the impact of the international economic system. Domestic groups are relatively powerless to protect their interests in the context of a highly interdependent world. Finally, the various intergovernmental institutions have not yet developed the ability or the will to represent effectively the concerns of these domestic groups. Thus, there is a need to develop new forms of international cooperation among like interests within the global economy.

The lack of a systematic investigation of this phenomenon requires us to illustrate these developments by means of specific examples. The Council of the Americas is a business-oriented group that is somewhat analogous to a lobbying organization in that it seeks to promote actions by Latin American governments that favor multinational corporations. The Council also seeks to aid and educate American corporations regarding the problems and prospects of doing business in Latin America. In addition to the Council and a number of other similar organizations, there are various international trade associations of some importance. More broadly, the International Chamber of Commerce has made a significant effort to develop a set of guidelines for multinational corporations, parent governments, and host governments. Quite clearly, the Chamber hopes that its ideas will be largely incorporated by similar efforts mounted by states or international organizations. Another interesting example of private international cooperation was the March, 1972 meeting in Versailles between American and European businessmen. The purpose of the meeting was to exchange views about some of the crucial economic issues dividing Europe and the United States and to try to reduce the resulting frictions. Government officials as well as the press were barred from the sessions.

As a response to the many business-oriented organizations in this emerging international system, some groups are seeking to develop a countervailing force to the multinational corporation. The efforts of international labor union organizations in this regard are most revealing, for the patterns of response which these union organizations are developing may prove to be a model for the actions of other groups. The various national labor movements often feel helpless in the face of the international mobility, flexibility, and strength of the multinational corporations. For a variety of reasons, the strategies and tactics used by unions on domestic employers are frequently ineffective when used on multinational employers.[46]

To overcome this disadvantageous relationship, unions have designed a number of activities to exert some control over the corporations. At the national level, unions from two or more states have cooperated to aid one another in their conflicts with the same multinational employer. At times, this has entailed meetings to exchange information and plan a common strategy for eventual confrontations with management. In other instances, coordinated action has actually been taken against the employer in several different countries. At the regional level, groups of unions have formalized their efforts to coordinate actions taken toward corporations. Through the leadership of the European Metalworkers' Federation, representatives of unions from several states have met with the management of such multinational employers as Philips, AKZO, VFW–Fokker, and others to discuss various issues. Moreover, when a union in one country has struck a multinational employer, counterpart unions in other countries have sometimes refused to work overtime to take up the slack caused by the disruption in production or have applied similar types of pressure to the common employer.

Similar activities have occurred at the international level. A number of the international trade secretariats (international union organizations organized according to type of industry), such as the International Metalworkers' Federation and the International Chemical and General Workers' Federation, have formed company councils composed of many of the unions associated with the same multinational employer. Information exchange, consultation and planning, and joint solidarity actions have been planned and coordinated by these international trade secretariats.

Although these activities do not represent the prevailing pattern of union responses to multinational corporations and the international economic system, they do represent both formal and informal efforts to

---

[46] For a discussion of trade union weaknesses and their responses, see David H. Blake, "Trade Unions and the Challenge of the Multinational Corporation," *The Annals,* Vol. 403 (September, 1972) 34–35; and David H. Blake, "The Internationalization of Industrial Relations," *Journal of International Business Studies,* III (Fall, 1972) , 17–32.

confront multinational corporations on a regional and international level. To a limited but increasing extent, industrial relations are being internationalized. One consequence of this type of activity by labor is the establishment of still another internationally organized nongovernmental interest-group activity, which may reduce the ability of a single state to control its economic affairs. A Canadian cabinet minister expressed dismay to one of the authors over the fact that a wage settlement hammered out by the international United Auto Workers and Chrysler, a settlement that was applicable to Canadian and American employees, meant that the Canadian government could do little to moderate the inflationary nature of the contract.

This type of development, which is stimulated by multinational corporations, is leading to the emergence of a truly international economic and political system. Processes and procedures formerly limited to nations are necessarily being introduced at the regional and international level because of the international nature of these firms. Although this is clearly a slow trend, there is enough evidence to suggest that it may well be one of the most important long-run effects of the multinational corporations. These enterprises have provoked an operational internationalism that has not yet been achieved by formal political mechanisms.

POLICIES FOR CONTROL

It is natural that some attempts (particularly by host states) would be made to control the extensive impacts of multinational corporations on domestic interest groups, parent and host states, and regional and international organizations and systems. These efforts vary greatly in nature and in degree of success. Some states have not bothered to institute any controls at all, other than those already existing for domestic enterprises. At the other extreme is outright nationalization, whereby the host state obtains total ownership and control of the corporation and the foreign investment is completely eliminated. Between these two extremes is a wide variety of control mechanisms designed to preserve foreign investment while increasing the benefits received by the host state and reducing the associated disruptions and costs.

Overall, the substance of these control policies is quite varied and incorporates most of the concerns expressed by host states. Regarding balance-of-payments questions, some host states insist upon a specific degree of export activity by the multinational enterprise. In addition, they may impose barriers on the import of goods and the repatriation of profits to the foreign headquarters. Local-content regulations require the products of the foreign enterprise to have increasing amounts of domestically produced components or raw materials, and naturally this will add to a state's balance of payments surplus.

In terms of exerting local control over foreign enterprises, host states often establish requirements about the number and position of both foreign and local employees and managers. Some states require a majority of host-country citizens on the enterprise's board of directors. Other states go much further, insisting that the foreign enterprise share ownership—in varying proportions with national enterprises, local citizens, or government agencies.

Some of these measures and others as well enhance the domestic benefits of the foreign investment. Increasing tax rates or the pretax governmental share of profits is a common way by which host countries seek to enlarge their benefits. A few states have actively sought to have foreign investors conduct research and development in the host state, thereby increasing the opportunities for local scientists and enhancing the indigenous research and development capability of the host country.

Of course, there are many other measures that host states have adopted in order to exert some kind of control over the multinational corporation. Some of these efforts to increase the benefits and reduce the costs for the host state take the form of barriers to or requirements for entry. Multinational corporations seeking to invest must meet the specific demands of the host state, often through long, complex negotiations. Some of these provisions may apply to all foreign concerns; others may be ad hoc and specific to the particular investment.

Host-state control is also increased through the establishment of new requirements, which must be met by existing foreign enterprises. The firms must then decide whether compliance or withdrawal is the best course to follow. Having made the initial investment and incurred the costs associated with starting a new venture, it is difficult for a corporation not to respond in a fashion that allows it to continue making a profit and at the same time comply with the demands of the state. However, if the operation is marginal at best, or if the process can be easily closed down and opened up in another country, the bargaining power of the state is reduced. As with requirements for entry, these new measures may be applied generally or may be designed for a specific firm.

Just as it is impossible to examine all the types of incentives offered by host states, so it is impossible to discuss the many types of controls placed on foreign investment by host states. As we suggested earlier, the complexity and severity of these restrictions vary widely. States such as Belgium, the Netherlands, Great Britain, and a fairly large number of developing countries are quite receptive to foreign investment and impose few regulations. However, this attitude can easily change, as illustrated by the efforts of the Spanish government to increase their control over and benefits from foreign investment.

Other states have a much more stringent set of controls. For a long time, Japan made it exceptionally difficult for many multinational corporations to establish investments in that country. This policy has been liberalized considerably since 1971, but the change was a consequence of the pressure of the United States government and its multinationals. Mexico is another state that has traditionally controlled foreign investment in pursuit of its own national objectives. Although Mexican laws regarding foreign investment have been applied rather flexibly, some of their provisions specify not only a majority share of Mexican ownership but also a high degree of Mexican, as opposed to foreign, management. Coupled with these requirements are regulations overseeing the nature of technology transfers between Mexican enterprises and the subsidiaries of foreign firms and foreign business concerns. The registration of all technological contracts allows the Mexican government to determine whether the arrangement is in the best interests of Mexico. In spite of these restrictions, which are applied selectively, foreign investment thrives in Mexico.

Other states have taken an even more restrictive posture on foreign investment, exhibiting a basic reluctance to welcome multinational corporations, but this stand is tempered sometimes with an awareness of the necessity of having some foreign investment in certain specified industries. The terms for admission and operation are much stricter than in Mexico, for instance. Salvador Allende's Chile exhibited this tendency, as did Indonesia in 1965 and Ceylon in 1962 and 1963. Interestingly, the Soviet Union and some of the Eastern European countries are seeking to attract foreign investors, but under clearly specified limitations. Some multinational corporations are willing to operate under these more difficult conditions, but such restrictions, particularly if coupled with governmental instability, tend to scare off many potential investors. Thus, there is the interesting anomaly of President Allende nationalizing investments from the United States and other countries, and at the same time attempting to attract foreign investment without much success. On the other hand, multinational corporations of many nationalities find the huge Soviet market and the stable Soviet investment climate to be exceptionally attractive in spite of the extensive restrictions on business activities.

The success of host-state efforts to control the activities and impact of multinational corporations while still obtaining desired benefits varies with such factors as the nature of the controls, the stability of the investment climate, the size of the market, dependence on the raw material, and of course the specific nature of the foreign investment. To put it in different terms, the multinational enterprise weighs the costs of doing business under restrictions with the possible benefits to be received. Nations perform the same type of calculus, but from a different perspective. Speaking generally, the restricted Soviet environment is attractive because of the very large market, in terms of population and stage of industrial development, and the existence of important raw materials. A much smaller and poorer market, even with less onerous and cumbersome restrictions, may be far less attractive to many manufacturing firms. However, if this smaller and poorer country has scarce and critical raw materials, the extractive multinational may put up with the governmental controls in order to gain access to the raw material. In sum, a set of restrictions that control, without driving out, foreign investment in one country or in a specific industry may be ineffective and disastrous in another country or in a different industry in the same country.

Parent states have also attempted to control the impact of multinational corporations, but almost exclusively from the perspective of enhancing parent-state benefits and reducing costs. Since World War II, almost all of the current capital-exporting countries have at one time or another imposed controls on outward-bound capital investment. These measures were designed to preserve scarce currency. Other types of controls have been established in response to concerns about antitrust, national security, protection of domestic industry and employment, and punishment leveled at specific countries, such as Rhodesia.

Rarely, though, have the control efforts of the parent state been designed to insure that its multinationals behave in an appropriate fashion in host countries. Recently, Japan has become quite concerned about the poor Japanese image and hostile relations stimulated by the expanding and insensitive presence of Japanese firms in Asia. Japan has established a set of guidelines in response. Both Sweden and the United States have provisions in their investment-guarantee programs that try to foster good behavior. But although Sweden has an extensive list of "social conditions," the impact of such efforts seems quite limited. However, as foreign investment grows and pulls parent governments into difficult situations, more parent states may seek to regulate their own multinationals.

Thus far, we have discussed control efforts undertaken by nations acting alone. An alternate control strategy is concerted action by a group of states regarding the conditions under which multinationals are allowed to operate. Because of the commonly agreed-upon rules and regulations for foreign investment adopted by a specific group of states, their coordinated efforts tend to overcome to some degree the advantages of mobility and flexibility enjoyed by the corporations. These groupings may be organized basically along geographic and regional lines, as is the case with the Andean Common Market and the European Economic Community, or they may involve cooperation because of a common natural resource, as in the case of OPEC.[47]

The Andean Common Market is an interesting example of a regional effort to control the actions and effects of multinational corporations and still obtain the desired benefits. With respect to control, the six member states have agreed upon a relatively stringent set of rules regarding foreign investment. With respect to benefits, they have joined together as a common market, so that investors abiding by their rules can produce and sell in a market of six states with a combined population of approximately 66 million people. Therefore, from the perspective of the investor, the costs of operating in a more controlled environment need to be measured against the benefits of doing business in a much larger market with a significant reduction of intraregion tariffs.

The Andean experiment is quite unique in its comprehensiveness, and, thus, a brief look at some of its provisions regarding foreign investment may be instructive. First, foreign investment is prohibited in a number of industries, including banking, insurance, broadcasting, publishing, and internal transportation. Second, new investment and most existing investment must divest itself of majority ownership (the fade-out formula) within 15 years in Chile, Colombia, Peru, and Venezuela and within 20 years in Bolivia and Ecuador, so that national investor participation will be at least 51 percent. Third, annual earnings repatriated by the foreign firm cannot exceed 14 percent of the investment. Fourth, a foreign subsidiary may not pay its parent company or other affiliate for the use of intangible technological know-how; in addition, clauses or practices that tend to restrict competition or production or otherwise increase the cost of the technology to the host state are prohibited. The Andean code contains other provisions, but these four suggest the extent to which the Andean countries are attempting to control the actions and impact of the multinationals. Clearly, these six states desire foreign investment, but on their own terms.

At the international level, there have been no successful attempts to impose controls on foreign investment. However, there is quite a bit of activity and concern in such places as the International Labor Organization, UNCTAD, the Economic and Social Council of the United Nations, and the Organization for Economic Cooperation and Development (OECD). Although studies are being conducted and suggestions for establishing international rules and regulations have been made, little of a concrete nature has been achieved. However, a 1974 United Nations

---

47 OPEC is discussed in some detail in Chapter 7.

report has recommended the consideration of a move toward the establishment of codes of conduct.[48] It is interesting to note that a number of executives and business organizations have recommended the development of an international code to regulate not only the multinational corporations but also host states and parent states.

In assessing the effectiveness of attempts to control the behavior and impact of multinational enterprises, a few general patterns can be observed. The efforts to control multinational corporations focus primarily on their relationship with host states and domestic interests within the host states. Parent states have imposed controls in order to advance their own economic interests, but parent states have made few attempts to regulate the foreign behavior of these firms. The issue of the impact of foreign investment on the relations among states has received scarcely any systematic attention, and there have been no suggestions for remedying any of the resulting problems.

With respect to the efforts to control multinationals and their actions in host states, much evidence indicates that these firms are willing to operate under stringent conditions as long as it is profitable for them to do so. In other words, many states can more effectively harness the activities of these enterprises towards national objectives with the corporations readily adapting to the new environment. However, not all states are in this fortunate position, and the adaptability of industries and specific firms varies quite widely. Again, the decision to adapt or not depends largely upon management's assessment of the benefits to be gained from continuing operations versus the costs to be incurred.

Undeveloped states and small countries without the benefit of deposits of scarce natural resources are not in a position to exert significantly greater control over foreign investment without threatening to drive away the investments. Basically, the larger and richer state has the best chance to impose controls since this type of state has the most to offer the multinational corporation. As with trade and monetary matters, it appears that most developing countries are less able than the more advanced states to obtain the greatest amount of benefits from foreign investment. This peripheral relationship may be improved by joint action, but the obstacles to such efforts are great.

Of course, if one rejects the objective of industrialization and growth, there is no need for a state to accept investment by multinational

---

48 For a discussion of the efforts of international organizations along these lines, see Robert S. Walters, "International Organizations and the Multinational Corporation: An Overview and Observations," *The Annals,* vol. 403 (September, 1972), 127–38. See also United Nations, Department of Economic and Social Affairs, *The Impact of Multinational Corporations on Development and on International Relations* (E/5500/Rev. 1, ST/ESA/6), 1974.

corporations. Furthermore, if one views the relationship between host states and these firms in strict zero-sum terms—meaning that corporate benefits are offset by host-state costs—then the implied policy is to nationalize all existing investment and prohibit the entrance of new operations. However, if the relationship is viewed in positive-sum terms, then the challenge for host states is how best to maximize the benefits and reduce the costs associated with foreign investment.

THE MULTINATIONAL CORPORATION AS A LIGHTNING ROD

In the late 1960s and the 1970s, the issue of the multinational corporation has been a critical one for host states and for the United States as the largest parent country. Trade unionists, academics, journalists, politicians, bureaucrats, and ideologues have focused their attention on the multinational corporation. It may be the case that this enterprise is serving as a lightning rod, drawing to it attacks that are associated with the more general frustration caused by the impact of the global political economy on states and on groups within states. With the increasing dependency and interdependency caused by the internationalization of most economies, it is more difficult for states and domestic interests to control their own destiny effectively. As we pointed out in Chapters 2 and 3 with respect to trade and monetary matters, international and foreign developments interfere directly with domestic patterns and policies. Moreover, policies designed to alleviate the disruptions caused by adjustment to an internationalized economy are often hindered and made unworkable by external events and the actions of other states.

Of course, we readily admit the seriousness of the issues raised by many regarding the impact of foreign investment. Indeed, we suggest that there are other problems that are not adequately aired. However, it does seem that in some instances multinational corporations are being attacked primarily because they are the most visible manifestation of the limits on national autonomy imposed by the global political economy. It is very difficult for union leaders, business executives, legislators, and politicians in the United States and elsewhere to focus anger on something as abstract as trade flows or the monetary system. These targets are most elusive and complex, and therefore not very useful in stimulating concern and action. However, multinational corporations are tangible and almost irresistible targets of discontent.

With respect to the developing nations, their major problem may not be the actions of multinationals but rather the fact that the global economy is emerging largely in disregard and ignorance of their interests.

In terms of trade, monetary affairs, and investment, the major issues for the advanced states just do not involve the developing countries, with the possible exception of access to raw materials.

Perhaps the lightning-rod analogy is inappropriate. But it may be that the basic cause of host and parent states' concerns is their difficulty in making the necessary internal and international political and economic adjustments to the emerging global political economy.

5

Aid Relations
Between
Rich and Poor States

Until recently, foreign aid[1] figured prominently in all analyses of relations between advanced industrial states and less-developed countries.
Although it still constitutes an important and unique dimension of
relations between rich and poor states, other economic channels, such as
trade and investment, have assumed greater importance. Export earnings
account for 80 percent of less-developed countries' foreign exchange
earnings, and of the remaining 20 percent, private-investment flows have
in recent years exceeded net official-aid flows to poor states from Western
states. These economic facts are reflected in the contemporary political
dialogue between the center and periphery of the global economy, a
dialogue in which the stress is now placed primarily upon the terms of
trade and the rights of ownership associated with direct foreign investment in poor states. Until the mid 1960s, the dialogue focused on the
volume and terms of aid flows. Nevertheless, aid flows continue in substantial amounts, and the political issues surrounding this economic link
between advanced industrial states and less-developed states remain important—even if they are not as determinate of overall relations as they
once were.

The volume of economic aid flowing from Western states to less-

---

[1] This discussion, consistent with the focus of this volume, will be confined to
economic assistance and will exclude military aid. By economic assistance, we
mean flows to less-developed countries and multilateral institutions provided
by governments for the ostensible purpose of development; such flows are
concessional in character, relative to commercial terms (lower interest rates,
longer repayment periods, grace periods, and so forth) .

developed countries and to multilateral aid institutions during the period 1962–1972 is summarized in Table 5-1. The net aid disbursements of $8.6 billion in 1972 from these states constituted about 85 percent of the total aid flowing to states in the Third World that year. Beyond this, the major sources of aid were the Communist states, which disbursed an estimated $800 million in economic assistance in 1971. The data in Table 5-1 reflect some major trends in economic assistance. The United States remains the largest single aid donor by a wide margin. However, its aid disbursements have remained at virtually the same level throughout the last decade. The increases in aid flows since 1961 have come from countries other than the United States. Germany and Japan, in particular, have emerged as major new sources of aid over the past decade.[2] As a consequence, the United States, which accounted for 59 percent of total Western aid in 1961, accounted for only 39 percent in 1972. American spokesmen argue that this 39 percent is not an inappropriate share of total Western aid flows, since the United States accounts for 40 percent of the total GNP of non-Communist advanced industrial states.

More generally, however, the data in Table 5-1 reflect a declining

TABLE 5-1.   **The Volume of Aid: 1962, 1967, 1972 (In Millions of American Dollars)[a]**

Country	Aid Flows[b]			Aid as a Percentage of Donor's GNP		
	1962	1967	1972	1962	1967	1972
France	945	826	1,321	1.27	0.71	0.67
Germany	405	508	808	0.45	0.41	0.31
Japan	85	379	611	0.14	0.31	0.21
United Kingdom	421	485	608	0.52	0.44	0.40
United States	3,182	3,472	3,349	0.56	0.43	0.29
TOTAL DAC[c]	5,438	6,536	8,654	0.52	0.42	0.34

Source: OECD, *Development Cooperation, 1973 Review* (Paris, 1973), pp. 181, 189.

[a] Current United States dollars.

[b] Net official development assistance to less-developed countries and multilateral agencies. This excludes, for example, private direct investment and portfolio investment, as well as public and private export credits and guarantees.

[c] Total aid for all states represented in the Development Assistance Committee (DAC) of the Organization for Economic Cooperation and Development (OECD). In addition to the states specified in the table, these include Australia, Austria, Belgium, Canada, Denmark, Italy, the Netherlands, Norway, Portugal, Sweden, and Switzerland. Column entries do not add up to the total.

[2] The data in Table 5-1 understate Japanese aid flows, since Japan extends large amounts of export credits ($856 million in 1972), which are not included as official development assistance in OECD statistics.

aid commitment on the part of Western states over the past decade. Although Western aid has risen from $5.4 billion to $8.6 billion between 1962 and 1972, it should be noted that the high rate of global inflation since 1970 has absorbed most of the dollar increase in the amount of aid flows since 1967. The major Western states' commitment to economic assistance programs clearly appears to be in decline when aid disbursements are considered as a proportion of the donors' GNP. For Western states as a whole, this proportion has dropped from 0.52 percent to 0.34 percent over the period 1962–1972. By this measure of the aid burden, the United States has dropped since 1962 from third to twelfth place among the sixteen Western aid donors in OECD.

THE DONORS' RETREAT FROM AID

Several factors help to account for the decline of donor interest in economic assistance, particularly in the case of the United States. Primary among these is the gradual evolution of Soviet-American relations from cold-war competition to limited détente. The cold war had provided the basic rationale for American economic assistance programs, a rationale that was especially useful as a means to mobilize domestic political support for large aid appropriations. The emergence of a limited superpower détente removed a major incentive for the United States and the USSR to compete with each other in offering aid to states throughout the Third World. Just as important in the case of American economic aid flows, détente deprived the aid program of its cold-war rationale, which earlier had given the aid effort its sense of urgency and a direct link with America's national security. With the erosion of its cold-war logic, American economic assistance has enjoyed diminishing domestic political support.

Additionally, the experience of the Vietnam war gave rise to serious doubts about the ultimate consequences of vigorous aid efforts among those Congressional liberals who had previously been major supporters of American economic aid. Senator Fulbright, Chairman of the Senate Foreign Relations Committee, and other long-time advocates of aid came to view it as a program that deeply involved the United States in the internal affairs of its aid recipients—even to the point of compelling the United States to make extensive military commitments of questionable value to legitimate American interests. In short, Congressional liberals who were among the strongest advocates of an internationalist posture for the United States in its relations with less-developed countries, began to argue for a lower profile, one that recognized limits to the desirability and capacity of America to shape the political fabric of states throughout the Third World. Since economic assistance was so crucial in establishing intimate bilateral ties between the United States and less-developed countries, Congressional liberals became severe critics of massive aid flows.

There were also other developments over the past decade that made it increasingly difficult to mobilize domestic political support for a large economic assistance effort by the United States. During the 1960s and 1970s, a number of domestic problems received intense political attention—new welfare measures such as Medicare and national health insurance, civil rights, public transportation, urban decay, environmental improvement—and all involved major commitments of public capital. The simple fact that Americans became preoccupied with the enormity of the tasks confronting their own society was probably more important than the actual flow of resources into new programs designed to deal with these social problems. In any event, relative to the 1950s the economic assistance program now faces substantially greater political competition for its share of the national budget. Evidence of the decline in domestic political support for aid can be seen in the fact that Congressional cuts of Administration requests for aid appropriations averaged 31 percent in the period 1968–1972, compared with 18 percent in the period 1963–1967.

The economic challenges that face the United States and other Western countries in the 1970s, as well as the capital outlays required by new domestic legislation, make the opportunity costs of contemporary economic assistance much greater than during the 1950s and 1960s. For example, food exports to less-developed countries are one thing when the United States enjoys large grain surpluses; they constitute quite another matter when grain reserves are very low and rising food prices in the United States are a major component in producing this country's highest rate of inflation during peacetime. Thus, proposals for increased food aid to numerous less-developed countries that faced severe famine in 1974 were confronted by tough opposition in the United States on the grounds that massive grain exports, even for famine relief, would aggravate the inflation in the American economy. The problem posed for aid flows extends far beyond this particular example. By 1974, all advanced industrial states faced chronic inflation, stagnation in real economic growth, and, with the exception of West Germany, balance-of-payments deficits as a result of increases in their energy-import bills. In this economic context, increases in aid to poor states can come only after concessions are wrung from consumer interests who are preoccupied with the effect of aid-financed exports on inflation. Also to be overcome are the fears of manufacturers and organized labor about the loss of jobs and production to less-developed countries industrializing with the help of aid. As a result, economic assistance programs are likely to be casualties of the simultaneous pursuit of neomercantilist and anti-inflation foreign economic policies by advanced industrial states. In this sense, successful negotiations of a new global trade and monetary order, as well as strong domestic economic growth, may be a prerequisite for increases in the rich states' commitment to economic aid programs.

To account for the erosion of support for economic assistance, we must also note the emergence of "donor fatigue," particularly on the part of the United States. Most major aid donors deny that they expect gratitude or allegiance from less-developed countries as a condition for economic assistance. Nevertheless, they resent the fact that long-time aid recipients so seldom evidence either in sufficient measure. Relative to the early years of economic assistance efforts, there is considerably less conviction in Western states that aid programs bring with them clearly identifiable influence over a recipient country's foreign policy orientation and its domestic political-economic processes. Over the years, all major aid donors have witnessed votes against their position on crucial issues before the United Nations, as well as public displays of hostility (such as attacks on embassies or other facilities) within the less-developed countries, to which much of their economic aid has flowed. This holds true for Communist aid donors as well as Western states. The Soviet Union has seen anti-Soviet rallies held in stadia constructed with Soviet aid. During the Cuban missile crisis in 1962, Guinea refused to permit Soviet aircraft bound for Cuba to land for refueling at the Conakry airport, which had been constructed with Soviet aid. After years of experience with aid programs, the accumulation of incidents such as these inevitably gives rise to skepticism about the political returns from economic assistance. This is true even if donors insist that no political obligations are connected with development assistance.

In addition to frustration with the foreign policy results of economic aid, the United States and other Western countries have lost confidence in their capacity to determine the development path of poor states through aid programs. Relative to a decade ago, for example, aid donors are much less confident of their ability to produce predictable political, social, and economic results in poor states through transfers of technology,[3] population control programs, duplication of Western public education and health systems, and capital flows designed to increase the GNP of aid recipients. There is, in addition, much more reluctance on the part of aid donors than there was a decade ago to argue that economic assistance is linked in any clearly direct manner to the forging of Western democratic political systems in recipient states. In short, those officials in donor states who see economic assistance as a means of guiding

[3] For a discussion of the politics of transfers of technology, see Chapter 6.

the development efforts of poor states towards preconceived social, economic, and political ends are more sensitive to their limitations than in the past. They are also less prone to exaggerate claims about results to be expected from aid programs. These uncertainties about economic assistance make it more difficult in rich states to secure additional resources for economic aid programs.

A similar erosion of confidence in the developmental results of aid is evidenced in appraisals of aid by Soviet analysts. They have expressed doubts about the results of Soviet aid to the state sector in non-Communist less-developed countries, as well as about the consequences of Soviet aid recipients' precipitously nationalizing the private sectors of their economies.[4] Soviet spokesmen have also expressed more general doubts about the nature of socialism espoused by many leaders of Third-World states and about the profound differences between these forms of socialism and the "scientific socialism" of Moscow.

The decline in donor states' support of economic assistance efforts is explained largely by these changes in the international political environment, by the erosion of domestic political support for aid appropriations, and by the emergence of "donor fatigue." In spite of these developments, Western states continue to have sufficient interests in less-developed countries to maintain economic assistance programs—albeit at reduced levels in relation to their economic capabilities. Economic aid will continue to be a valuable instrument in the diplomacy of advanced industrial states. For example, large requests for aid were an integral part of the Nixon Administration's military withdrawal from Indochina and its efforts to settle the Middle East conflict. Two weeks after Secretary of State Kissinger's marathon negotiation of an Israeli-Syrian troop disengagement, and one week before President Nixon's visit to the Middle East in 1974, the administration requested $100 million in economic aid to rebuild Syrian towns along the disengagement line, $350 million in economic aid to Israel, $207 million for Jordan, and $250 million for Egypt. Similarly, France has over the years sustained a large economic aid program designed to maintain political and extensive cultural (education) ties between itself and its former colonies. Economic aid will be maintained as a permanent instrument employed by rich states in pursuit of their disparate political goals in less-developed countries, whatever the alterations in the philosophical underpinning of their aid efforts or the trend in overall aid flows.

Rich states will also continue economic assistance programs in an effort to promote their national and private economic interests in the

---

[4] See Robert S. Walters, *Soviet and American Aid* (Pittsburgh: University of Pittsburgh Press, 1970) , pp. 65–67.

Third World. The scarcity in global supplies of certain mineral resources emerged as a clear constraint to the prosperity of all advanced industrial states following oil shortages in 1973. More than ever before, rich states can be expected to use economic aid, along with other incentives, to secure access to vital raw materials in less-developed countries. Japan, for example, made massive aid commitments to oil-producing states in the Persian Gulf and to Indonesia in the aftermath of the Arab embargo on oil shipments during 1973 and 1974.

Rich states also use aid to finance their exports to less-developed countries. Japan and Germany, in particular, have relied heavily upon export credits as a major component of their total resource flows to less-developed countries. As long as neomercantilism continues to be an important part of advanced industrial states' overall trade policies, rich states are likely to continue economic assistance to poor states as a means of improving their balance of trade. For example, in the early 1970s about one third of the imports of India, Pakistan, and Indonesia were financed from aid.

The connection between economic assistance and the creation of a hospitable climate for direct private foreign investment is still another reason for the continuation of aid programs by Western states. The United States and other Western aid donors have frequently spoken of economic assistance in the forms of resource surveys, feasibility studies, and infrastructure projects in less-developed countries (ports, communication facilities, roads, rail transportation, electric power networks, and so forth) as crucial in creating the necessary preconditions for poor states to finance their future development through private resource flows. In these and other ways (such as investment guarantees for firms operating in poor states, and the threat of denying future foreign aid to less-developed countries that nationalize private foreign investment without adequate compensation), economic aid programs are an integral part of securing investment opportunities for firms in donor states. In an age of burgeoning private foreign investment, most Western states will continue to have a vested interest in supporting aid programs on this ground alone.

Finally, advanced industrial states will continue to engage in economic aid efforts because they contribute a unique type of resource transfer to less-developed countries. Export earnings and private foreign investment combined may dwarf aid flows to less-developed countries, but export earnings and private investment flow, in the first instance, to firms and individuals in poor states. Economic assistance, on the other hand, supplies new investment capital directly to governments in poor states for their use in priority development activities. Thus, systematic improvements in agriculture, education, health, and a variety of other activities crucial for economic development are much more likely to be produced through aid than through revenues generated by trade or private investment.

The importance of aid in a poor state's overall development is greater than one would expect from looking at the volume of aid flows, shown either as a proportion of total foreign exchange receipts or as a proportion of total investment by less-developed countries. It is politically unfeasible for advanced industrial states today to deny their interest in the development of the Third World. Because of aid's unique characteristics, rich states that claim to have an interest in poor states' development must continue aid disbursements, notwithstanding their doubts about the political and economic results.

CONCERNS OF AID RECIPIENTS

So far, our attention has been focused on the concerns of donor states. After years of reliance upon economic assistance from a variety of multilateral and bilateral sources, less-developed countries remain particularly concerned about a number of issues. The debt-service burden (repayments to service and retire past loans) is most prominent in this regard. The total external debt of less-developed countries has increased at a rate of 13 percent a year, from $38 billion in 1965 to $80 billion at the end of 1971.[5] In order to service this debt, less-developed countries repaid $6.8 billion in principal and interest to rich states in 1971. Annual repayments of past debts by poor states as a whole are growing about twice as fast as their export earnings, from which these debts must be serviced. Hence, in years to come an increasing proportion of poor states' foreign exchange earnings must be spent to retire past debts rather than to fund new development.

The debt-service problem does not face all less-developed countries equally, of course. One half of these debts were concentrated in only ten states in 1971.[6] India is particularly affected by debt-service problems. Its repayments on past loans in 1971 exceeded aid flows in the same year into that country from eight bilateral donors and the International Bank for Reconstruction and Development (IBRD). India's debt service over the next fifteen years is likely to absorb an average of 22 percent of its export earnings. Though India is presently an extreme case, it exemplifies the threat to the development of many poor states posed by continued use of

5 OECD, *Development Cooperation, 1973 Review* (Paris, 1973), pp. 67, 70.

6 India, Brazil, Pakistan, Mexico, Indonesia, Iran, Argentina, South Korea, Yugoslavia, and Turkey. Ibid., p. 68.

aid and other loans that carry relatively short repayment periods and interest rates higher than one or two percent.

Although development aid is a major component of less-developed countries' overall indebtedness, the extensive use of public and private export credits is the major contributor to the present level of debt-service payments by less-developed countries. Export credits account for one third of the poor states' total debt, but 57 percent of their current debt-service payments.[7] At a minimum, advanced industrial states and less-developed countries must soon find lower-cost alternatives to the reliance upon export credits to finance poor states' imports from the West.

If present trends continue, numerous less-developed countries will be unable to avoid financial collapse under a crushing debt-service burden unless their major creditors agree to postpone or to write off their financial obligations. Progress along these lines requires joint action by advanced industrial states that are competing with one another economically and politically in less-developed countries. Moreover, export credits are an integral part of the neomercantilist foreign trade policies pursued by advanced industrial states. Thus, states that rely heavily upon export credits as a stimulus to domestic production and a favorable balance of trade are unlikely to curtail their use unless a comprehensive multilateral agreement assures that a reduction in the use of export credits will not leave a rich state at an economic disadvantage relative to its major competitors. Similarly, rescheduling or canceling debt repayments from poor states must involve all major creditors; otherwise, the generosity of one creditor merely allows a poor state to meet its payments on financial obligations to less sensitive creditors. There have been numerous examples of multilateral agreements among rich states to reschedule the debt-service payments of particular less-developed countries facing financial crises, and discussion of the debt-service implications of continued reliance upon export credits to poor states is under way. It is important to realize, however, that a comprehensive solution to the Third World's debt-service problem involves more than just the development interests of poor states. It must also take into account the conflicts of interest among creditor nations that inhibit the joint action that is necessary to meet the general needs of less-developed countries.

Another issue of increasing political importance in relations between rich and poor states is the maldistribution of income among and within states. Of course, this has long been a major concern of less-developed countries, a concern that aid donors have believed they could partially remedy by their transfer of resources to poor states. Today, the political salience of the issue lies in the now almost universal realization

[7] Ibid., pp. 67–68.

TABLE 5-2.   The Gap Between Rich and Poor States

	Less-Developed Countries' Average	Advanced Industrial States' Average	United States
Per Capita GNP	$230	$3,085	$4,756
Population (millions)	1,850	664	207
Population growth rate	2.6%	1.1%	1.1%
Literacy	40%	97%	98%
Per capita annual grain consumption[a]	400 lbs.	———	2,000 lbs.
Life Expectancy	52 years	71 years	72 years
Persons per Physician	3,400	700	620
Per Capita Power Consumption (annual KWH output per person)	200	5,140	8,000

From Overseas Development Council, *The United States and the Developing World, Agenda for Action* (Washington, D.C., 1973), p. 123.

[a] Lester Brown, "The Next Crisis? Food," *Foreign Policy*, No. 13 (Winter, 1973/74), 5.

that after decades in which tens of billions of dollars in economic assistance have flowed from rich to poor states, income disparities appear to be greater than ever. This is true despite the substantial economic progress less-developed countries have made since World War II. For example, less-developed countries as a group achieved an average annual GNP growth rate of 6 percent in the period 1967–1972. This is the growth target demanded for less-developed countries in the strategy for the United Nation's Second Development Decade (1970–1979). In spite of this remarkable overall performance by less-developed countries, a number of development gaps remain so pronounced that they cast doubt upon the whole aid enterprise.

There is, of course, the gap between states in the center and the periphery of the global economy. This is *The Gap* that has long been the focus of all observers of development politics and economics. Some indicators of the magnitude of the disparity between standards of living in rich and poor states are presented in Table 5-2. The existence of this gap, despite decades of aid in an era of high development expectations, has created an increasingly conflictive political relationship between rich and poor states.[8] It is a situation producing in poor states extreme resentment

8 For a translation of these statistics into alterations in the standard of living an American would have to make were he or she to live in a less-developed country with a per capita income equivalent to that experienced by most people in the world, see Robert Heilbroner, *The Great Ascent* (New York: Harper Torchbooks, 1963) , pp. 23–27.

and frustration that could become explosive, particularly since this gap is, by all projections, growing wider every year.

In addition to the staggering inequalities between rich and poor states' income levels and standards of living, there are great disparities in economic performance among the less-developed countries themselves. Assertions that less-developed countries enjoyed an overall GNP growth rate of 6 percent in recent years conceal massive differences in economic growth. When increases in population are reflected in indicators of economic growth, a startling picture emerges. Among the less-developed states the poorest countries, with 67 percent of the Third World's population, are hardly witnessing economic growth at all: increases in per capita GNP have averaged only 1.5 percent a year over the period 1960–1970. On the other hand, less-developed countries that are major oil exporters or that have a per capita GNP of $500 or more, enjoyed growth rates three to four times higher during the same period;[9] these countries have only 11 percent of the Third World's population. In short, the creditable average growth of the Third World in recent years is very misleading. For the most part it has beeen absorbed by population increases, leaving standards of living practically unchanged. Moreover, real per capita economic growth in the Third World is concentrated in relatively few less-developed countries; these states constitute only a small fraction of the total population of poor states. Not only is the gap between rich and poor states growing, but the gap between poor and very poor states is also growing.

The most alarming maldistribution of income is found *within* poor states—even those that have been major aid recipients. A recent study of income distribution patterns in over forty less-developed countries found that in 1960 the richest 20 percent of the population in these states had an average share of 56 percent of the national income; the poorest 60 percent of the population accounted for an average share of only 26 percent of the national income.[10] There is reason to believe that in many poor countries these disparities are not only continuing, but are growing more pronounced. For example, in Brazil between 1960 and 1970 the share of the national income received by the poorest 40 percent of the population declined from 10 percent to 8 percent, whereas the share of the richest 5 percent grew from 28 percent to 38 percent.[11] The same general condition appears to characterize Mexico and India.[12]

[9] Address by Robert McNamara, President of the International Bank for Reconstruction and Development, Santiago, Chile, April 14, 1972, p. 3.

[10] Ibid., p. 5.

[11] Ibid., p. 4.

[12] Ibid.

Inequalities in income distribution are now the subject of great concern to decision makers and observers in rich as well as poor states. It is not that such inequalities did not exist in the past. Rather, these inequalities are now documented more precisely, and they not only persist but seem to have worsened during the very period when aid programs were enjoying their heyday. Universal recognition of the increasing economic disparities between rich and poor states, moderately poor and very poor states, and rich and poor segments of the population within less-developed countries makes maldistribution of income all the more salient as a political issue within the global economy. It is clear that economic assistance efforts must change drastically if aid is to play an important role in arresting these trends. Similarly, vigorous social and economic reforms by governments in less-developed countries, not just aid, are essential to reduce income inequalities within poor states.

In addition to the debt-service burden and maldistribution of income, less-developed countries that rely heavily on economic assistance fear political and economic subordination to donor states. Acceptance of economic assistance gives donor states a major, sometimes decisive, voice in the recipients' investment decisions, which in turn directly affect all aspects of domestic relations (social, economic, and political). Since most aid flows are tied to purchases from the donor state, less-developed countries also find aid commitments to be an important constraint on their choice of major trading partners among advanced industrial states. Moreover, aid commitments are often contingent upon a recipient's adoption of policies favorable to foreign investment by firms in the donor state. For example, the Hickenlooper Amendment for years prohibited the extension of American economic assistance to any country that nationalized American foreign investments without adequate compensation. In a more directly political vein, less-developed states sometimes find aid contingent upon their interrupting relations with the donor's enemies. Thus, during the 1960s American aid was prohibited to any state that supplied goods other than food or medical supplies to North Vietnam and Cuba. Less-developed countries resent these types of constraints on what they feel to be their own national prerogatives in establishing basic domestic and foreign policy. Although they covet the resources transferred through economic aid channels, less-developed countries fear that these programs afford donor states a means to penetrate and subordinate the political and economic system of aid recipients.

This by no means exhausts the concern of less-developed countries over the implications of aid relations, but the issues we have discussed indicate that recipients as well as donors are wary of aid. The terms that accompany economic assistance, the end uses of such assistance, and expectations concerning its consequences require, and are slowly beginning to receive, careful reexamination by states in the center and in the periphery of the global economy.

MULTILATERAL AID

Between 1967 and 1972, the share of multilateral aid relative to total aid flows from Western states increased from 11 to 22 percent.[13] In 1972, $1.9 billion in aid flowed through multilateral agencies to less-developed countries—primarily via the IBRD and the United Nations Development Program (UNDP). There are contradictory explanations as to the reasons for and the significance of this trend from bilateral to multilateral aid. One view is that multilateral aid is a means by which both donors and recipients can eliminate some of the more nettlesome problems they each associate with bilateral economic assistance. Another view (the radical perspective) is that multilateral aid is merely a more subtle and effective means than bilateral aid of enabling Western states to exercise their domination and exploitation of less-developed countries.

According to the first view, multilateral aid substantially removes politics from economic assistance; consequently, it is preferred by both donors and recipients to bilateral aid. Multilateral aid is a way to continue economic assistance with less direct involvement on the part of a donor state in the internal affairs of recipients. Thus, liberal United States Congressmen can support multilateral aid as a means of maintaining an internationalist orientation and simultaneously reduce a specifically American presence in less-developed countries; a former colonial power such as the Netherlands can give multilateral aid and thereby avoid charges that its aid efforts are merely an attempt to reimpose its dominance over former colonies. From the donors' perspective, multilateral aid permits a rich state to demonstrate its commitment to the development of poor states in a way that minimizes political attacks from aid critics at home and abroad. In addition to these attractions of multilateral aid to rich states, the very nature of aid-related problems, such as how to untie aid and ease the debt-service burden of less-developed countries, requires increased multilateral cooperation by donors. Any donor state would be disadvantaged by significant unilateral steps toward these ends.

Recipients, too, can see some major advantages to multilateral aid. Development assistance can be separated more clearly from the narrow political and security interests of various donors if aid is disbursed through an international organization. Even if multilateral aid disburse-

[13] OECD, *Development Cooperation, 1973 Review*, p. 43.

ments are conditioned upon specified policy changes by a recipient, it is easier for a less-developed state to accept these conditions from an international institution of which it is a member than to accept them from another state. Membership in the international agencies that disburse aid also gives less-developed countries a voice in establishing the criteria for aid allocations. However small their voice, compared with that of rich states in these institutions, it is greater than the voice they have in shaping the bilateral aid policies of donor states. Hence, mutlilateral aid is attractive to both donors and recipients because it places an international organization between the parties to buffer what is usually a bittersweet aid relationship.

From the radical perspective, Western aid—multilateral as well as bilateral—has never been designed to facilitate the development of poor states. Indeed, in this view aid is merely another instrument that ensures the subordination of states in the periphery to Western states that control the capitalist global economy. This exploitation is crucial for the indefinite continuation of the rich states' prosperity. International economic institutions are purportedly essential to the efforts of rich states to subordinate and exploit less-developed countries. The radical perspective with regard to aid is entirely consistent with their view of the function international organizations perform in trade and monetary relations, which we discussed in Chapters 2 and 3. Rich states remain fully in control of the aid policies of international institutions by virtue of their budgetary contributions and voting power, whereas the participation of poor states merely creates the illusion of a genuinely multilateral aid enterprise.

The International Monetary Fund and the International Bank for Reconstruction and Development are the focus of radical critiques of multilateral aid. Rather than serving any positive purpose for poor states, these two institutions are viewed as the keystones of international imperialism.[14] As the major sources of multilateral short-term credit for less-developed countries having balance-of-payments difficulties and of long-term development loans, the IMF and IBRD impose stringent conditions on their borrowers, conditions that open the door for their penetration by the trade and investment of rich states. Less-developed countries not willing to conform to IMF and IBRD suggestions find themselves denied not only loans from these institutions but also credit through private channels or bilateral aid programs. Thus these and other multilateral aid agencies are merely a subtler and more effective means of attaching poor states to the international imperialist system than the cruder devices of bilateral aid, military conquest, and explicit political control.

---

14 For further discussion of the IMF as it affects less-developed states, see Chapter 3, pp. 66–73.

The tone and substance of radical contentions about the basic character of economic assistance and about international loans from rich to poor states are illustrated in these remarks by Cheryl Payer.

> The [international loan] system can be compared point by point with peonage on an individual scale. In the peonage, or debt slavery, system the worker is unable to use his nominal freedom to leave the service of his employer, because the latter supplies him with credit (for overpriced goods in the company store) necessary to supplement his meager wages. The aim of the employer-creditor-merchant is neither to collect the debt once and for all, nor to starve the employee to death, but rather to keep the laborer permanently indentured through his debt to the employer. The worker cannot run away, for other employers and the state recognize the legality of his debt; nor has he any hope of earning his freedom with his low wage.
>
> Precisely the same system operates on the international level. Nominally independent countries find their debts, and their continuing inability to finance current needs out of imports [*sic*], keep them tied by a tight leash to their creditors. The IMF [and IBRD] orders them, in effect, to continue laboring on the plantations, while it refuses to finance their efforts to set up in business for themselves. For these reasons the term "international debt slavery" is a perfectly accurate one to describe the reality of their situation.[15]

Here, Payer refers specifically to IMF policies, but from the radical viewpoint her discourse could apply as well to the designs and behavior of rich states generally—particularly to their use of international lending institutions to supervise the subjugation of less-developed countries. Income maldistribution and the debt-service burden facing poor states are seen by radicals as the logical consequences of aid. To radicals, the effectiveness of multilateral institutions in securing these imperialist ends accounts for increases in aid through multilateral channels. Radicals place no stock in the argument that multilateral aid offers advantages to recipients as well as to donors. The trend towards multilateral aid through existing institutions horrifies them.

CONCLUSION

The radicals' assessment of multilateral assistance overstates the extent to which the dilemmas faced by poor states in their aid and other economic relations with rich states are the result of the virtually flawless execution of a grand design by the United States and its capitalist allies. It under-

---

[15] Cheryl Payer, "The Perpetuation of Dependence: The IMF and the Third World," *Monthly Review*, XXIII, 4 (September, 1971) , 40. Copyright © 1971 by Monthly Review Inc. Reprinted by permission of the editors of Monthly Review Inc.

states conflicts of interest among Western states as creditors. It tends to ignore the capacity of less-developed countries to exert some influence on the policies of multilateral agencies. It underestimates the ability of these countries to execute domestic reforms conducive to the achievement of their own development goals—whether this entails maximum aggregate economic growth or more equitable income distribution at home. Nevertheless, the radical perspective is helpful in alerting us to the profound degree of helplessness and frustration found among most Third World states as they strive to develop economically and to achieve a greater capacity for economic action that is independent of the preferences of rich states and international economic institutions.

Although these and other aspects of aid relations will continue to raise sensitive political problems, it is likely that economic assistance will be less and less the focal point of political-economic relations between advanced industrial states and less-developed countries. The political dialogue between the center and the periphery in the contemporary global political economy has been broadened beyond the subject of aid to include the gamut of international investment, trade, service, and monetary relations. In this broader context, aid flows appear to be among the least promising channels through which less-developed countries can secure access to substantially greater amounts of foreign exchange for development goals.

6

Technology, Ecology, and World Politics

The international implications of developments in science and technology are only beginning to receive widespread attention by political analysts. Political scientists have examined the effect of technological advances on the global strategic balance and on the defense postures of various states. The study of political development has generated interest in technology gaps. But more relevant to our concerns, emerging science- and technology-related questions will have an increasingly important impact on international political and economic relations. The political dimensions of such developments as weather modification capabilities, the exploitation of mineral resources on the sea bed, and the global ecological challenge require analysts of world politics to address a gamut of science and technology issues more directly than in the past.

TECHNOLOGY GAPS

The existence of a technology gap between rich and poor states has long been a universally recognized phenomenon. Most poor states presently lack the capital and human resources necessary for anything more than limited research and development efforts. It has been estimated that among Latin American and Asian states expenditures on research and development amount to about 0.1 to 0.5 percent of GNP, compared with 3.2 percent for the United States and 1 to 2 percent for most European states.[1] Understandably, the less-developed countries must rely on im-

[1] Lester Pearson, *Partners in Development* (New York: Praeger Publishers, 1969), p. 66.

ports of foreign technology, the costs of which are substantial. In 1968 payments for technology imports[2] by thirteen less-developed countries, representing 65 percent of the total population and 56 percent of the total gross domestic product of developing states, was estimated at approximately $1.5 billion.[3] This was equivalent to over one half the annual flow of direct foreign investment to all less-developed countries during the same year.[4] The acquisition of foreign technology could cost less-developed states $9 billion annually by 1980. This would be equivalent to about 15 percent of their anticipated export earnings.[5] These statistics are indicative of the magnitude of the technology gap facing poor states and are the source of their demands for international policy measures designed to help bridge it.

In the mid 1960s a technology gap emerged as an important political issue among advanced industrial states. Europeans, particularly the French, took note of the seemingly unassailable scientific and technological predominance of the United States relative to other Western states. In the decade 1957–1966, the United States devoted over three times the resources to research and development ($158 billion) as did all the industrialized states of Western Europe combined ($50 billion).[6] From 1951 to 1969, scientists in the United States received 21 of 38 Nobel prizes in chemistry and 23 of 40 Nobel prizes in medicine and physiology.[7] Giant American-based multinational firms such as IBM and Kodak are capable of devoting resources to research and development that are equal in magnitude to the gross sales of their competitors in Europe.[8] Indeed, IBM spent as much on the development of its model 360 computer ($5 billion) as the French government planned to spend on the *Force de Frappe,* its nuclear deterrent, from 1965 to 1970.[9] In short, over the past decade advanced industrial states (particularly France) have come to

2 Technology imports in the form of payments abroad for patents, licenses, know-how and trademarks, and management and service fees.

3 United Nations, *Multinational Corporations in World Development* (New York, 1973) , ST/ECA/190, p. 50.

4 Ibid.

5 *Transfer of Technology,* Report by the UNCTAD Secretariat, TD/106, November 10, 1971, pp. 17–18.

6 OECD, *Gaps in Technology,* Analytical Report (Paris, 1970) , p. 115. During the middle 1960s American expenditures on research and development were fifteen times those of West Germany and ten times those of Britain. Raymond Vernon, *Sovereignty at Bay* (New York: Basic Books, 1971) , p. 90.

7 Vernon, *Sovereignty at Bay,* p. 90.

8 Kenneth Waltz, "The Myth of National Interdependence" in *The International Corporation,* ed. C. Kindleberger (Cambridge, Mass.: M.I.T. Press, 1970) , p. 217; and John Dunning, "Technology, Unitied States Investment and European Economic Growth," in *The International Corporation,* p. 165.

9 Waltz, "The Myth of National Interdependence," p. 217.

perceive themselves, relative to the United States, as victims of a technology gap, much as less-developed states perceive themselves as disadvantaged in relation to all advanced industrial states.

The international political controversies surrounding these technology gaps are centered in the universal desire of states to exercise control over science and technology—as opposed to acquiring it from external sources, however accessible the technology or generous the terms. All states want to harness science and technology to national economic, social, and security policies. This is widely perceived to require national control over research and development, which in turn can be assured only with a broad-based, indigenous science and technology capability. To the extent that a nation lacks this capability, feelings of acute economic vulnerability and outright resentment toward foreign sources of technology are likely to arise. These feelings can lead to severe international tension, particularly in cases where states find it beyond their capacity to produce internally the technology necessary for innovation in economic sectors that are vital to their national autonomy and international economic competitiveness. Resource-rich developing countries need the most advanced techniques for processing mineral resources, and a country such as France needs the latest computer technology for its political and economic policies.

Indigenous scientific and technological capability is widely associated with great power status in world politics. The French in particular have made this connection. Robert Gilpin summarizes the French position.

> Today Great Power status accrues only to those nations which are leaders in all phases of basic research and which possess the financial and managerial means to convert new knowledge into advanced technologies. In the case of the two superpowers, eminence in science and technology go hand-in-hand, and it appears unlikely that any nation or group of nations can ever again aspire to a dominant role in international politics without possessing a strong, indigenous scientific and technological capibility. International politics has passed from the era of traditional industrial nation states to one dominated by the scientific nation states.[10]

On no occasion was the validity of this general position manifested more clearly to France than in its efforts to develop an independent nuclear force during the 1960s. The vulnerability of even an advanced industrial state that is dependent upon an ally for foreign sources of technology was revealed when the United States government initially

[10] Robert Gilpin, *France in the Age of the Scientific State.* Copyright © 1968 by the Princeton University Press, published for The Center of International Studies, p. 25. Reprinted by permission of Princeton University Press.

prohibited the French purchase of certain IBM computers required for its *Force de Frappe* on the grounds that the nuclear test ban treaty forbade America's assisting a nonnuclear power to obtain nuclear weapons.[11] In the eyes of the French and numerous other states on the wrong side of the technology gap, the achievement of a greater degree of self-sufficiency in science and technology is a prerequisite for the capacity to forge an independent stance in global political and economic relations.

Particularly high stakes seem to be associated with technological dependence upon the United States, or any foreign country, in the field of electronics. Jean-Jacques Servan-Schreiber states the case very dramatically.

> Electronics is not an ordinary industry: it is the base upon which the next stage of industrial—*and* cultural—development depends. In the nineteenth century the first industrial revolution replaced manual labor by machines. We are now living in the *second industrial revolution* and every year we are replacing the labor of human brains by a new kind of machinery—computers.
>
> A country which has to buy most of its electronic equipment abroad will be in a condition of inferiority similar to that of nations in the last century which were incapable of industrializing. Despite their brilliant past, these nations remained outside the stream of civilization. If Europe continues to lag behind in electronics, she could cease to be included among the advanced areas of civilization within a single generation.[12]

Thus, technology gaps have a profound impact on states' economic, political, military, and cultural status. These gaps can produce a visceral reaction in states in which vital national, political, and economic aspirations are perceived to be dependent upon access to foreign technology; for this means that national aspirations are also vulnerable to sabotage by states or corporations beyond national control. As such, technological dependence is an issue that rapidly becomes transformed into one of intense nationalist feelings.

Proposals for dealing with technology gaps fall nicely into the pervasive clash between liberal economic thought and radical thought on numerous issues of international political economy. Liberal thought (embraced in this dialogue by most technological "haves") generally stresses the desirability and economic efficiency of sharing technology

---

11 Ibid., p. 54. These IBM computers were to be purchased from the French affiliate of IBM. This case is a good example of the political implications of multinational corporations for host state–home state relations. These implications are discussed in Chapter 4 of the present volume.

12 J.-J. Servan-Schreiber, *The American Challenge* (New York: Avon Books, 1969), p. 42. Italics in original.

among states through public aid programs, direct foreign investment, or purchases of privately controlled technology. Radical thought (embodied in the position of many technological "have-nots") emphasizes the need for national control over technology, rather than mere access to it. The primary value of national self-determination can be achieved only if a state has the capacity to establish research and development priorities, to affect the timing for the introduction of new technology, and to affect the pace at which new technology is diffused. In short, radical thought sees a genuine solution to the technology gap only in an indigenous capacity for innovation, not in access to technology that is supplied from abroad.

How can the technology gaps be eliminated? Economic assistance programs from rich states to poor states since World War II have typically included a strong technical assistance component. Such efforts have been viewed by aid donors as a major instrument to bridge the technology gap between themselves and less-developed countries. Early technical assistance efforts, such as President Truman's Point Four Program, were based on the notion that with minimal expense advanced industrial states could, and should, share their technology with less-developed states by demonstrating their proven techniques of industrial and agricultural production to aid recipients. It soon became evident to all, however, that technology cannot be transferred from advanced industrial societies to less-developed ones without extensive adaptation to meet the particular needs of the aid recipient. For example, the capital-intensive technology underlying most American production processes is not well suited to the needs of capital-short, labor-abundant societies of the Third World.

Recognition of the complexities of successful transfers of technology to poor states has led to more impressive results in recent years. Undoubtedly, the most successful application of technology to problems of less-developed countries has been the development of new strains of rice and wheat, which, compared with traditional strains, are more responsive to fertilizers[13] and more adaptable to varying growing conditions. This technological breakthrough was responsible for a quantum jump in the previously stagnant rice and wheat yields of the densely populated states of Asia that were threatened with famine in the mid 1960s. Notwithstanding the social, economic, and political strains that have accompanied this "green revolution,"[14] it is an outstanding example of the

---

[13] This responsiveness to fertilizer has proved to be a double-edged sword, however. It makes grain production in these states highly sensitive to the availability of fertilizer. Thus, the green revolution is in danger of becoming a casualty of the high prices of energy in the 1970s, for chemical fertilizer production depends upon the availability of natural gas, which is now in short supply.

[14] See Lester Brown et al., "The Social Impact of the Green Revolution," *International Conciliation*, No. 581 (January, 1971), entire issue.

benefits to be derived from research and development on problems that face less-developed countries. The research was funded by private foundations in the United States, and the fruits of the research were diffused among poor states through foreign aid programs.

Less-developed countries are most interested in receiving technology from advanced industrial states, but they are presently much more aggressive than they used to be with regard to the technology to be shared. Most technology transferred from rich to poor states incorporates research and development that is oriented basically to the problems of advanced industrial societies. In various international forums, primarily within the United Nations, demands are now being raised for rich states to devote a specified percentage (5 to 10 percent) of their public expenditures on research and development to projects of special concern to less-developed countries.[15] Examples of research desired by less-developed countries are the development of new uses and markets for primary products such as jute and rubber that face increasing competition in world markets from synthetic substitutes produced in advanced industrial states. Demands are also being made for the location of research centers in the Third World and the development of a scientific and technological infrastructure within and among less-developed countries. Some of these states insist that multinational corporations locate research and development facilities in the host state as a requirement for the entry of their investment. Through international organizations such as the United Nations Conference on Trade and Development, less-developed countries request that governments of states in which parent firms of multinational corporations are located help transfer technology to less-developed states by providing certain fiscal and financial incentives that would make such transfers more attractive to the firm and less expensive for the importer of technology.[16] In general, poor states simply are no longer content to acquire only that technology that advanced industrial states would on their own accord supply to Third-World states through public and private channels.[17]

Though the less-developed countries are becoming more assertive in the dialogue on the technology gap between rich and poor states, it is unlikely that advanced industrial states will respond to the above demands in a manner that is acceptable to poor states. Over the years, the radical position that less-developed countries must develop an indigenous scientific and technological capability to bridge the technology gap will

15 Pearson, *Partners in Development*, p. 205.

16 United Nations, *The Declaration and Principles of the Action Program of Lima* (Geneva, 1971) TD/143, p. 66.

17 For a concise summary of less-developed countries' demands concerning technology transfers, see United Nations, *The Declaration and Principles of the Action Program of Lima*, pp. 66–72.

probably gain more support than proposals that are more consistent with liberal economic thought—that is, proposals that stress reliance upon external sources for innovation and diffusion of technology. Yet it is not at all clear how poor states can in fact develop a broad-gauged scientific and technological capability without depending on sustained support from advanced industrial states and multinational firms.

As in so many other aspects of international economic relations, the multinational corporation has emerged as a focal point in disputes over the cause of, and remedy for, technology gaps. These institutions figure prominently in the politics of the technology gap between the United States and other advanced industrial states, as well as that between rich and poor states. In contrast, economic aid programs as an instrument for bridging the technology gap are relevant almost exclusively to poor states.

The advocates of multinational corporations see them as constituting the most effective agent of technological innovation and the diffusion of technology among states. Modern industrial innovation increasingly requires the existence of large and complex organizations, extremely large amounts of capital, and a long-range commitment to the development of a major product or process.[18] Accordingly, research tends to be concentrated in a relatively few large firms; in 1964, for example, just 28 firms accounted for 63 percent of the total research and development expenditures by the business sector of the United States.[19] The giantism of multinational corporations makes them well equipped to generate technological innovation.

Moreover, multinational firms are vigorous agents for the diffusion of technology among states. Multinationals not only bring production into the host state, but also provide a continuing flow of technology through research conducted by their affiliates within the host state as well as through their imports of technology from the parent firm. Various studies indicate, for example, that foreign affiliates of American manufacturing firms in Britain,[20] Australia, and Canada[21] spend more on research and development than their host-state competitors. Intracompany exchanges of technology are also a major channel for the diffusion of technology across national boundaries. Nearly 75 percent of United States sales of technology and managerial skills are made to foreign affiliates of American firms.[22] These characteristics of multinational corporate behavior indicate the central role these firms play in the international

---

[18] See Vernon, *Sovereignty at Bay*, pp. 92–96.

[19] OECD, *Gaps in Technology*, Analytical Report, p. 152.

[20] Dunning, "Technology," p. 162.

[21] Jack N. Behrman, *National Interests and the Multinational Enterprise* (Englewood Cliffs, N.J.: Prentice-Hall, Inc., 1970) , p. 64.

[22] OECD, *Gaps in Technology*, Analytical Report, p. 243.

circulation of technology. Adherents of liberal economic thought will point to such data as evidence of how the operations of multinationals reduce technology gaps among states.

Decision makers and analysts sharing the radicals' world view of the global political economy, and critics of the enterprises generally, see multinational corporations as a cause of, rather than a cure for, technology gaps among states. Even if multinationals are vigorous agents of technological innovation and diffusion, they undertake these tasks in order to advance their global corporate interests rather than as a response to the research and development priorities of host states. In addition, even when multinational corporations are willing to transfer technology of vital interest to a host state, the exchange can be thwarted by intervention by the home state of the firm. The IBM transaction with France concerning the *Force de Frappe* is a case in point. The problem of relying on these firms for technology is that the host state is unable to assure itself of the acquisition of technology of the sort, and with the timing, that is most appropriate to its economic, social, and security problems.

Not only do technology transfers through private channels leave technological have-nots vulnerable to foreign firms and governments, there is also a widespread conviction that multinational corporations share technology in ways that exacerbate gaps in technology between the home and host states of the firms. Most multinational corporations concentrate their research and development activities in the country in which the parent firm resides. In 1966, for example, only 6 percent of the total research and development budget of American-based multinational corporations engaged in manufacturing was spent abroad.[23] Even in cases where such firms establish research and development facilities in host states, the critics of multinationals cite numerous ways in which a technology gap is widened. Multinational firms are frequently able to offer host-state scientific talent higher salaries, better research facilities, and greater opportunities for advancement than indigenous scientific establishments can. This can result in the multinational corporations' acquisition of the best local scientists—thereby preempting the development of a nationally controlled technological capability. New ideas generated by research in foreign affiliates are typically sent back to the parent firm for exploitation and development.[24] Much of the research and development effort of local affiliates of multinational corporations consists primarily of adapting parent research to the local market.[25]

The combined effect of these aspects of multinational corporate

---

23 United Nations, *Multinational Corporations in World Development*, p. 50.

24 Behrman, *National Interests*, p. 63.

25 Ibid., pp. 63–64.

behavior is, according to their critics, to stifle the creation of a broad-based indigenous capacity for technological innovation in host states. The result of such behavior is to give parent firms and their home governments immediate access to and control over research conducted by local scientific talent in foreign affiliates around the globe. The effect is to condemn host states to perpetual dependence upon the United States (as the home of the majority of multinational firms) for basic and applied research in science-based industries. Note is taken in all quarters of the fact that "[technology] gaps exist significantly in those industries where the multinational enterprise is active."[26] To critics of multinational corporations, this is all unambiguous evidence that such firms perpetuate and enhance the technological dominance of their home states rather than reduce asymmetries in technology among states.

Assessment of the technology gap typically leads to proposals for a group of states—for example, Europeans—to fully integrate their economies and emulate the giantism of American-based multinational firms.[27] Such an effort is likely to succeed only to the extent that European states also shed their national identities and their desire for the capacity to conduct foreign policy and provide for national defense independent of one another. Until this occurs, European states will duplicate, and compete with one another for, research and production facilities in the leading science-based industries. The resulting ineffi-ciency could well undermine the basic strategy of emulating the giant American firms. For example, the contracts for the joint British-French supersonic transport Concorde were carefully divided between the two states, and duplicate production lines were maintained despite the higher costs of doing so.[28] Such problems led a European research director to suggest, "If America wishes to close the technology gap with Europe, all she needs to do is erect 51 different sets of custom barriers, tax systems, space and defense programs, science policies and public buying arrange-ments; the gap will be gone in a year!"[29] Moreover as a radical critic of the existing global economy insists, "If these strong and developed Euro-pean economies cannot find a European solution to the real develop-mental problem posed by the technological gap . . . , what hope do the weak and underdeveloped economies caught in the same system have to find a solution?"[30]

26 Ibid., p. 57.

27 For example, see Servan-Schreiber, *The American Challenge,* pp. 150ff.

28 Behrman, *National Interests,* p. 168.

29 Quoted in Dunning, "Technology," p. 166.

30 Andre Gunder-Frank, "Sociology of Development and the Underdevelopment of Sociology," in J. Cockroft, A. I. Frank, and D. Johnson, *Dependence and Underdevelopment* (Garden City, N.Y.: Doubleday, 1972) , p. 367.

WEATHER MODIFICATION AND THE SEA BED

In addition to the controversy surrounding asymmetries in technological capacity among states, increasing international political conflict is likely to result from the sheer scale and boldness of activities now within the technological capacity of states and large firms. For example, a Soviet scientist has proposed that the USSR could increase its production of grain and other agricultural products by climate modification designed to produce colder, shorter winters and longer, warmer summers in the USSR. He argued that this could be accomplished by damming the Bering Strait and pumping warm Pacific water into the Arctic Ocean to melt the polar ice cap. There is considerable disagreement over the global ecological impact of such a project, but it is generally conceded that the Soviet Union has the capital and engineering resources to undertake this task.[31] Admittedly, the scale of this project is larger than most, but 53 nations conducted weather modification programs of some sort during 1973. As these efforts increase, severe political conflict will inevitably emerge among states that are competing to project upon others the disadvantages of climate alterations while keeping the benefits for themselves.[32]

Weather modification is also likely to emerge as an explicit weapon of statecraft and warfare. States with the capacity to divert or suppress hurricanes might well refuse to employ this capability on behalf of others facing a severe storm, or they might agree to divert it only after securing an explicit political-economic quid pro quo. The United States actually employed weather modification techniques in the Vietnam war. It attempted to inhibit the mobility of Communist supplies and troops by producing torrential rains in Vietnam. The United States also created highly acidic rainfall in Vietnam for the purpose of fouling enemy radar equipment.[33] The intended and unintended effects upon others of climate modification provide a dramatic example of a newly emergent science and technology issue that will have an increasingly important impact on international political and economic relations.

Exploitation of the sea bed, particularly beyond the continental margin, is another technology-related issue that is generating political

31 Robert McLaughlin, "They Stole Our Rain," *VISTA*, IX, No. 1 (August, 1973), 19; Eugene Skolnikoff, "The International Functional Implications of Future Technology," *Journal of International Affairs*, XXV, No. 2 (1971), 269.

32 McLaughlin, "They Stole Our Rain," p. 50.

33 Ibid.

conflict among states. In particular, there is currently great interest in mining the plentiful ferromanganese nodules (which contain valuable metals such as manganese, copper, nickel, and cobalt) that exist at various locations on the ocean floor at depths of 12,000 to 20,000 feet. An ocean resources official in the United States Department of Interior claims that opening just three ocean mines would give the United States "12 percent of the manganese it now imports, 41 percent of the copper, 54 percent of the nickel, and three times the current imports of cobalt."[34]

Political controversy surrounds the exploitation of this potential wealth because, among other things, only states or firms possessing the most advanced technology and large capital resources are able to exploit these mineral resources. Not only would they capture the lion's share of this sea-bed wealth, but the scale of mining operations that is foreseen would seriously disrupt existing international mineral-commodity markets, upon which numerous states rely for foreign exchange earnings. Also, there is presently no legal basis to establish clearly who has jurisdiction over the ocean floor and its resources beyond the continental shelf. By a General Assembly resolution of 1970, states and companies are supposed to refrain from moving unilaterally even to stake out claims on the sea bed until an international authority is established by treaty to resolve jurisdictional disputes and to distribute internationally a portion of the income generated from exploitation of the sea bed. But intense disagreements prevented the creation of an international authority at either the Caracas (1974) or Geneva (1975) sessions of the Law of the Sea Conference.

There is obviously potential for severe conflict in the absence of an international legal and political framework with which to resolve disputes over control of the sea bed.[35] As commodity prices rise and as the world begins to think of mineral resources in finite terms, there will be immense pressure for states and firms to claim and exploit unilaterally the sea bed's resources prior to the creation of an international authority—notwithstanding the General Assembly resolution. Several United States firms have invested heavily in developing the technology for extracting and processing manganese nodules on the ocean floor at great depths (the Summa Corporation of Howard Hughes, Kennecott, and Deepsea Ventures at Tenneco). They all wish to begin operations soon in order to exploit their technological lead. It is believed that at least three commercial mines could be operating by the end of the 1970s.

Weather modification and exploitation of the sea bed are symptom-

34 *The Wall Street Journal*, September 21, 1973, p. 1.

35 See Evan Luard, "Who Gets What on the Seabed?" *Foreign Policy*, No. 9 (Winter, 1972/73), 132–47.

atic of the international political problems posed by new technology and science capabilities. The scale of operations made possible by advances in technology virtually assures that the ecological, economic, and political interests of numerous states and other actors will be affected by activities undertaken unilaterally by technologically advanced states and firms.[36] Technological advances have thus substantially increased international interdependence and all its attendant political problems and opportunities.

THE ECOLOGICAL CHALLENGE
AND THE GLOBAL POLITICAL ECONOMY

Many analysts believe that technological progress has not merely increased international interdependence but, more important, has brought the world to a point approaching the carrying capacity of the planet. The world's population, consumption of food and mineral resources, and pollution of water, air, and soil are all growing exponentially, perhaps approaching levels that threaten global survival. Medical science and technology have contributed to the population explosion by a dramatic reduction of mortality rates in less-developed countries. It took the world until the mid 1970s to reach a population of four billion; present trends indicate that this figure will double within 35 years. Modern industry already consumes staggering amounts of ultimately finite mineral resources. Global demand for minerals will be five times greater in 25 years than it is now. A by-product of industrial growth is increased water, soil, and air pollution, which is reaching proportions that threaten to upset the ecological balance of large areas of the planet.

The provision of global food requirements was the most acute planetary danger in the early 1970s, however. Global food demand has reached near-crisis proportions as a consequence of rapid population increases in poor states and unprecedented levels of affluence in advanced industrial states. Food production has not kept pace with increased demand: global reserve stocks of grain have dropped from 26 percent of consumption in 1961 to only about 8 percent in 1974. These dangerously low reserve stocks are concentrated almost entirely in the United States and Canada, which together are now the breadbasket of the world. Both countries are subject to the same weather cycles, and with global reserves so low a poor crop season in North America would produce mass famine in many parts of the world. The tightness of the

---

[36] Most less-developed countries lack the technological capacity and the capital resources to engage in these types of activities on a large scale.

world's grain market has led to skyrocketing food prices in the early 1970s. These prices will place even subsistence food needs beyond the reach of millions of people in less-developed countries unless bold new efforts in food aid materialize quickly.

Population growth, food demand, growth in world production, consumption of mineral resources, and pollution are, of course, interdependent phenomena. The Club of Rome's now famous report, *The Limits to Growth*,[37] takes explicit account of the interdependencies among these factors in an ecological model of the world. Their analysis concludes that present trends of exponential growth of all these phenomena will result in collapse of the global economic and/or ecosystem before the year 2100.

Considerable controversy surrounds the precision of the data and the appropriateness of the specific assumptions underlying this and other warnings about global disaster as a consequence of rapid industrial growth.[38] However, a burgeoning literature on the subject agrees on one key point. In the long run, technological "progress" is more likely to result in planetary disaster than in improved living standards unless its direction changes dramatically. In particular, the universal worship of economic growth must give way to wide recognition of the need for near-zero-growth economies that emphasize conservation, not increased consumption.

Kenneth Boulding's contrast of "cowboy" and "spaceman" economies goes to the heart of the matter. The cowboy economy is based on a frontier-like perception of limitless supplies of the raw materials necessary for production as well as a limitless assimilation capacity of the environment for pollutants generated by production processes. It is an economy that worships growth in consumption and production. Economic success is measured by increases in "throughput"—the quantities of goods that are extracted from raw material reservoirs, processed, consumed, and ultimately discharged into reservoirs of pollution. The spaceman economy is based on a perception of finite supplies of raw materials as well as severe limits on the capacity of the environment to absorb pollutants. The notion of such an economy is derived from viewing the earth as a single spaceship. It is an economy in which the primary concern is the maintenance of limited raw material reservoirs, upon which continued production rests, and environmental reservoirs into which pollutants from production can be discharged. Success is measured in terms of the extent to which these vital reservoirs are

[37] Donella Meadows et al., *The Limits to Growth* (New York: Signet Books, 1972). Also see "Blueprint for Survival," *The Ecologist*, January, 1972.

[38] See H. S. D. Cole et al., *Models of Doom* (New York: Universe Books, 1973).

preserved by minimizing production and consumption.[39] Present technology is oriented toward a cowboy economy. The plea of *The Limits to Growth,* and of environmentalists generally, is for the development of a technology and life style appropriate for the spaceman economy into which they see the world headed. Only if we are able to do this, they argue, will the world be able to avert the disaster caused by our attempt to live beyond the carrying capacity of the planet.

The transition to a spaceman economy will be a long and difficult process. Until, for example, it is absolutely clear that specific mineral resources are in danger of being exhausted, most people, nations, and corporations will resist abandoning the relative comfort of a consumption-oriented economy. Although it seems incontrovertible that at some point the planet's resources will be exhausted, current data on the reserves of specific mineral resources are not of a quality that allow accurate prediction of when that time will come. Table 6-1 presents the estimates of resource availability used in *The Limits to Growth* model. But these and all other such figures should be viewed with caution. For example, in a paper delivered before the American Economic Association convention in January, 1974, available supplies of aluminum were assessed in terms of limits to growth:

> According to the table [in the paper] . . . known reserves of aluminum could last 23 years at current consumption rates. But "total crustal abundance" (all there is in the known world) could keep the system running 38.5 *billion* years.
> Somewhere in between . . . lies the "economically relevant measure, ultimate recoverable resources," and that . . . gives us 68,066 more years of aluminum to go.
> But . . . the last number is "the most uncertain, especially because it involves estimates of what future prices and technologies will be."[40]

It is unlikely that fundamental alterations in consumption patterns and production techniques in a manner consistent with a spaceman economy will occur until the limits to growth imposed by availability of resources are considerably clearer than they are now.

Notwithstanding the imprecision of the data available to us, existing trends make it imperative to develop an increased sensitivity to the need for controlling global consumption of raw materials and pollutants being pumped into the earth's atmosphere and water supplies. What are some of the likely political and economic consequences of various national and international efforts to accomplish these goals?

39 Seen Kenneth Boulding, "The Economics of the Coming Spaceship Earth," in *Environmental Quality in a Growing Economy,* ed. H. Jarrett (Baltimore: Johns Hopkins Press, 1966) , pp. 9–10.
40 *The New York Times,* January 6, 1974, Sec. 3, p. 17. Emphasis ours. © 1974 by The New York Times Company. Reprinted by permission.

TABLE 6-1. Nonrenewable Natural Resources

Resource	Exponential Index[a] (Years)	Exponential Index Using Five Times the Known Reserves[b] (Years)
Aluminum	31	55
Chromium	95	154
Coal	111	150
Cobalt	60	148
Copper	21	48
Gold	9	29
Iron	93	173
Lead	21	64
Manganese	46	94
Mercury	13	41
Molybdenum	34	65
Natural Gas	22	49
Nickel	53	96
Petroleum	20	50
Platinum Group	47	85
Silver	13	42
Tin	15	61
Tungsten	28	72
Zinc	18	50

The Limits to Growth: A Report for The Club of Rome's Project on the Predicament of Mankind by Donella H. Meadows, Dennis L. Meadows, Jørgen Randers, William W. Behrens III. A Potomac Associate's book published by Universe Books, New York, 1972.

[a] The number of years that known global reserves will last assuming that consumption grows exponentially at the average annual rate of growth.

[b] The number of years that five times the known global reserves will last assuming that consumption grows exponentially at the average annual rate of growth.

With regard to global efforts to control pollution, it is important to note the cleavage already apparent between advanced industrial states and less-developed countries. Spokesmen for poor states[41] see the present emphasis on pollution control as a projection onto the rest of the world of the rich states' peculiar environmental problems. They see little merit in massive expenditures to prevent further deterioration of the environment in nonindustrialized areas of the world that are capable of absorbing more effluents at relatively little short-term risk. Development is a higher value than clean air and water to most people in poor states. In the face of constant capital shortages, the addition of pollution control devices to economic projects is thought to raise the costs of development

[41] For example, see Joao Augusto de Araujo Castro, "Environment and Development: The Case of Less Developed Countries," *International Organization*, XXVI, No. 2 (Spring, 1972), 401–18.

and to curtail it unnecessarily. Moreover, to the extent that rich states give priority to costly maintenance of environmental standards at home, this priority is likely to be used as a pretext for reducing the volume of economic assistance they make available to less-developed countries. Thus, less-developed countries tend to see global pollution control efforts as a threat to their development progress.

These fears are seen in the argument by less-developed countries that pollution is a concomitant of highly industrialized societies. Pronouncements about the negative aspects of industrialization and rapid economic growth have a distinctly hollow ring when they come from those who already enjoy the fruits of modern industry. To less-developed countries, the appeal for the poor to avoid the environmental evils of industrialization constitutes a reintroduction of Rousseau's "happy savage" enjoying the blessings of backwardness.[42] "The implementation of any worldwide environmental policy based on the realities of the developed countries tends to perpetuate the existing gap in socio-economic development between developed and developing countries and so promote the freezing of the present international order."[43] For these reasons less-developed countries will be most reluctant partners in a global attack on the problems of pollution, which they believe rich states created in the first place.

In the short run, serious efforts at environmental improvement will be concentrated among the advanced industrial states where pollution problems are most severe. But, there are some serious impediments to a successful attack upon these problems, even if most advanced industrial states are convinced of the need for action. One impediment is illustrated in the logic of collective action, as discussed by Mancur Olson.[44] Collective or public goods (such as military defense, clean rivers, superhighways, and so forth) go to everyone in a region, regardless of disparities in their contributions to obtaining the goods. By their nature, collective goods cannot be denied to those individuals in the region who paid nothing for them. For example, a person who refuses to pay taxes nevertheless secures the same protection as a solid taxpayer from a country's nuclear deterrent force. Olson suggests that because of the nature of these goods, individuals (or states or firms working in a common effort) act most rationally by making as small a contribution as possible towards provision of a collective good; for once it is provided, the collective good benefits the smallest contributor just as much as the largest.

In a continent such as Europe, which comprises numerous indus-

---

42 Ibid., p. 406.
43 Ibid., p. 401.
44 *The Logic of Collective Action* (New York: Schocken Books, 1968).

trial states, cleaner air and water are collective goods (shared by all states), which, when achieved, cannot be denied to particular countries in the region that contribute less than others to environmental improvement. It is rational behavior for each state to reap the benefits of environmental improvements by virtue of other states' actions, while seeking to minimize the economic burden connected with its own pollution control efforts. In light of this fact alone, it is likely that pollution control efforts will have less than optimal results.

This logic of collective action is reinforced by the sensitivity of international economic interdependence. Multinational corporations, for example, will be very sensitive to disparities among various states' pollution control standards, which affect production costs and competitiveness in international trade. To the extent that these disparities develop, they will have a substantial impact on investment decisions by corporations and on the trade position of various states. Asymmetries in national environmental improvement efforts will thus alter international capital and trade flows, and their attendant balance-of-payments and political consequences. In these circumstances, states can be expected to compete with one another to attract investment and increase export earnings by maintaining relatively lenient pollution control standards. The combined effect of this behavior and that associated with the provision of collective goods is to give every state interested in environmental improvement the incentive to work just a little less vigorously than its neighbors to control pollution. In view of these problems, an effective assault on global pollution will require advanced industrial states to harmonize their environmental control standards as well as the timing with which they are put into effect. Efforts in this direction are under way in the Organization for Economic Cooperation and Development as well as in other international institutions, but the issues are immensely complex and progress is slow.

In the meantime, as various states take measures to improve the environment, a number of specific international economic and political difficulties can be anticipated. There is little doubt that states will erect various tariff and nontariff barriers to protect domestic producers whose competitiveness deteriorates as a consequence of increased costs imposed by compliance with environmental control standards. An even more nettlesome problem will arise, however, as states impose new trade barriers for neomercantilist purposes under the guise of environmental protection. For example, a recent law in West Germany restricts the lead content of gasoline to 0.15 grams per liter:

> Ostensibly, the law was passed to reduce lead emissions from automobiles in West Germany although it has the simultaneous impact of restricting

sales of other countries' automobiles in West Germany, which is clearly
a nontariff trade barrier. West German vehicles can easily be adjusted
to low lead gasolines, but several major Italian and French automobile
makers' high compression engines cannot be so easily adjusted.[45]

Is such a law designed primarily to reduce foreign auto sales in West
Germany or to improve the air quality? In the future, significant international political and economic clashes are bound to arise as different states
arrive at different answers to this type of question.

Manipulation of national environmental control standards is likely
to become an important new instrument of foreign policy. As part of the
American response to Libya's nationalization of American oil firms in
1973, President Nixon ordered a relaxation of environmental regulations
preventing the use of fuel oil with a high sulfur content. Though this
move was designed primarily to ease overall energy supplies available to
the United States, it was also a means of reducing the particular attractiveness of Libyan crude oil, which has a low sulfur content, to American
importers. In short, the alteration of pollution standards was a step
making it easier for the United States to consider a boycott of Libyan oil
as a response to the Libyan nationalization of American oil properties.
The Middle Eastern war of 1973 and the subsequent global energy crisis
superseded this more narrow Libyan oil problem in American foreign
policy. However, events prior to the war illustrate how domestic environmental regulations can become important instruments of foreign policy.

The political and economic consequences of environmental control
efforts by advanced industrial states will not be confined to these countries alone. Even if less-developed countries opt out of international
efforts at environmental improvement, they will find both new economic
opportunities and new problems as advanced industrial states implement
their own environmental programs. There are a number of ways in which
less-developed countries stand to gain from increased attention by rich
states to environmental quality. Primary products of less-developed countries that have been displaced by synthetic substitutes manufactured in
industrialized states may enjoy a strong resurgence in world markets. For
example, reaction against the environmental impact of manufacturing
synthetic rubber and paper products, as well as the high costs necessary to
control pollution associated with synthetic rubber and paper processing,
may lead to increased demand in advanced industrial states for the
primary products that these synthetics replaced.

The expense of conforming to environmental control standards in

---

[45] Ralph C. d'Arge and Allen U. Kneese, "Environmental Quality and International Trade," *International Organization*, XXVI, No. 2 (Spring, 1972),
438.

rich states may also lead to increased investment in less-developed countries willing to import pollution. This could involve more local processing of raw materials supplied by less-developed states, as well as increased investment in manufacturing facilities generally. Brazil's planning minister has said that Brazil would welcome industries that because of their pollution might be unacceptable elsewhere. They "do not want such an industry in an already polluted region, but it would be acceptable in an area where its discharges were tolerable and if it would make a clear contribution to development."[46]

Some less-developed countries have already found ways to increase export earnings by their willingness to import pollution. Malaysia, for example, exports all of its locally produced crude oil at premium prices, which are obtainable because of this oil's low sulfur content, and imports for domestic use cheaper, high-sulfur crude oil from the Middle East.[47]

This is not to suggest that less-developed countries will reap only opportunities for gain as a result of environmental control efforts by advanced industrial states. Less-developed states already voice concern about a further deterioration in their terms of trade with industrial states as the latter tackle their pollution problems. It is assumed that increased production costs associated with compliance to strict environmental control standards in center states will be passed on to the consumer. Thus, because of their heavy dependence upon imports of industrial goods from center states, less-developed countries see a direct link between environmental policies, more costly industrial imports, and the longstanding issue of the terms of trade between rich and poor states.

More important, less-developed countries are likely to face difficult export problems as advanced industrial states impose environment control standards. Product standards designed to alleviate ecological problems in rich states will have to be met by less-developed countries that export to these markets. For example, they may find it impossible to export to the United States foodstuffs treated with DDT. Less-developed countries are likely to face fragmented international markets that require elaborate labeling schemes to assure compliance with varying national ecological standards as a precondition for market access. Some less-developed countries found it difficult in a similar situation to take advantage of preferential tariff reductions on their exports of manufactured and semimanufactured goods offered by European states in 1972 because of technical problems they faced in supplying proper certificates of origin demanded by the rich states. These certificate-of-origin diffi-

---

46 Thomas Sanders, "Development and Environment: Brazil and the Stockholm Conference," American Universities Field Staff, *Fieldstaff Reports, East Coast South American Series*, XVII, No. 7 (June, 1973), 8.

47 *The Wall Street Journal*, October 10, 1973, p. 46.

culties are much less complex than those associated with certification of compliance with ecological standards. This fact augurs poorly for the export capacity of less-developed states in an ecologically oriented age.[48]

These are some of the trade, investment, and development impacts of movement towards pollution control by rich states. All of these economic issues are likely to generate strains in international political relations. This is not to suggest that national and international efforts at environmental improvement will not, or should not, be implemented. Nor is it to suggest that economic growth and environmental controls are always antithetical; control over pollution of the sea is required to maintain commercially productive fisheries, for example. The world must become more sensitive to ecological imbalances produced by modern production techniques. But meaningful action towards these ends will produce economic and political conflicts, which must be better understood before they can be managed.

Those who take an ecological view of world politics see an opportunity for new forms of international cooperation as the world faces the dangers of overpopulation, pollution, famine, and exhaustion of its mineral resources. Some see in the global ecological crisis a surrogate for the invasion from another planet to which world government advocates have traditionally pointed as the sort of external danger necessary to unify nations and reduce conflicts among them. Richard Falk has voiced this line of reasoning.

> Let us suppose we were lucky enough to discover that another planet was preparing to attack and destroy the earth. The discovery would have to be verified and assimilated in the various main capitals of the world. A stragey of planetary defense would then have to be devised. . . . The normal limits of what kinds of international cooperation are feasible might disappear for the duration of the war and the requirements of military necessity might overcome entrenched interests in the economic and social status quo. . . .
>
> For the first time the people of the earth are confronted by a common [ecological] danger, but it remains doubtful as to whether a situation as diffuse and abstract as the ecological crisis can arouse the political imagination sufficiently to serve as the equivalent of a personified enemy aggressor.[49]

Falk and other ecologists strive to make the ecological crisis widely perceived as "the equivalent of a personified enemy aggressor." The

---

[48] For an excellent summary of the challenges pollution control efforts pose for less-developed countries, see United Nations, *Impact of Environmental Policies on Trade and Development, in Particular of the Developing Countries,* TD/130, 1972.

[49] *This Endangered Planet* (New York: Vintage Books, 1971), pp. 12–13, 39.

benefits from such a campaign are not only the avoidance of planetary collapse but the possibility, indeed the necessity, of doing so through a structural revolution in world politics involving intense international cooperation of a sort that renders the nation state obsolete. According to their logic, the nation-state system is itself a generator of global conflict and an obstacle to success in efforts to deal with the ecological challenge confronting the world.[50] To the extent that they discuss the problem, ecologists tend to see great potential for increased harmony in global political and economic relations as a consequence of the ecological crisis.

Although the world might respond in this positive manner to the challenge of an ecological crisis, less constructive responses are at least as likely to occur. The conflict potential among states would probably be heightened substantially if the spaceman-economy (no-growth) philosophy is adopted as a means to avert global ecological disaster. There would undoubtedly be new international political relations binding states together; but as we shall see below, these relations might take the form of traditional empire rather than world federalism or other forms of voluntary economic and political unification.

There is much discussion of the desirability of a no-growth strategy to combat ecological problems, but the importance of economic growth to facilitate change and inhibit conflict within and among states can hardly be overestimated. Redistribution of income to improve the lot of the disadvantaged is much more likely to occur with a minimum of conflict if this can be accomplished by giving them a larger slice of an expanding economic pie. The expectation of economic growth is the foundation upon which most redistribution programs rest. For example, less-developed countries have through UNCTAD sought increases in their agricultural export earnings by having advanced industrial states grant them greater access to the rich states' domestic markets. Less-developed countries argue that this could be done without harm to domestic agricultural producers if the advanced industrial states merely set aside for less-developed countries a given percentage of the expected increase in the domestic market for agricultural products. A general expectation of economic growth is the key to such a proposal.

Within domestic societies a similar situation holds. Edward Woodhouse reports that a recent study of Singapore conducted by Peter Bush[51] found that "ethnic compatibility and system legitimacy were maximized

---

50 Ibid., pp. 37–56. Falk feels that the nation-state system accounts for the logic of collective action, discussed above, which operates as an impediment to effective action in controlling pollution or conserving rare resources. Ibid., pp. 48–49.

51 Peter Bush, "Political Unity and Ethnic Diversity: A Case Study of Singapore" (Ph.D. dissertation, Yale University, 1972).

when both the Chinese and the Malays perceived rapid economic progress for both groups."[52] Woodhouse's account is worth elaborating.

> The differences in political attitudes of subjects with different perceptions of the economic situation were so striking that one could expect a race war or major loss of system legitimacy to occur as a result of a cessation of economic growth. A substantial portion of social scientists' and citizens' indifference to income distribution derives from the assumption that things will be getting better for everyone. When it becomes clear that this assumption no longer holds, either egalitarian norms or inegalitarian practices will come under pressure both within and among polities. Ideological changes, the sharpening of cleavages and substantially increased conflict seem virtually inevitable.[53]

Along these lines, one wonders what the outcome would have been had the civil rights movement in the United States reached its peak in the early 1970s, when expectations of economic growth came into question, instead of a decade earlier, when there was widespread optimism that things would be getting better for everyone.

Advocates of a zero-growth approach to the ecological challenge tend to ignore or understate the link between economic growth and conflict resolution in domestic as well as international affairs. Such a situation transforms so many social, economic, and political relationships from positive-sum to zero-sum games. In a world of finite wealth, improvement in anyone's lot is perceived to result from others having to sacrifice their well being. Within a spaceman economy, marginal groups in domestic societies and marginal states in the global political economy will have little cause to hope for improvement of their status other than through confrontation. This is, of course, the basis of poor states' vigorous opposition to a zero-growth strategy in the world's response to its ecological challenge. A world of states and enterprises operating on the premise of limits to growth might well create an era of virulent domestic and international conflict rather than increased harmony in facing the common danger of planetary collapse. It is important to avoid projecting a zero-growth mentality as appropriate for state, corporate, and personal behavior unless the facts foreclose any alternative strategies for conserving resources and improving the environment.

This general problem can be understood more clearly by focusing

---

[52] Edward J. Woodhouse, "Re-Visioning the Future of the Third World: An Ecological Perspective on Development," *World Politics*, XXV, No. 1 (Copyright © 1972 by Princeton University Press), 32. Reprinted by permission of Princeton University Press.

[53] Ibid.

specifically upon probable international responses to a hypothetical widespread perception that the supply of certain critical mineral resources were so scarce as to limit the capacity for economic growth.[54] In these circumstances, states and corporations whose economic viability depend upon continued supplies of specific mineral resources could be expected to bid the price of these goods up to unprecedented levels. The high prices of goods produced from these mineral resources would affect adversely the standard of living even of people who could afford them. But more important, the mineral resources themselves and the goods produced with them might well be priced beyond the reach of numerous less-developed countries and marginal economic groups within advanced industrial societies. The latter may be aided by domestic income distribution programs, but such programs are unlikely to be very effective in relations among states. The majority of poor states may simply be priced out of industrial development.[55] On the other hand, the few less-developed countries that possess large reserves of critically short mineral resources are likely to become very rich and important actors in world politics by virtue of their strategic position in the global economy.

It is also likely that governments of states able to do so will seek to assure supplies of scarce mineral resources by bringing international exchange of these goods directly under public control. Thus, government-to-government arrangements will be negotiated between major consumer and supplier states for the purpose of organizing international markets for specific mineral raw materials. These types of government-to-government market arrangements will probably replace the present organization of private markets (that is, an oil market, a copper market, and so on) now dominated by oligopolies of giant firms. The result is likely to be a fragmentation of international trade, investment, and monetary relations. Those states unable to negotiate inclusion within these organized commodity markets will be acutely vulnerable to international economic and political pressures.

To the extent that the finiteness of critical mineral resources is thought to limit economic growth, even more drastic alterations than these are likely to occur in the international political economy. Powerful states will probably come to see that various financial and commercial agreements with suppliers of raw materials are insufficient to assure continued access to the critical resources. Immense domestic and interna-

---

[54] We could also use the availability of food supplies as the basis of the discussion that follows. Only then, the shortages imply not only decreases in production and living standards but also the question of survival.

[55] Woodhouse, "Re-Visioning the Future of the Third World," p. 13.

tional pressures will propel strong states toward increased reliance upon military conquest and territorial control as the only appropriate means to assure supplies of the mineral resources, upon which their economic prosperity depends. Thus, overt political control and traditional forms of empire may replace what less-developed countries and radical thinkers refer to as the neo-colonial relationships between center and periphery states. Under these circumstances, which will promote more drastic measures than those discussed above, underdeveloped states that are the major suppliers of critical raw materials will become primary objects of international conflict rather than important political and economic actors in their own right.

In all these ways the consequences of a zero-growth or spaceman economy, in which the finiteness of global mineral supplies is widely perceived, would appear to be an increased stratification among rich and poor states and increased inequalities in income within domestic societies. As much as we might hope for a positive global response of the sort that Richard Falk outlines, the international political economy under these circumstances is likely to look more similar to the world Lenin outlines in his theory of imperialism[56]

As in our discussion of pollution, the thrust of this argument is not that the world should or can avoid confronting the problem of conservation of mineral resource supplies. The trends that Falk, the authors of *The Limits to Growth,* and other ecologists have brought to the world's attention compel decisive action. But ecologists have prescribed as the primary strategy for coping with the global ecological crises a movement toward zero-growth economies, and this has frightening implications for domestic and international relations. The strategy may ultimately become necessary to avert planetary collapse, but it should be viewed as a last resort, not as a first choice, to cope with the challenge presented by global ecology.

A more sensible move at the present time is to maintain intense political pressure and attractive economic incentives for technological innovation in "resource-extending and pollution-suppressing" production processes.[57] Even efforts of this sort will be opposed, understandably, by poor elements of society throughout the globe on the grounds that the large expenditures involved will preclude development, more productive employment, and increases in the delivery of much-needed

---

56 All of these tendencies can be observed in the behavior or rhetoric of Western states as the dimensions of the oil crisis in 1973–74 became clear. In this case, however, the supply shortages were artificially created by the producing states.

57 For an argument along these lines, see Robert L. Heilbroner, "Growth and Survival," *Foreign Affairs,* LI, No. 1 (October, 1972) , 15.

welfare services. However, massive investments in research and development along these lines is preferable to the adoption of a zero-growth strategy. Zero-growth will marginalize the poor even further and will increase conflict throughout the world. Therefore, it should be embraced with caution, and only after other efforts fail.

7

Strategies for States in the Periphery of the Global Political Economy

In the view of most observers, less-developed countries have failed to maximize their position in global economic and political relations. Why this is true, however, is a matter of dispute. It may be the result of their own social-political-economic choices, or of a conscious policy on the part of advanced industrial states to exploit them over several centuries, or of the rich states' preoccupation with economic relations among themselves and their relative neglect of the impact of these relations on poor states. Whatever the explanation, it is important to examine alternative strategies that less-developed countries, acting individually and in concert, can employ to augment their share of the benefits from international economic transactions.[1] Success, of course, implies that Third World countries will simultaneously strengthen their political position in the international arena.

LIBERAL ECONOMIC STRATEGY

If the leadership of a less-developed country accepts the basic tenets of liberal economic thought, one way to enhance that state's benefits from global economic transactions is simply to attract more of those transactions to it. The strategy here is to forge national policies in a manner

---

[1] Less-developed countries' policies toward foreign investment will constitute the focus of this chapter, though other forms of economic transactions, such as trade and aid, will be discussed in passing. Strategies for poor states to secure greater gains from trade were discussed in Chapter 2.

designed to exploit the highly sensitive international economic interdependence characterizing the contemporary world.[2] Taking advantage of the sensitivity of multinational corporations to business opportunities all over the globe, a less-developed country can occasionally attract foreign capital, increase its exports, and otherwise channel foreign capital and technology in accordance with its national economic priorities by the use of selective economic incentives.[3]

Brazil has employed this strategy with great success since 1964. Through a combination of economic incentives and rigid domestic political controls, it has attempted to attract foreign capital and to harness it to the government's domestic and international economic aspirations. In regard to export expansion, for example,

> there is a pretty unanimous consensus among the Brazilian public and private sector of the part international companies can take in conquering world markets *for* Brazil. Both the government and local industrialists want international firms to come to Brazil, set up manufacturing operations—preferably in partnership with the domestic private sector—and export to the world market from their Brazilian production facilities.[4]

Through the extension of export and investment incentives[5] to domestic and foreign firms—at a time when many Latin American states are imposing constraints on foreign investment—Brazil has attracted multinational corporations that desire a production base for their operations throughout Latin America.[6]

Efforts have also been made through industrial incentives to promote investment for regional development of the destitute Brazilian Northeast. Under specified conditions, firms that invest in this area of Brazil can secure advantages that include a 50 percent reduction in income tax, a ten-year exemption on income tax and surtax, and an exemption from federal taxes on imported equipment.[7] In other countries and in various regional integration schemes, multinational corporations have acted more rapidly than indigenous firms to take advantage of

---

2 See Richard Cooper, "Economic Interdependence and Foreign Policy in the Seventies," *World Politics*, XXIV, No. 2 (January, 1972), 159–81.

3 For a more complete presentation of an "exploitatitve response" to international economic interdependence, see Cooper, "Economic Interdependence and Foreign Policy in the Seventies," p. 168.

4 *Brazil: New Business Power in Latin America* (New York: Business International Corporation, 1971), p. 42. Italics added.

5 For examples of these export and investment incentives, see *Brazil: New Business Power in Latin America*, pp. 38, 46.

6 Robert Moss, "The Moving Frontier: A Survey of Brazil," *The Economist*, September 2, 1972, p. 47.

7 *Brazil: New Business Power in Latin America*, p. 28.

such incentives,[8] and foreign investors have indeed moved into the Brazilian Northeast in response to these exceptional economic opportunities.[9]

These types of incentive schemes administered by a military leadership capable of managing inflation, suppressing wage levels, and generally assuring a stable political environment hospitable to foreign investment have made Brazil one of the most attractive locales for foreign capital. Foreign investment in Brazil totaled $3 billion in 1972,[10] and foreign firms accounted for 38 percent of the growth in Brazil's exports of manufactures from 1960 through 1968.[11] Foreign capital has contributed substantially to Brazil's increase in GNP of 8 to 10 percent each year since 1968. This growth rate surpassed even that of Japan and has made Brazil an important political actor, globally as well as regionally.

It would be misleading to conclude that the typical state in the periphery would necessarily match the achievements of Brazil if it adopted the same strategy. In addition to manipulable economic incentives and its political complexion, Brazil is particularly attractive to foreign sources of capital, technology, and services because of its immense wealth of natural resources and its large population. In contrast with most less-developed states, the sizable and growing Brazilian market plus the availability of local factors of production make it possible for a wide variety of multinational corporations to employ economies of scale in their Brazilian operations, even if the potential for exports is small. Also, because of its territorial and population size, a strong economic performance immediately gives Brazil an international political importance that few Third-World states would enjoy, even if, through similar policies, they were able to achieve growth rates approximating those of Brazil in recent years.

Short of emulating Brazil, however, less-developed countries can offer specific incentives to attract foreign capital, technology, goods, and services. This strategy has been employed in the past by states, whether developed or underdeveloped, in specific economic areas, such as shipping-registration incentives in Liberia and Panama, cheap labor for assembly of consumer goods in Taiwan and South Korea, and tax incen-

8 Raymond Vernon, *Sovereignty at Bay* (New York: Basic Books, 1971), pp. 245–46.

9 Among the international investors in the Brazilian Northeast are Phillips Petroleum, Union Carbide, Dow, DuPont. U.S. Steel, Asahi Chemical, Rhone Poulenc, and Mitsubishi Rayon. *Brazil: New Business Power in Latin America*, p. 32.

10 Robert Moss, "The Moving Frontier," p. 29.

11 "Foreign Investment in Brazil: A Survey of Its Impact on the Economy," *Business Latin America*, February 18, 1971, p. 52.

tives for the location of international corporate sales offices in Switzerland.[12]

This strategy to increase benefits from international economic transactions entails certain costs, however, which make it unpopular, or even politically impossible to sustain, in many less-developed countries. In order to maximize the state's attractiveness to potential foreign investors, a premium is often placed upon political stability and economic growth, at the expense of domestic social justice and income redistribution. These are major objections voiced by opponents of the authoritarian political controls employed by the military regime that has directed Brazil's recent economic boom. Also, to the extent that massive foreign capital is attracted to a less-developed country, the problem arises of foreign control over important areas of domestic economic and political life. In 1969 it was estimated that foreign firms operating in Brazil accounted for 72 percent of total investment in the capital goods sector, 78 percent of total investment in the consumer durables sector, and 53 percent of total investment in the consumer nondurables sector of the Brazilian economy.[13] Critics of the Brazilian military leadership point to such figures as evidence of the denationalization of Brazilian industry and the loss of national autonomy that follow logically from the pursuit of this type of economic strategy by any less-developed country.[14] Whatever the benefits of such a strategy in terms of increased export revenues and aggregate growth, these costs are held to be unacceptable by many less-developed countries and by all proponents of radical thought.

REGIONAL EFFORTS TO ATTRACT AND CONTROL INVESTMENT

The investment code of the Andean Common Market is an example of an attempt by six less-developed countries[15] to avoid the economic denationalization associated with the Brazilian experience while seeking the capital, technology, and services of multinational corporations. By the terms of this code, multinational corporations are to be excluded from key sectors of these states' economies.[16] Those firms operating in

---

[12] Richard Cooper, *The Economics of Interdependence* (New York: McGraw-Hill, 1968) , p. 101.

[13] "Foreign Investment in Brazil," p. 50.

[14] For a more elaborate assessment of the Brazilian economic "miracle" from the radical perspective, see Eduardo Galeano, "The De-Nationalization of Brazilian Industry," *Monthly Review*, XXI, No. 3 (July-August, 1969) , 11–30.

[15] Peru, Colombia, Ecuador, Chile, Bolivia, and Venezuela.

[16] The sectors are domestic wholesale and retail trade, communication, public utilities and transportation, and financial institutions.

other sectors are to be subject to very strict controls over various aspects of their operations: limited repatriation of profits, agreements on purchases of factor inputs, restricted access to local credit, review of licensing agreements, and evaluation of export marketing agreements. Multinational corporations are also required to turn over majority control to local capital within specified time periods.[17] All of these controls are designed to increase both the national autonomy of the Andean states and their share of the economic returns from foreign operations within their jurisdiction.

For most less-developed countries, concerted rather than individual action vis-à-vis foreign investors is likely to be necessary in order to attract multinational corporations under controls such as those in the Andean investment code. If a single state imposes strict investment controls, multinational corporations sensitive to differences in national regulation of their activities will avoid that state and locate elsewhere in the region.[18] If, on the other hand, a number of states in a region adopt an identical investment code, multinationals that wish to operate in the region will find it much more difficult, perhaps impossible, to avoid the constraints. The connection of such investment controls with movement toward a regional common market is a particularly interesting strategy because the prospect of an integrated regional market, rather than a number of small national markets, may offer the incentive necessary to attract foreign investment even under strict controls.[19]

NATIONALIZATION

The approach of the Andean Pact may appear as a halfway measure to economic nationalists in less-developed countries. The Andean states are, after all, still interested in attracting foreign investment, albeit under stringent conditions. Nationalization of major foreign operations within

17 This code is discussed further in Chapter 4. See also Peter Schlisser, "Restrictions on Foreign Investment in the Andean Common Market," *International Lawyer*, V, No. 3 (July, 1971), 586–98.

18 This is more the case for small states than for larger, more highly developed countries. For example, Mexico has attracted foreign capital quite successfully with investment controls similar in some respects to the Andean investment code. See Chapter 4 for a more detailed discussion of controls imposed on foreign investors by host states.

19 For an evaluation of consequences of the Andean investment code, see Raymond Vernon, *Restrictive Business Practices*, Study prepared for the United Nations Conference on Trade ond Development, 1972, p. 25; and M. Wionczek, "U.S. Reaction to the Andean Group System for Treatment of Foreign Capital," *Comercio Exterior*, XVII, No. 6 (Mexico), June, 1971, 27–30.

the state is sometimes prescribed as a more appropriate strategy for an individual less-developed country in its attempts to increase its share of benefits from global economic relations. The strategy of nationalization is likely to appear most attractive to those less-developed countries in which government revenues are generated largely from exports of primary products whose extraction and international sales are controlled by foreign capital.

This is true for several reasons. Foreign-owned extractive enterprises engaged in the exploitation and shipment abroad of finite natural resources give the appearance of removing national wealth rather than creating it, as a manufacturing enterprise does. Thus, foreign investment in extractive industry is particularly resented in less-developed countries, and it is more prone to nationalization than is foreign investment in the manufacturing sector, for example. In addition, the return on foreign direct investment in extractive industries is typically much higher than the return on investment in manufacturing industries.[20] Even though the host state's share of earnings from extractive enterprises controlled by foreign capital has increased substantially over the years, host states have a compelling urge to nationalize these enterprises and to gain *all* the earnings from these particularly lucrative investments. This movement is certain to gain strength as the limits to available mineral resources are appreciated throughout the globe and as the prices of these products begin to reflect this fact.

The nationalization of foreign investments in extractive enterprise is an extraordinarily appealing strategy for those less-developed countries fortunate enough to possess major supplies of primary products.[21] Nationalization holds the promise of increased government revenues and foreign exchange earnings in a way that appears to reduce the dependence of a poor state upon rich states and the multinational corporations operating from them. This policy has immense domestic political appeal in those less-developed countries in which the general population is highly sensitive to dependence upon, and perceived exploitation by, rich states and foreign firms.

Seductive as this policy may be for less-developed countries, it does not necessarily result either in increased revenues or in reduced depen-

[20] See U.S. Congress, Senate Committee on Finance, *Implications of Multinational Firms for World Trade and Investment and for U.S. Trade and Labor,* 93rd Cong., 1st sess. 1973, p. 445.

[21] We will focus our discussion of nationalization on extractive industry since this is such a salient export sector to many Third World states. It is very difficult to analyze the pros and cons of nationalization with any precision unless one focuses on particular economic sectors or products.

dence upon multinational firms. Unless a number of special circumstances are present, nationalizing local production of primary products for sale abroad is likely to place a less-developed country in the unenviable position of being a supplier of last resort. As a result, it faces great uncertainty in the amount of its export earnings and government revenues from year to year. Moreover, it is also likely to remain as dependent upon multinational corporations for marketing the product internationally as it had been previously dependent upon them for production of the primary product.[22]

The production and sales of most mineral resources, such as petroleum, copper, tin, and aluminum, are typically controlled by an oligopoly of vertically integrated multinational corporations that are at once the major producers *and* the major consumers of the mineral resource. Vertical integration is a compelling goal of large enterprises that seek to avoid risk either as suppliers or as consumers of mineral resources. A firm that begins as a producer of, say, copper creates affiliates that process and/or fabricate products from the mineral in an effort to assure its sales of copper in a buyer's market. A firm that begins as a producer of finished goods requiring massive amounts of copper inputs creates affiliates to produce copper itself in an effort to assure its supply of the mineral in a seller's market.[23] This behavior ultimately results in the oligopolistic control of international markets in mineral resources, a condition faced by almost any less-developed country contemplating nationalization of foreign-owned extractive industry. This situation often reduces the efficacy of nationalization as a strategy to enhance the economic returns and national autonomy of a less-developed country possessing valuable mineral resources.

Nationalization is likely to bring a steady increase of economic returns to a less-developed country to the extent that (1) the stage of production represented by a foreign firm's operations in the country is the greatest barrier of entry into the vertically integrated production and sales process,[24] (2) the state that nationalizes the foreign firm either con-

22 In addition to these problems, one must also take into account the effect that nationalization of extractive industry might have on efforts to attract foreign investment in other economic sectors or efforts to secure international loans. The discussion that follows relies heavily upon the work of Theodore Moran. In particular, see "New Deal or Raw Deal in Raw Materials," *Foreign Policy,* No. 5 (Winter, 1971/72), 119–36; "Transnational Strategies of Protection and Defense by Multinational Corporations: Spreading the Risk and Raising the Cost for Nationalization in Natural Resources," *International Organization,* XXVII, No. 2 (Spring, 1973), 273–88; and *Multinational Corporations and the Politics of Dependence: Copper in Chile* (Princeton, N.J.: Princeton University Press, 1974).

23 Moran, "New Deal or Raw Real in Raw Materials," pp. 122–23.

24 Ibid., pp. 124–27.

tinues to cooperate with, and participate within, the oligopoly controlling international distribution of the mineral resource,[25] or to develop
an international distribution capability of its own—one that is seen by
refiners, fabricators, and consumers of the mineral as a dependable source
of supply at stable prices.[26] Unless these circumstances prevail, the state
that nationalizes foreign-controlled extractive operations will find itself a
supplier of last resort, because multinational firms will seek "safer"
sources of supply.

If the stage of production represented by the foreign firms' operations within a particular less-developed country is not the greatest barrier
of entry into the vertically integrated production and sales process,
nationalization of the foreign operations will not result in increased
revenues or in control over marketable production of the mineral for
international consumers. If alternate sources of supply of the mineral can
be developed, the multinational firm whose mining operations are
nationalized will develop them. Even if these alternate deposits are more
expensive to develop, they will be attractive to multinational firms seeking to avoid risk in securing supplies of the mineral. Thus, in response to
the threat of nationalization of their mining operations in Chile and
other areas, large corporations in the copper industry have recently
focused their efforts on extracting copper from lower-grade ore deposits
in more "secure" areas of the world, such as Australia, Canada, and the
United States.[27] Copper is a mineral resource for which access to unprocessed reserves is the greatest barrier of entry to a vertically integrated
production and sales process. Even so, after nationalizing foreign-based
copper industries in 1971, Chile faced the loss of its major consumers and,
thus, reduced economic returns from its international sales of copper.
Attempts at nationalization by less-developed countries to maximize
revenues from international sales of other mineral resources, such as
aluminum and tin, are even less likely to succeed over the long run
because the greatest barrier of entry to the vertically integrated production and sales of these minerals is possession of highly sophisticated
processing technology and immense amounts of capital, not access to ore
deposits.[28]

The other major requirement a less-developed country must meet
in order to sustain increases in economic returns from the nationalization

---

25 Ibid., pp. 129–31.

26 Moran, *Multinational Corporations,* p. 242.

27 Ibid., pp. 32–33. For an interesting discussion of the corporate strategy employed by Kennecott in anticipation of and defense against nationalization of
its operations in Chile, see Moran, "Transnational Strategies of Protection
and Defense by Multinational Corporations."

28 Moran, "New Deal or Raw Deal in Raw Materials," p. 126.

of extractive industry is to maintain its reputation as a dependable supplier of the mineral to consumers abroad. This means continued participation within the international oligopoly of multinational firms which often control the bulk of international sales of mineral resources. In this way, the production of the nationalized operation continues to enjoy a sustained volume of sales at controlled price levels in international markets. Unless this is accomplished, or unless the less-developed country develops an international sales network of its own that is just as dependable in supplying the mineral at steady price levels, the income generated from nationalizing production is likely to be reduced or very uneven from year to year.[29] The development of its own sales and distribution network is often beyond a less-developed country's economic capacity or administrative skills; it is, in addition, always a long-term enterprise. The threat of interrupting supplies for political purposes is, in any case, not compatible with maximizing earnings from nationalized production over the long run. Thus, the country that nationalizes foreign-controlled production of its mineral resources finds that it must continue to cooperate with the same firms, or with firms similar to those it nationalizes at home, for the sales of its products abroad.

These facts pose a major dilemma for less-developed countries attempting both to maximize revenues from sales abroad and to reduce dependence upon multinational corporations (and their parent states) by nationalization of local operations of extractive industry. The government that chooses this policy will usually have to decide which of these goals to pursue, since they tend to be mutually exclusive. Policies designed to obtain steadily increasing, or even stable, economic returns from international sales of nationalized mineral exploitation require cooperation with, and continued dependence upon, multinational corporations. But this is politically difficult and often unacceptable for a regime whose domestic support rests upon its confrontation with foreign firms over the production and sale of these economic resources. Refusal to cooperate with multinational firms may minimize dependence upon them (and their parent states), but a less-developed country will thereby most likely suffer great fluctuations in its receipts from international sales. The regime may feel that a redistribution of income within the country and a sense of national identity and pride accompanying nationalization are more than adequate compensation for the loss of stable or increased export earnings. Our point, however, is simply that nationalization of foreign capital in local extractive industry seldom results in *both* increased revenues and reduced dependence upon foreign firms.

However, if global demand for a particular mineral resource con-

29 Ibid., pp. 129–33; and Moran, *Multinational Corporations*, pp. 240–41.

tinually exceeds production and if there are no economically feasible synthetic or natural substitutes, certain less-developed countries may find success in nationalization without risking continued dependence upon foreign firms for international sales. To the extent that the world begins to approach the limits of global mineral resources, such a situation could conceivably emerge in regard to numerous products in the not too distant future. At present, petroleum is the product enjoying this market situation, but even in this case the oil-producing states have pursued a strategy that differs in several crucial respects from unilateral nationalization of the sort we have been discussing.

This analysis of nationalization as a strategy for less-developed countries suggests in most cases that it is not likely to produce all the results that at first glance make it attractive to economic nationalists. We have focused upon nationalization of extractive industry, but our basic argument can, with minor adjustments, be applied to the nationalization of numerous types of production marketed internationally. Of course, a very different situation and calculus exist with regard to the efficacy of nationalization of foreign firms that produce only for consumption within the domestic market of a less-developed country.

COMMODITY PRODUCER CARTELS

If, in general, nationalization of foreign-controlled extractive industry by individual less-developed countries has little chance of yielding all the benefits claimed, unified action by a group of less-developed countries that together possess the major deposits of the same mineral resource should offer greater hope of success. In this case, the strategy involves concerted action by major producer states confronting an industry or oligopoly as a whole, rather than a single producer state confronting only the firm (or firms) located within its borders. If less-developed countries possessing the major sources of a particular mineral resource can maintain a common front vis-à-vis all the major multinationals in that industry, none of these states can be relegated to the position of a supplier of last resort. Collectively, they would still be able to exert considerable weight in international distribution and sales. This is, of course, the strategy that has been employed quite successfully by oil-producing states through the Organization of Petroleum-Exporting Countries (OPEC).[30]

OPEC was formed in 1960 in an effort to represent more effectively

[30] OPEC is composed of Iran, Kuwait, Saudi Arabia, Iraq, Venezuela (the original members), Qatar, Libya, Indonesia, Algeria, Nigeria, Ecuador, United Arab Emirates, and Galon.

the interests of the oil-producing states in their dealings with the few giant oil firms—especially on the question of host-state revenues. After the closure of the Suez Canal in 1967, which enhanced the bargaining position of the oil-producing states, they were able through coordinated efforts to increase their share of the revenues from crude-oil sales, on the average, from about 50 percent to over 90 percent. The most dramatic evidence of their enhanced bargaining position and cohesiveness was their increase in the posted (official) price of oil from $2.59 to $11.65 per barrel during 1973, production cutbacks, and a selective embargo on oil shipments to the United States and some other Western states by the Arab members of OPEC following the Arab-Israeli war. Even more important is the relative ease with which the oil-producing states are taking control of the oil companies' operations on their soil. Particularly interesting in this regard was the successful negotiation in concert by Saudi Arabia, Qatar, Kuwait, Iraq, and Abu Dhabi of a participation agreement with 23 international oil companies. Concluded in 1972, the participation agreement called for a gradual increase in the producing states' share of the concessions within their borders until they acquire majority (51 percent) control in 1983. Their bargaining position is now so strong that these and other oil-producing states will not in fact wait until 1983 to assume majority control, and their share will undoubtedly approach 100 percent.

The participation agreement differs in some fundamental respects from the nationalization policies discussed above, and it is worthy of attention in its own right as a strategy for less-developed countries. Knowledge of these differences is crucial in understanding why participation (or what at least began as participation) may produce more economic and international political payoffs for less-developed states than does outright nationalization. Participation is an arrangement whereby the oil multinationals are pushed into a minority ownership position without being forced to disengage from the oil-producing states. The companies give up majority (perhaps even minority) control over their concessions, but they remain the operators of these concessions and continue, for the time being, to distribute and market the oil-producing states' petroleum internationally. In this way, the producing states gain control over their natural resources and determine prices and production levels (which used to be determined by the oil companies), while still securing the benefits of the corporations' technological expertise, managerial talent, capital, and distribution and sales networks. Sheik Yamani, the Saudi Arabian Minister of Oil and Minerals, who negotiated the participation agreement for the producing states, frequently refers to the arrangement as establishing a "Catholic marriage between the producer countries on the one hand and the consumers and the major or independent oil companies on the other hand by linking them to a state where it is almost impossible for any of them to divorce."[31] It is clearly a marriage, however, that the producing states forced upon reluctant parties and in which they hold the upper hand. Recognizing this fact, oil-industry spokesmen have referred to it as a "shotgun wedding."[32]

Nationalization seeks to expel foreign firms from the host state, whereas participation seeks to exploit them. Nationalization leads to open conflict with foreign firms upon which the less-developed country often depends for new technology, capital mobilization, and international sales. Participation is designed to forge continued cooperation between the less-developed countries and the multinational corporations at all stages of the production and sales process, and the host states are firmly in control of the terms of the relationship.

What circumstances have allowed the oil-producing states to force this arrangement upon the oil multinationals? What are the manifestations and international implications of these less-developed countries' new-found economic and political strength? Among other things, the OPEC states were able to obtain multinational corporations' agreement to participation arrangements because they control the lion's share of global production and reserves of the mineral, and because they maintained a united front. OPEC states accounted for approximately one half of global petroleum production during 1972,[33] 90 percent of the oil entering international trade during 1972,[34] and 67 percent of the world's proven oil reserves.[35] This position of OPEC in present and anticipated global production and sales makes the international oil companies hostages of the producing states as long as they coordinate policy through OPEC.

Through OPEC the oil-producing states have secured control over production, and they receive the dominant share of economic benefits derived from international sales of crude oil. Combined with the rapid increase in global oil demand (8 percent annually during the period 1967–1972),[36] this situation seems certain to assure the oil-producing states, particularly those in the Middle East, a dramatic increase in their economic wealth and international political position. Europe and Japan have always relied heavily upon imports to meet their oil needs, but now even the United States has joined them as a major oil importer from

31 *The New York Times,* October 8, 1972, Sec. 3, p. 7.

32 Ibid., Sec. 4, p. 3.

33 Table 7-1.

34 *The New York Times,* July 8, 1973, Sec. 3, p. 7.

35 Table 7-1.

36 *Statistical Review of the World Oil Industry, 1972,* British Petroleum Company Limited, 1972, p. 8.

Table 7-1.   Global Distribution of Oil Reserves, Production, and Consumption
in 1972 (Percentage of World Total in Parentheses)*

Country	Oil Reserves[a] (billions of barrels)		Oil Production[e] (millions of barrels per day)		Oil Consumption[e] (millions of barrels per day)	
OPEC States	447	(67)	25[a]	(47)	n.a.[g]	
Middle East[b]	355	(53)	18	(37)	1	(2)
United States	37	(6)	9	(18)	16	(30)
Western Europe	12	(2)	—[f]	(0)	14	(27)
Japan	——[c]	(0)	—[f]	(0)	5	(9)
Communist States	98[d]	(15)	9	(18)	8	(15)
Others	73	(11)	9	(18)	9	(17)
World Total	667	(100)	53	(100)	53	(100)

*Figures have been rounded.

[a] Source: The Oil and Gas Journal, LXX, No. 52 (December 25, 1972), 82, 83.

[b] Abu Dhabi, Iraq, Kuwait, Qatar, Saudi Arabia, Libya.

[c] Less than 500 million barrels.

[d] USSR (75 billion barrels), China (20 billion barrels), Eastern Europe (3 billion barrels).

[e] Source: Statistical Review of the World Oil Industry—1972, British Petroleum Company Limited, 1972.

[f] Less than 500,000 barrels per day.

[g] Not available from these data sources, but negligible as a proportion of the world total.

the Middle East.[37] In 1973, the Middle East states were the source of 20 percent of total American oil consumption.[38] It was predicted, prior to the events in late 1973, that by 1980 the Middle East states would provide 35 to 40 percent of America's oil consumption.[39] American oil imports, together with great increases in Europe's and Japan's consumption of oil from the Middle East over this decade, will generate massive revenues for these oil-producing states. Indeed, after purchasing all the development and the military capability they can absorb, the oil-producing states in the Middle East will probably have accumulated in excess of $250 billion in foreign reserves by 1980.

This massive wealth, in addition to their physical control over the bulk of global oil production, gives these oil-producing states dramatic new strength in international economic and political relations. Following the production cutbacks and the oil export embargo applied to the United States, the Netherlands, and Portugal for their support of Israel in the 1973 Middle East war, the Arab states (indeed, all major oil-produc-

[37] Compare the oil production and the oil consumption of these states in Table 7-1.

[38] James Akins, "The Oil Crisis: This Time the Wolf is Here," Foreign Affairs, LI, No. 3 (April, 1973), 463.

[39] Ibid.

ing states) have been actively courted by all major oil-consuming states. Through the use of the oil weapon in 1973 and 1974, they produced a noticeable change in American policy in the Middle East—from a clearly pro-Israeli stance to the posture of a mediator between Israeli and Arab interests. Europe and Japan virtually embraced the Arab position in the conflict in order to assure access to oil from the Middle East. Within four months after the Arab oil embargo, delegations of Western and Japanese governments and businesses had concluded or were negotiating $11 billion in deals with Middle East states for long-term oil contracts. The Middle East states have and will continue to make demands upon Europe, Japan, and the United States for preferential trade treatment, increased receptivity toward direct and equity investment they might wish to make in oil-consuming states, an increase in Western investments within their borders at terms attractive to the host states, and an enhanced role in international monetary decision making by virtue of their strong reserve position. In 1974, the nine European Common Market countries offered the Arab states a long-term economic, technical, and cultural cooperation plan that is designed to accommodate these demands.

The new strength of the Middle East oil states will also produce more general political and strategic dilemmas for Western states. Their desire to insure uninterrupted oil supplies will drive the various major oil-consuming states into intense competition with one another for access to Middle East oil on an individual basis, or toward politically charged negotiations among themselves as to the appropriate terms upon which a common Western position on oil consumption can be forged. The wealth and size of some oil-producing states, such as Iran, will permit them to emerge as significant regional military powers, with which the center states must forge new relationships. Western states are also coming to view the security of tanker routes out of the Persian Gulf and the cultivation of friendly relations with states along these routes as an important new strategic concern. In all these economic, political, and military respects, concerted action by the OPEC states can be seen to have moved a number of previously less-developed countries out of the periphery of global relations.

The Western states are currently searching for responses appropriate to this new challenge posed by the oil-producing states. In the long run, the United States and others are looking toward the development of alternate energy sources such as solar power, nuclear power, and coal liquification and gasification. In addition, they are pushing the development of technology that would enable economically feasible exploitation of oil-shale and tar-sand deposits in the United States and Canada, which could yield as much oil as present Persian Gulf reserves. In the meantime, however, the OPEC states will retain a stranglehold on global energy resources. To decrease their vulnerability in the short run, the major oil-consuming states are attempting to reduce consumption, reduce the level of oil imports, coordinate efforts to negotiate a reduction in oil prices, and institutionalize a scheme to share petroleum supplies in the event of future threats of supply interruptions (particularly when directed at a single state) by oil-producing states. These state policies have become imperative because the international oil companies are no longer strong enough to protect the interests of consumers in their bargaining with oil-producing states.[40]

Another strategy for oil-consuming states has been proposed by M. A. Adelman and T. Moran among others.[41] They argue that oil consumers would benefit from, and should therefore encourage, outright nationalization by the OPEC states of the international oil companies' crude oil production. A complete takeover of oil production by the oil-producing states would place the burden of maintaining the oil suppliers' cartel completely upon the states themselves. In the past, this burden has been borne by the major international oil companies. Maintenance of the cartel would require the various oil-producing states to establish and abide by agreements on production levels and international sales prices. According to this line of argument, political cleavages among the oil-producing states and the political demands within these states for maximizing oil revenues would make it very difficult for the oil-producing states to maintain these agreements on production and prices. There would be intense pressures on individual states to increase their revenues, at the expense of others in the cartel, by exceeding their production quota and/or by shaving prices for major oil consumers. Such behavior would benefit consumers in the Western states more than the present arrangements between the oil-producing states and the major oil companies—arrangements wherein the state increases its revenues by demanding higher taxes on the oil companies, which in turn pass the larger tax bill on to consumers in the form of price increases.

The emerging monetary reserve position of numerous oil-producing states might undermine the logic of Moran and Adelman, however. As we have seen, it is estimated that the Middle East states will have immense foreign reserves by 1980. If this is the case, the pressures to exceed produc-

---

40 See Walter Levy, "An Atlantic-Japanese Energy Policy," *Foreign Policy*, No. 11 (Summer, 1973), 159–90. For some of the problems arising in these efforts, see *The New York Times*, June 22, 1973, p. 43; and *The Washington Post*, February 14, 1974, p. 1.

41 M. A. Adelman, "Is the Oil Shortage Real?" *Foreign Policy*, No. 9 (Winter, 1972/73), 69–107; T. Moran, "Coups and Costs," *Foreign Policy*, No. 8 (Fall, 1972), 129–37.

tion quotas and cut prices in order to increase oil revenues may not be as great as Moran and Adelman suggest.[42] At least, those oil-producing states that accumulate massive amounts of foreign reserves during this decade (Kuwait, Libya, Saudi Arabia, Qatar, and the United Arab Emirates) would seem quite capable of maintaining an oil suppliers' cartel even if nationalizing oil production placed the burden of honoring production controls and price levels directly upon them.

Among the various alternatives available to Western states in response to the new strength of the oil-producing states in the Middle East, military conquest is certainly the most drastic. It is raised here not because it is a highly probable response now, but because more will be heard about it to the extent that Western states generally, and the United States in particular, perceive the oil-producing states in the Middle East to be too unstable or too hostile for assured deliveries of petroleum. Indeed, prior to the Middle East War of 1973 Senator Fulbright noted the possibility of a military solution to America's energy needs.

> The United States might come to the conclusion that military action is required to secure the oil resources of the Middle East to secure our exposed jugular. The United States might avoid direct military intervention and leave the action to militarily potent surrogates such as Israel or Iran.[43]

Since that war and the oil embargo, there has been open speculation among government-connected American scholars about the efficacy of a military seizure of key oil fields in the Persian Gulf as a means to break OPEC and lower the price of oil.[44] Secretary of State Kissinger himself raised the threat of military action should the Arab oil-producing states adopt policies (presumably another embargo) that would lead to an "actual strangulation of the industrialized world."[45]

Military action is not likely in the short run. However, its suggestion by American officials is designed to give OPEC states pause in contemplating another embargo or in drastically increasing oil prices as

---

42 As an example of the political and economic flexibility such reserves give an oil-producing state, Libya's reserves of $2 billion in 1970 (during its negotiations for higher oil revenues) would have enabled Libya to cover its import bills and government expenditures for four years without any further oil income. Akins, "The Oil Crisis," pp. 470–71.

43 *The New York Times,* July 8, 1973, Sec. 4, p. 3.

44 See Robert Tucker, "Oil, The Issue of American Intervention," *Commentary,* LIX, No. 1 (January, 1975) , 21–31; and Miles Ignotus, "Seizing Arab Oil," *Harpers,* CCL, No. 1498 (March, 1975) , 45–62.

45 Interview in *Business Week,* January 13, 1973, p. 69.

they did in 1973. In any event, the suggestion of military action in connection with oil supplies in the 1970s lends credence to the suggestion in Chapter 6 that military conquest is a likely response of great powers should mineral resource scarcities threaten their economic prosperity.

The nature of the alternative responses being discussed among advanced industrial states is itself evidence of the extent to which OPEC has enhanced the economic and political position of the oil-producing states. It is not surprising, therefore, that the united-front approach of OPEC is cited as a model of behavior for less-developed countries that possess large deposits of mineral resources other than oil. It is a viable strategy for peripheral states generally, to the extent that (1) access to the product in its primary stage constitutes the greatest barrier of entry into the vertically integrated production and sales process; (2) the dominant portion of the world's supply of the mineral is concentrated in a very limited number of peripheral states whose political outlook and economic situation are sufficiently congruent to make concerted economic action possible; (3) global demand for the product is rising steadily over the years; (4) natural and synthetic substitutes are not available or are extremely costly to employ; (5) production cutbacks to hold or increase prices do not significantly increase unemployment in the producing states; and (6) financial reserves are large enough to allow limits in output without seriously curtailing imports necessary for development. Unfortunately, from the point of view of less-developed countries seeking to alter their position in the global economy, very few resources other than petroleum meet all of these criteria.

Copper and bauxite are the two mineral resources that lend themselves most to an emulation of OPEC. There is now a permanent institutional structure linking the major exporters of copper—Chile, Peru, Zambia, and Zaire—and a similar structure linking the major aluminum exporters—Guinea, Australia, Guyana, Jamaica, Sierra Leone, Surinam, and Yugoslavia. But even though these states account for the bulk of copper and bauxite exports, most of the other conditions that made it possible for the oil-producing states to reap massive gains through OPEC are not present. Concerted action by producers of bauxite, copper, tin, and a few other mineral resources will most likely consist of efforts to force advanced industrial states and international firms to pay considerably more for access to mineral deposits, to locate processing facilities in the mineral-supplying states, and to share ownership with the host states. These mineral-producing states are not likely to have much success with production cutbacks, selective embargoes, and direct control over world market prices, in the manner of the oil-producing states in 1973. In general, although concerted action by the oil-producing states has been most successful, it is unlikely in the near future that peripheral states exporting minerals other than oil will secure anything like the economic and political leverage possessed by the OPEC states.

UNIVERSALIST EFFORTS TO REFORM
THE GLOBAL ECONOMY

OPEC exemplifies a strategy whereby states in the periphery cooperate and bargain along industry lines to enhance their economic and political position in international relations. There are also numerous multilateral efforts structured along regional and universal lines by less-developed countries that extend well beyond confrontation with a particular global industry. Such efforts are seldom dramatic, but they are an important dimension of less-developed countries' attempts to extract more benefits from their economic relations with rich states, and multinational corporations.

Since its creation in 1964, the United Nations Conference on Trade and Development (UNCTAD) has provided the institutional framework for the most persistent universal efforts by less-developed countries to reform the global economy. The cleavage between periphery and center states in the global economy is formalized in UNCTAD by a group system[46] in which nearly 100 poor states have repeatedly adhered to a common position in proposing alterations in the conduct of international economic relations. The poor states are given political, legal, and economic backstopping in their efforts by a secretariat infused with the economic orientation of Raul Prebisch, UNCTAD's first secretary-general.[47]

Through UNCTAD the states in the periphery secured an agreement with the center states whereby the latter would grant preferential access for a wide variety of less-developed countries' exports of manufactures and semimanufactures. Proposals have also been generated for commodity agreements and financial schemes designed to compensate for what all less-developed states view as a secular decline in their terms of trade with advanced industrial states.[48]

In monetary affairs, UNCTAD has played an important role in dramatizing the exclusion of less-developed countries' participation in international monetary decision making. Partly because of UNCTAD's efforts in this regard, the poor states were brought into the monetary

---

[46] For a discussion of the group system, see Branislav Gosovic, "UNCTAD: North-South Encounter," *International Conciliation*, No. 568 (May, 1969), pp. 14–30.

[47] See Chapter 2 for a discussion of Prebisch's orientation.

[48] See Chapter 2 for a discussion of these proposals.

negotiations begun in 1972 under the auspices of the Group of Twenty. UNCTAD has also been important in keeping alive the proposal to forge a link between allocations of new liquidity created in the form of Special Drawing Rights and development assistance for poor states.[49]

UNCTAD has pressed hard for alterations in the terms upon which shipping services controlled by merchant marines of center states are provided to less-developed countries.[50] In the field of economic assistance, UNCTAD has established targets for the volume and terms of aid from all rich states as well as focusing attention upon debt-service problems and the costs of tied aid to donors and recipients. With regard to foreign investment, UNCTAD has examined restrictive business practices such as export license contracts, use of patent rights, use of trademarks, and the transfer of technology as they affect exports and the general development prospects of Third World states. Increasingly, this organization is serving as a forum where less-developed countries can share information and propose unified action to deal with their common concerns as weak states playing host to multinational corporations.

Together, these activities of UNCTAD constitute a broad-gauge assault on the existing norms of behavior and division of benefits in economic relations between the center and periphery of the global economy. Through its activities, UNCTAD has done more to identify and dramatize systemic constraints on national development efforts of poor states than to produce significant transfers of economic resources or to enhance the international decision-making role of less-developed countries. Nevertheless, UNCTAD provides a good example of the value of universal efforts through international organizations to structure communication between rich states and poor states on the gamut of economic issues that are of primary importance to the latter.[51]

In spite of the value of UNCTAD to peripheral states, there are several major limitations on what it can accomplish to enhance the position of less-developed countries in the global economy. Of foremost importance, UNCTAD decisions are not legally binding on states or other actors. Hence, even though within UNCTAD the less-developed countries as a group pursue a bargaining stance of confrontation with rich states, concrete results from UNCTAD deliberations ultimately rest upon

---

[49] See Chapter 3 for an elaboration of these demands.

[50] In 1961, the poor states paid over $6 billion for shipping services. For a description of UNCTAD activities related to shipping policy as they affect less-developed countries, see Iqbal Haji, "UNCTAD and Shipping," *Journal of World Trade Law,* VI, No. 1 (January/February, 1972) , 58–118.

[51] Regarding this point, see Robert S. Walters, "International Organizations and Political Communications: The Use of UNCTAD by Less Developed Countries," *International Organization,* XXV, No. 4 (Autumn, 1971) , 818–35.

the willingness of rich states to unilaterally grant various economic concessions to poor states out of humanitarianism or enlightened self-interests. Needless to say, major alterations in the distribution of resources in favor of the Third World are unlikely to be produced in such a context.

Second, even if the rich states were to make major economic concessions to poor states, the problem of asymmetrical distribution of income between the center and periphery of the global economy would be transformed into a problem of the asymmetrical distribution of greater income *within* the periphery. In other words, proposed reforms in international economic relations inevitably favor some poor states at the expense of others. The general preference scheme negotiated within UNCTAD yields benefits primarily to only a dozen or so of the most advanced among the 95 less-developed countries of the world. A link between the creation of Special Drawing Rights and development assistance through the International Development Association (IDA) would exclude many Latin American states from receiving any benefits because they are not eligible for loans from this soft window of the World Bank. Thus, even should the rich states comply with poor states' demands in UNCTAD, the politics of distributing the new economic gains will produce conflicts among states in the periphery. Even if, in the aggregate, this means a larger slice of the global economic pie is placed in the hands of the poor, it is unlikely they will find it easy to harmonize their disparate interests.

The success of the oil-producing states provides a useful illustration of the dilemma posed for less-developed countries in general when a few less-developed countries are capable of extracting price or other concessions from the rich states or multinational corporations. As a result of OPEC's success, the many oil-consuming states within the Third World face vastly higher energy import bills, just as the rich states do. Also, assuming that the prices of industrial exports reflect the higher cost of energy inputs, the terms of trade facing most less-developed countries will deteriorate even further. Accordingly, the benefits that accrue to a few oil-producing states from their capacity to keep oil prices high carry with them balance-of-payments and development problems for most other states in the periphery.[52] This will be the case even if the oil-producing states establish aid programs to help other Third World states, since such aid programs will cover only a fraction of the increased oil import bills now burdening less-developed countries. OPEC's success, in a word, has been something of a nightmare for other poor states.

Similar dilemmas will be posed when major economic concessions

[52] See Chapter 3, p. 68.

are secured by certain less-developed countries, whether through UNCTAD activities or deliberations elsewhere. Anticipation of these problems is likely to prevent the maintenance of group cohesion among less-developed countries in UNCTAD, except on the very broad questions concerning relations between the center and the periphery.[53] Problems of the equitable division of gains among poor states is a major obstacle to successful employment of universalist strategies by less-developed countries in their efforts to gain increased benefits from international economic transactions. Indeed, these problems may themselves generate new political and economic conflicts among poor states.

Regional efforts may prove to produce more concrete results for poor states than universal efforts, though the two are not necessarily incompatible. A small number of states having geographic proximity, enjoying cultural and historical ties, and facing common economic threats and opportunities are more likely to be able to adopt concerted policies on specific economic problems than 95 less-developed countries all over the world. Concerted action may be particularly important for those states whose small populations and economic weakness place them at a disadvantage in their bilateral dealings with rich states or multinational corporations. A myriad of regional integration efforts by less-developed countries over the past two decades reflects the appeal of regional action to Third World states. We have seen, for example, how the Andean states have sought to strengthen their position vis-à-vis multinational corporations through the creation of a regional common market and through regional cooperation on an investment code. It is interesting to note that these concrete actions taken at a regional level occurred at a time when universal efforts by less-developed countries to deal with multinational corporations were confined to the production of general studies on the problem.

RADICAL STRATEGIES

With the exception of nationalization, this discussion of alternative strategies for states in the periphery seeking to improve their position in the global political economy has focused on a positive-sum view of international economic relations. That is, both poor and rich states are believed to secure benefits from their various economic transactions; the

---

53 For a discourse on the efficacy of UNCTAD's activities, see Michael Lipton, "UNCTAD SCHMUNCTAD: Why Not Start Again from Scratch?" *The Round Table*, No. 247 (July, 1972), 297–309; and Robert Walters, "UNCTAD: Intervener Between Poor and Rich States," *Journal of World Trade Law*, VII, No. 5 (September/October, 1973), 527–54.

struggle is over attempts to increase the relative share of these benefits going to the poor states. Radical thinkers see the global economy in zero-sum terms, however. Benefits secured by rich states in their economic transactions with states in the periphery are seen as a direct measure of the economic loss suffered by the poor states. In short, the contemporary poverty of states in the periphery is seen by radicals as the product of their continued economic relations on present terms with advanced industrial societies. When prescribing strategies by which less-developed countries might reduce losses or increase benefits from international economic relations, radicals emphasize the need to interrupt economic transactions with rich Western states—indeed, to rebel against the existing global system.

Consistent with this logic, a less-developed country might choose to withdraw from international economic relations to the maximum extent possible. Such a strategy is an insulatory response to a situation in which a poor state associates economic exploitation and political and cultural penetration with active participation in the contemporary global economy. Tanzania, for example, has adopted a variant of this basic posture in its insistence upon self-sufficiency. It has minimized international economic contacts and subordinated the values of rapid economic growth and development of heavy industry to the values of national autonomy, self-reliance, and the preservation of traditional social relationships. This strategy may involve the nationalization of foreign assets, but it differs from the typical strategy of nationalization. Nationalization is usually proposed not as a means to withdraw from, or minimize reliance upon, international economic relations, but rather as a means to increase the returns from these relations. In the case of the withdrawal or self-sufficiency strategy, the choice between rapid economic growth and national autonomy has been faced and resolved in favor of the latter. As we have seen, proponents of nationalization often fail to see that these values might be incompatible.

When taken to its logical conclusion, the radical position implies an aggressive strategy of confrontation between states in the periphery and the center states.[54] The United States and other Western powers are seen as owing their commanding economic and political position in the world to their capacity for continued access to and exploitation of states in the periphery. The only way for less-developed countries to improve their lot significantly is to act in concert to destroy existing exploitative economic relations and the present American role in the world economy. Radicals

[54] See, for example, Andre Gunder-Frank, "Sociology of Development and Underdevelopment of Sociology," in J. Cockroft, A. G. Frank, and D. Johnson, *Dependence and Underdevelopment* (Garden City, N.Y.: Doubleday & Co., 1972), pp. 321–98.

imply that this could be done by denying the United States and other Western countries the export markets, investment opportunities, and raw materials of the Third World upon which the center states' prosperity depends. Unlike the other strategies for which one can find some empirical referent, this strategy is exclusively theoretical at the present time. Because of this, we will address only briefly the question of the extent of the center states' dependence upon Third World states and the economic capacity and political efficacy of this proposed action. Since most of the relevant literature pictures the United States as the linchpin of contemporary international economic relations, this examination will be confined to the United States as the target of the Third World.

There is scant evidence to support the notion that the export market of Third World states affords them much leverage over the American economy. In 1971, total exports amounted to only 4 percent of the United States' gross national product, and less-developed countries purchased only 31 percent of American exports in 1971.[55] Moreover, their share of total American exports has been dropping over the past two decades. These figures suggest that American prosperity is not critically dependent upon its aggregate exports to states in the periphery, and that these states have relatively little capacity to alter American policies through concerted action to prohibit American exports from access to their markets.[56] It must also be remembered that most less-developed countries are in fact clamoring for more trade with the United States rather than contemplating a denial of their markets to American exports.

It would also appear that investment opportunities in less-developed countries are not the mainstay of American economic prosperity. Direct investment abroad by United States firms represented approximately 9 percent of domestic investment in 1972.[57] During the same year, American firms' earnings on direct foreign investment amounted to 12 percent of profits from domestic corporate activity.[58] These figures are

55 U.S. Bureau of the Census, *Statistical Abstract of the United States: 1972*, (93d edition), Washington, D.C., p. 778.

56 Radicals argue that aggregate data do not allow us to see the real importance of export markets in the Third World to the United States' economy. Instead, they focus attention upon the vital importance of these export markets to *particular American industries*, which, if badly harmed by denial of these markets, would damage the overall American economy far more than figures on exports as a percentage of GNP would indicate. For an analysis that concludes that the radicals' contentions on this point are overdrawn, see S. M. Miller, R. Bennett, and C. Alapatt, "Does the U.S. Economy Require Imperialism?" in *International Politics: Anarchy, Force, Imperialism*, ed. R. Art and R. Jervis (Boston: Little, Brown, 1973), p. 353.

57 Calculated from U.S. Department of Commerce, *The Survey of Current Business*, August, 1974, Part II, p. 16, and December, 1974, p. SF2.

58 Calculated from *The Survey of Current Business*, August, 1974, Part II, p. 23; and U.S. Bureau of the Census, *Statistical Abstract of the United States: 1974* (95th edition), Washington, D.C., p. 489.

for *total* direct foreign investment by American firms. Only 28 percent of total American direct foreign investment is located in less-developed countries (compared with 37 percent in 1950).[59] In 1972, American direct foreign investment *in less-developed states* constituted only 2 percent of domestic investment, and earnings on foreign investment in Third World states during 1972 were only 4 percent of domestic profits.[60] On the basis of these data, it would appear that the less-developed countries occupy a small and declining role in overall American investment as it relates to general economic prosperity. Also, as in the case of trade, most less-developed countries are in fact seeking to attract American and Western foreign investment under conditions more compatible with the interests of the host state, rather than seeking to deny the access of this capital to states in the periphery of the global economy.

It can be argued that in spite of these aggregate data, the return on American direct foreign investment in less-developed countries is higher than on American investment at home or in other advanced industrial states. This might lead to the conclusion that this portion of earnings from total American investment is critical to the American economy despite the relatively small portion of American investment in Third World states. The difference in returns on American investment in industrialized and nonindustrialized states is explained primarily by the high earnings rates in petroleum and extractive industries generally: in 1972, 61 percent of the earnings on foreign investment in less-developed countries came from petroleum.[61] Earnings rates on manufacturing investments in industrial and nonindustrial areas of the world differed by less than 1 percent during the 1960s.[62] Since most new American investments in less-developed states are in manufacturing rather than extractive industry, it is likely that these overall disparities in rates of return will decline in the future. In the meantime, it is hard to visualize American economic prosperity as critically dependent upon its returns from investment in extractive industries in less-developed countries, as opposed to

[59] Senate Committee on Finance, *Implications of Multinational Firms,* p. 97.

[60] Calculated from *The Survey of Current Business,* August, 1974, Part II, p. 20, and December, 1974, p. SF2; and *Statistical Abstract of the United States: 1974,* pp. 489, 781.

[61] *The Survey of Current Business,* August, 1974, Part II, p. 23. The rate of return on petroleum investments by American firms in less-developed states during 1972 was 23.3 percent, compared with rates of return of 12.4 percent on manufacturing investments in the same states. Ibid.

[62] Robert Tucker, *The Radical Left and American Foreign Policy* (Baltimore: Johns Hopkins Press, 1971), p. 128. We wish to express our debt to Tucker for the basic structure of the arguments in these two paragraphs, which we have updated with 1972 data. In 1972, American foreign investment in manufacturing yielded a return of 13.9 percent from advanced industrial states versus 12.4 percent from less-developed countries. *The Survey of Current Business,* August, 1974, Part II, p. 23.

the lower rates of earnings on investment in all sectors at home and in other industrial societies—where the overwhelming bulk of American investment is concentrated.

The capacity of less-developed states to secure global economic reform by threatening to withhold mineral resources appears more impressive than their capacity to do so through the denial of their markets to American exports and capital. For example, Harry Magdoff lists six critical materials necessary for the production of jet engines and points out that imports account for 75 to 100 percent of American consumption of four of these materials (columbium, nickel, chromium, and cobalt).[63] By means of this illustration Magdoff very dramatically makes the point raised by many radicals that the overall American economy is highly dependent on raw material imports that in many cases are supplied by less-developed countries. It is a small step to conclude that concerted action by the Third World to deny these resources to the United States would indeed accomplish the goal of forcing the United States to agree to major alterations in the terms upon which it conducts foreign economic relations.

The major problem in implementing a collective denial of mineral resources vital to the American economy is the extremely remote possibility that major suppliers would agree to such a policy. Table 7-2 explains why. It is unlikely that states such as Brazil, Canada, Mexico, the Philippines, and Malaysia would elect to cooperate in this endeavor. To implement a concerted strategy of denying mineral resources to the United States would require the emergence and cooperation of radical regimes in most of the states listed in Table 7-2. But even radical regimes might not wish to take such action. Those states that have individually nationalized foreign-owned extractive enterprises have usually done so to increase their returns from sales of the mineral resources to advanced industrial states rather than to halt deliveries to major consumers and purposefully disrupt the global economy. This is true notwithstanding the Arab oil embargo of the United States in 1973 and 1974. It must also be realized that the United States retains considerable capabilities of its own to which it could resort should a direct confrontation along these lines be attempted by producers of mineral resources. "The United States and Canada today control a larger share of the world's exportable supplies of grain than the Middle East does of oil."[64] It is hard to conceive the form that "victory" would take should a commodity war erupt between the Third World and the United States.

Short of actually denying raw materials to the United States, there

63 Harry Magdoff, *The Age of Imperialism* (New York: Monthly Review Press, 1969), pp. 51–52.

64 Lester Brown, "The Next Crisis? Food," *Foreign Policy*, No. 13 (Winter, 1973/74), p. 21.

TABLE 7-2. Major Suppliers of Mineral Resources of which 50 Percent or More of American Consumption Is Imported

Mineral	Percentage of Consumption Imported	Major Sources, 1966–1969, as a Percentage of American Imports
Manganese	90	Gabon (31), Brazil (26)
Bauxite	90	Jamaica (59), Surinam (26)
Asbestos	80	Canada (92)
Chromium	80	Republic of South Africa (40), USSR (24), Philippines (17)
Fluorspar	80	Mexico (75), Spain (14)
Nickel	70	Canada (90)
Platinum Group	70	United Kingdom (43), USSR (26)
Beryllium	70	Brazil (36), India (27)
Cobalt	70	Congo (Kinshasa) (43), Belgium–Luxembourg (30)
Tin	60	Malaysia (66), Thailand (27)
Zinc	60	Canada (51), Mexico (18)

Source: Nazli Choucri, "Population, Resources, and Technology: Political Implications of the Environmental Crisis," *International Organization*, XXVI, No. 2 (Spring, 1972), 209.

are possibilities for securing changes of American policy on longstanding issues of economic importance to less-developed countries through the leverage afforded by OPEC states. Radicals would like to see the oil-producing states demand in concert the construction of a new economic order that would be more beneficial to all poor states as the *quid pro quo* for assurances of adequate supplies of oil at reduced prices to the United States and other rich states. In addition, should less-developed countries successfully institute producer cartels in commodities other than oil, the opportunity would be present for a confrontation between *coalitions* of commodity producer cartels and advanced industrial states. This would add even more leverage to demands for radical reforms in the conduct of global economic and political relations.

Radical thinkers are prone to assert that aggregate data on the Third World's portion of American export trade, foreign investment, and raw material supplies both understate American economic dependence on the poor states and miss the point. They hold that the economies of advanced industrial nations, particularly the United States, "are so intricate that the removal of even a small part, as in a watch, can stop the mechanism."[65] Most evidence suggests, however, that the leverage the less-developed countries have is basically that of raising costs and producing some major, but probably manageable, adjustments throughout the American and global economies. Pursuit of concerted action of this sort

[65] Gabriel Kolko, *The Roots of American Foreign Policy* (Boston: Beacon Press, 1969), p. 50.

might result in increasing a few less-developed countries' share of the benefits in various types of international economic transactions, but it is likely overall to produce further stratification among rich and poor states. Moreover, except in the broadest terms radical thinkers fail to identify the mechanisms through which, and the terms upon which, international trade, capital, technology, and services will be conducted should this strategy succeed in revolutionizing the existing global economy.

CONCLUSION

In order to bring greater coherence to the themes of this chapter, the alternative strategies are summarized in Table 7-3.

The strategies shown in the first two columns of the table rest upon an assumption consistent with liberal economic thought that global economic relations are essentially positive-sum in character—that is, that

TABLE 7-3.   Alternative Strategies for States in the Periphery of the Global Economy

	Taking Advantage of the Existing Global Economy	*Securing Reforms within the Existing Framework of the Global Economy*	*Revolutionizing, or Insulating Oneself from, the Global Economy*
Individual State Action	Exploit sensitivity of international economic interdependence (Brazil)	National effort to attract foreign economic activity under strict control of host state (Mexico)	(a) Nationalize assets of foreign firms (Chile— copper) (b) Minimize participation within global economy (Tanzania)
Concerted State Action	Exploit majority control of mineral resources vital to global economy (OPEC)	(a) Regional attempts to attract foreign capital under strict control of host states (Andean Pact) (b) Universal attempts to redistribute income to poor states (UNCTAD)	Deny export markets, investment opportunities and raw materials to the United States and center states, on existing terms (radical theorists)

poor as well as rich states benefit from economic cooperation.[66] The main difference we wish to convey between the strategies in the first and second columns is that in the case of the former, the less-developed countries are for various reasons in a position of greater strength than most poor states in their relations with rich states or multinational firms. Hence, they will be less wary of contacts with the established global economy than will states pursuing the strategies labeled as attempts to secure reforms within the existing framework of the global economy. The third column, in contrast, contains strategies that rest upon assumptions consistent with radical thought: that national autonomy is a supreme value and that global economic relations between rich and poor states are essentially zero-sum. This typology may exaggerate the disparities between various strategies, but it is useful in providing an overall perspective of diverse modes of economic and political behavior.

Less-developed countries never rely exclusively on a single strategy to improve their position in the global political economy. Often, the simultaneous pursuit of different strategies can lead to mutually reinforcing results. For example, the regional investment code of the Andean states may help stimulate universal oversight of multinational corporate behavior through UNCTAD, which in turn would strengthen the hand of many less-developed countries struggling with foreign investment policy. However, a special difficulty arises for a less-developed country when it approaches one economic sector (such as extractive industry) in zero-sum terms, and at the same time wishes to cooperate within other economic sectors (manufacturing or service industries) on the basis of positive-sum assumptions. Thus, Chile's nationalization of copper was inconsistent with its efforts through its membership in the Andean Pact to attract foreign capital in other economic sectors.

It would be gratifying if on the basis of this discussion a general policy prescription could be suggested that would dramatically enhance these states' position in the global political economy,[67] but it would be a

---

[66] The reader may wish to refer back to the general discussion of the differences between liberal economic thought and radical thought presented in Chapter 1.

[67] This is not to say that less-developed states employing these and other strategies are unlikely as a whole to increase their economic or political position in the global economy. Advanced industrial states and multinational firms can expect to find states in the periphery extracting a greater share of the benefits from international economic transactions than they were able to do prior to the 1970s. The era of low prices for primary products and virtually complete control of international commodity markets by Western firms has passed. However, notwithstanding some alteration of the less-developed states' general position in the global political economy, these states are unlikely overall to secure economic and political gains, *relative to advanced industrial states,* that will even approach the magnitude that will be necessary to alter their perception that they must function in a global economy in which they are relegated unjustly to a peripheral position.

mistake to do so. Some presently less-developed countries such as Brazil and some oil-producing states will indeed become rich and politically important. Other poor states may in the future be catapulted into a position of wealth and political potence should they sit astride mineral resources that are subject to the intense global demand of the sort we see for petroleum today. Dankwart Rustow's observations about political modernization seem compelling as a general assessment of the problem.

> When one starts searching for causes, a country's rapid progress will always turn out to be closely related to very special and very favorable circumstances in its location or heritage [or in international market conditions]. The most admirable achievement seems least susceptible of imitation. . . . What is encouraging is the length and diversity of the list. . . . There is no reason to search for a single universal recipe, and even less to despair if any of its alleged ingredients are missing. Instead, each country must start with a frank assessment of its particular liabilities and assets; and each will be able to learn most from those countries whose problems most closely resemble its own.[68]

In efforts to prescribe policies by which less-developed countries might obtain greater benefits from global economic relations, it is important to make explicit the values that are to be maximized (for example, aggregate economic growth or national autonomy), the costs (social and economic) involved in the pursuit of these values, the political and economic conditions at home and abroad that must obtain for the successful pursuit of a specific policy, and the probability that such conditions are likely to be present or produced. These considerations will generate different assessments of the prospects for different countries, and even for the same country as it operates in different economic sectors. Proponents of both liberal economic thought and radical thought would do well to focus on these basic considerations instead of indulging their penchant to propose policies that are deduced from prior assumptions and that are seen as generally applicable to all states in the periphery and to all varieties of their economic transactions.

---

68 *A World of Nations: Problems of Political Modernization* (Washington, D.C.: The Brookings Institution, 1967), pp. 275–76.

8

The Dominant State
in the Global Economy:
The Policy Process
in the United States

The United States is the leading economic and political power among the center states and within the global economic system. Its hegemony is by no means unchallenged; it frequently is unable to get its own way; and in some regions of the world other states exercise more economic influence than the United States. Yet in terms of the breadth and intensity of its economic and political links throughout most of the world, it is the dominant state in the global economic system. Developments within the United States as well as specific American policies are likely to have widespread implications for countries throughout the world. Consequently, any analysis of the politics of the global political economy requires an examination of the policy-making process in the United States. This will be done by juxtaposing radical and pluralist perspectives of the American foreign policy process.

THE RADICAL PERSPECTIVE

The Substance of Foreign Policy

Our purpose is to examine the foreign economic policy-making process within the United States. From the perspective of various radical analysts, however, a fundamental assumption must first be made about the substance of United States foreign policy. Basically, though with some variation, radical critics feel that the foreign economic and political interests of the United States are synonymous. Therefore, the process by which foreign policy is made is essentially the same, regardless of whether the issue is an economic or a political one. Indeed, for most radicals a distinction between the two is not appropriate.

On this question, and others as well, there is some disagreement among radical analysts. One group, of a Marxist-Leninist orientation, tends to feel that the capitalist system of the United States largely determines its political concerns and that capitalism demands international economic and political involvement in order to overcome its many domestic shortcomings. According to this view, perhaps best represented by Harry Magdoff, capitalism is a system that inequitably withholds from its workers their fair share of income and wealth. Consequently, the limited purchasing power of the proletariat, coupled with an insatiable appetite for growth by corporations, results in a surplus of manufactured goods and investment capital. The domestic United States market cannot absorb enough new production to sustain corporate growth since the proletariat is not earning enough to purchase more goods. Less new investment capital is needed and less is able to be employed profitably in the United States. Therefore, the capitalist American system needs foreign outlets for its excess goods and investment capital. The foreign political and military policy of the United States is designed to secure and maintain these foreign markets for the benefit of the American economy. As Magdoff states, "the underlying purpose [of imperialism] is nothing less than keeping as much as possible of the world open for trade and investment by the giant multinational corporations."[1]

Magdoff and others go beyond this relationship to point out how dependent the United States is upon a host of critical raw materials found elsewhere in the world. Because these natural resources are necessary for the continued functioning of the highly developed American economy, American foreign policy seeks to safeguard the sources of these materials. This leads quite naturally to an expansionist and adventuresome foreign policy that knows few geographical or political limits.[2] Because of natural resource dependency and the need to have foreign markets absorb goods and capital, the foreign political policy of the United States is designed primarily to serve and advance its economic interests.

Another group of radical critics, especially Michael Hudson, feels that American economic interests and policy are really servants of an

---

[1] Harry Magdoff, *The Age of Imperialism* (New York: Monthly Review Press, 1969), p. 14. See Vladimir I. Lenin, *Imperialism* (New York: International Publishers, 1939) for the classical Marxist-Leninist view of imperialism.

[2] This issue has been examined in greater depth in Chapters 6 and 7.

expansionary political policy.[3] He observes a self-assertive United States government that seeks to dominate other countries or at least to insure their compatibility with the American system. The expansion of American investments and trade is a conscious policy fostered by a government that is anxious to enhance the overall power of the United States. This outward thrust of state capitalism is based on a different cause-and-effect relationship than that advanced by Magdoff, but in both cases foreign economic policy and foreign political policy are thought to be so highly correlated as to be synonymous.

Richard Barnet combines the two previous radical positions when he ascribes American expansionism to its society and institutions. Like Hudson, he emphasizes the importance of the national security managers (officials in the State Department, Defense Department, National Security Council, CIA, and so forth) who have decision-making authority in foreign policy matters. However, Barnet, like many other radicals, stresses the business background of these officials and the dominance of business interests and attitudes in the government and in the society more generally. The crux of the relationship as he views it is that "the corporations continue to exercise the dominant *influence* in the society, but the *power* keeps passing to the state."[4] The congruence of foreign economic and political interests in American international relations is once more clearly indicated.

Regardless of differences among them, radical critics rarely make a distinction between the American foreign-policy-making process regarding political and security matters and the process for economic issues. Since the interests and objectives of business and government regarding both economic and security matters are basically similar, separate policy-making processes do not exist. In other words, decisions on Cuba, arms limitation agreements with the Soviet Union, security treaties with Japan, trade reform, and revision of the international monetary order spring from the same fountainhead of policy making.

The Formulation of Foreign Policy

Admitting the differences among radical analysts but recognizing their shared conviction that American foreign economic and political interests are similar, their views of how foreign policy is made in the United States can now be examined. It is important to note that discussions of the foreign-policy-making process by radical analysts focus almost

[3] *Super Imperialism: The Economic Strategy of American Empire* (New York: Holt, Rinehart and Winston, 1968) .

[4] Richard J. Barnet, *The Roots of War* (Baltimore: Penguin Books, 1972) , p. 185.

exclusively on the procedures by which policy is made on political, security, and military issues. Magdoff and others discuss the *substance* of American economic policy, but they fail to explore specifically the process by which foreign economic policy is made. Consequently, an examination of how radical analysts view the formulation of foreign economic policy must of necessity be based upon their statements regarding the policy process associated with political and security issues. However, because of their perception of the congruence of American economic and political interests, it is reasonable to assume that the policy processes in both issue areas will be similar.[5]

Radical thinkers perceive a United States foreign-policy-making process that is primarily a reflection of and a response to the interests of big corporations. It is a system in which economic and political interests, as defined and advanced by large business enterprises, dominate the substance of political and economic policy as well as the process by which foreign and domestic policies are made.

Radical analysts argue that business dominance is achieved as the result of the congruence between what is good for the United States and what is good for its large business concerns. Radical critics often rely upon statements by policy makers and corporate executives that appear to prove their point. One of the most often-quoted remarks is that of Assistant Secretary of State Dean Acheson in 1944 before a Congressional committee concerned about postwar economic planning. Drawing upon the frightening possibility of a new depression after the war, Acheson said, "We have got to see that what the country produces is used and sold under financial arrangements which make its production possible. . . . You must look to foreign markets."[6] The prospect of limiting production only to what could be consumed in the United States "would completely change our Constitution, our relations to property, human liberty, our very conceptions of law. . . . Therefore, you find you must look to other markets and those markets are abroad."[7] Thus, he continued, "We cannot have full employment and prosperity in the United States without the foreign markets."[8] Businessman Bernard Baruch was more suc-

---

[5] One further caveat is that we are attempting briefly to describe views of a number of analysts as if there were no differences among them. Of course, there are; thus, what follows is a short synthesis of the thoughts of many.

[6] Quoted in William Appleman Williams, "The Large Corporation and American Foreign Policy," in *Corporations and the Cold War*, ed. David Horowitz (New York: Monthly Review Press, 1969), p. 95. Copyright © by the Bertrand Russell Peace Foundation. Reprinted by permission. Parts of this passage have also been quoted in David Horowitz, *Empire and Revolution* (New York: Random House 1969), pp. 233–34; and Lloyd C. Gardner, *Architects of Illusion* Chicago: Quadrangle Books, 1970), p. 203.

[7] Williams, "The Large Corporations and American Foreign Policy," p. 96.

[8] Ibid.

cinct when he emphasized the "essential one-ness of United States economic political and strategic interests."[9]

Business influence over the foreign-policy-making process is insured by the recruitment of foreign policy officials from the highest ranks of the corporate and financial elite. Consequently, many of the national security managers not only represent business interests but in essence are corporate officials serving the government for a few years in the foreign policy apparatus. In the process, of course, they also further the interests of their corporations and of business in general. G. William Domhoff and Richard J. Barnet present analyses of foreign policy managers in the White House and the Departments of State, Defense, and Treasury that reveal that a significant proportion of these officials held top-level positions in corporations, financial institutions, and related corporate law firms prior to their recruitment into government service. Barnet points out, for example, that between 1940 and July, 1967, seventy of the ninety-one secretaries and undersecretaries of defense and state, secretaries of the three branches of the armed forces, chairmen of the Atomic Energy Commission, and directors of the Central Intelligence Agency came from large corporations and leading investment houses.[10] Thus, the link between business and foreign policy is forged by a direct sharing of executives by government and business.

More indirectly, but just as critical, is the unrepresentative social and educational background of many of the most important foreign policy officials and their counterparts in business. The similarity in their backgrounds would tend to provide them with basically the same outlook on many economic and political issues. They are likely to move in similar social and intellectual circles. Many of them share the characteristics of significant family wealth, membership in exclusive clubs, listing in *The Social Register,* attendance at select private preparatory schools, and graduation from Ivy League–type colleges. For example, a study by the Brookings Institution revealed that 32 percent of the political appointees to the Departments of State, Treasury, Defense, Army, Navy, and Air Force (all of which are important in the making of foreign policy) attended a select list of eighteen private preparatory schools.[11] Political appointees to cabinet departments, regulatory agencies, and other commissions that are less involved in foreign policy matters were much less

[9] Quoted in Benjamin J. Cohen, *The Question of Imperialism: The Political Economy of Dominance and Dependence* (New York: Basic Books, 1973) , p. 125.

[10] Richard J. Barnet, "The National Security Managers and the National Interest," *Politics and Society,* February, 1971, p. 260.

[11] These figures were derived from Table D.9 in David T. Stanley, Dean E. Mann, and Jameson W. Doig, *Men Who Govern* (Washington: The Brookings Institution, 1967) , pp. 124–25.

likely to have attended these prep schools (only 11 percent of them did so).

All of this means that this corporate-based power elite will find it quite easy to move between business and government positions, thereby insuring a foreign policy posture that is compatible with and supportive of big business interests. In the words of a leader in this type of analysis of the elite, "American foreign policy during the postwar era was initiated, planned, and carried out by the richest, most powerful, and most international-minded owners and managers of major corporations and financial institutions."[12] Thus, the unrepresentativeness of foreign policy managers in terms of socioeconomic background and previous positions in and allegiances to corporate America suggest strongly that big business interests help determine the foreign-policy-making process.

According to the radical view, the influence of big corporations on the foreign-policy-making process is further enhanced by the activities of a number of important groups that serve to transmit the business point of view to government officials. These transmission belts include a few of the large foundations based on corporate wealth, special blue-ribbon presidential advisory committees, and a small number of research and discussion committees. The Ford Foundation, the Carnegie Corporation, and to a lesser extent the Rockefeller Foundation have been active supporters of programs at universities and of foreign-policy-related groups that represent business concerns in the foreign-policy-making process. The special presidential committees are blue-ribbon citizens groups selected largely from corporate elites to analyze and to make recommendations regarding specific foreign policy issues. These committees have reported on such things as the nature of American military preparedness and the direction of its foreign aid programs. Seven of the eight most important committees concerned with foreign policy matters were chaired by corporate executives; the eighth chairman was the president of the Massachusetts Institute of Technology.[13] The research and discussion groups referred to are organizations such as the Council on Foreign Relations, the Committee for Economic Development, the Foreign Policy Association, and RAND, many of whose members and boards of directors come from a big business background.

All of these groups act as links between corporations and government officials, and they ostensibly provide expert but nonbiased advice from nongovernmental sectors. In fact, though, the interests, perspectives,

---

12 G. William Domhoff, "Who Made American Foreign Policy 1945–1963?" in *Corporations and the Cold War*, ed. Horowitz, p. 25. Copyright © 1969 by the Bertrand Russell Peace Foundation. Reprinted by permission of Monthly Review Press.

13 Ibid., p. 46.

and alternatives advantageous to business are conveyed to governmental decision makers through the activities of these groups. These transmission belts sponsor formal face-to-face meetings that allow their largely business membership to exchange ideas and information with American and non-American foreign policy officials. These information and access advantages, combined with good organization and competent staffs, mean that these groups are able to develop thoughtful and comprehensive recommendations about foreign affairs. Indeed, there are almost no other sources outside of the government that can consistently provide such well-informed and coherent analyses of foreign policy issues of direct relevance to foreign policy officials. In other words, these transmission belts enjoy a virtual monopoly of effective interest representation regarding foreign economic and political policy. Moreover, the similar background characteristics of business and government elites insure the receptivity of the latter to the concerns of the former.

This influence relationship is fostered as a result of the social, intellectual, and value similarities between foreign policy officials and the active membership of these transmission belts. This both follows from and leads to these groups serving as a major source of recruitment for high-level foreign policy officials. As an example of the two-way flow of personnel, prior to becoming secretary of state for President Kennedy, Dean Rusk was president of the Rockefeller Foundation. In the opposite direction, McGeorge Bundy left his position as National Security Advisor to the White House to become president of the Ford Foundation. There are many more such examples.

Domhoff suggests that the Council on Foreign Relations is probably the most important transmission belt for foreign policy matters. The large foundations and a number of major corporations provide the prime financial support for the Council. In addition, top corporate executives are members of the board of directors of the major foundations and are also members of the Council on Foreign Relations. Thus, according to Domhoff, it should not be surprising that the Council consciously attempts to increase the interaction between Washington officialdom and its largely corporate membership. These efforts have obviously paid off. For example, John J. McCloy, who has been among many things chairman of the board of Chase Manhattan Bank, high commissioner for Germany, and coordinator of American disarmament activities, once remarked, "Whenever we needed a man [to help direct foreign policy activity during World War II] we thumbed through the roll of Council members and put through a call to New York."[14]

14 Quoted by Joseph Kraft, "School for Statesmen," *Harper's Magazine*, July, 1958, p. 67.

To stimulate this interaction, the Council arranges off-the-record speeches and question-and-answer sessions by important foreign policy officials of the United States and other countries. The information learned, the insights gained, and the views exchanged draw together more closely corporate interests and Washington officials. In addition, the Council publishes a number of important books, reference works, as well as the prestigious journal, *Foreign Affairs*. The latter frequently contains articles by foreign policy officials.

However, Domhoff feels that the most important activity of the Council is the discussion and study groups that examine a specific issue in great detail. Twenty-five businessmen, government officials, a few military officials, and a small number of nonradical scholars conduct extensive discussions, often off the record, which eventually result in a book that presents a thorough statement of the problem. Some of the topics considered by these study groups have been instrumental in shaping United States policy regarding the nature of the United Nations Charter and the development of the Marshall Plan for European recovery, and in the early 1970s a full scale reassessment of American relations with China. In sum, the Council, along with the other groups mentioned, serves to encourage business participation in the formulation of foreign policy and to transmit business influence to foreign policy officials in multiple ways. At the very least, such institutions provide an important means of access to and maintenance of contacts with foreign-policy makers.

The basic argument of the radicals is that American foreign policy reflects and represents the interests of big corporations in foreign affairs. Whether governmental political objectives conveyed through state capitalism lead to foreign economic involvement, or vice versa, is not a crucial distinction for our purposes. Either way, the result is a foreign policy that is linked closely and substantively to the interests of corporate America through a foreign policy formulation process that is subject to immense and almost exclusive influence from big business on the executive branch of the government. Congress, the radical analysts feel, is a largely impotent body in foreign policy matters since it often meekly upholds the policies and actions of the executive without acting as an alternate decision-making center. Consequently, corporate efforts to influence foreign policy are logically directed primarily to the executive branch.

Radical analysts feel that business dominance of the policy-making process is enhanced because of the lack of influence of other countries on this process. The United States, as the premier power of the world, is largely unconstrained by the interests and concerns of other countries and thus enjoys a correspondingly wide decisional latitude. American political and military policies, in conjunction with foreign economic policies that change economic partners into economic dependents, have enabled the United States to insure the compliance of most states to its wishes. The radical literature is replete with examples of how the United States has imposed its will on recalcitrant friends and enemies in order to enrich itself and its corporations and to extend its global dominance at the expense of other countries. Thus, the United States has consciously attempted to structure and use the global economic system in a way that promotes its economic and political hegemony and the subjugation of other states. As a result of this process, American policy is largely unfettered by the wishes and constraints that are imposed by other countries. This gives American business interests free rein to develop and implement the kinds of policies that will advance their interests the most.

A CRITIQUE OF THE RADICAL VIEW

Admittedly, this brief sketch of the radical conception of the American foreign-policy-making process fails to do full justice to both the richness of the argument and the many significant differences that do exist among radical analysts. Nevertheless, it is appropriate to raise questions about the substance of this radical view, the methodology used to develop these positions, and how each contributes to an understanding of the foreign-economic-policy-making process.

Of particular concern is the almost total lack of attention paid by radical thinkers to the process by which American foreign economic policy is made. Instead, they have focused almost exclusively on political, security, and military topics in reaching their conclusions about the dominant role of business interests in American foreign policy. By building their argument on these types of issues, the radical critics are making their observations on and drawing conclusions from a limited and special set of circumstances. Moreover, most radical critics are content to specify the parameters that limit the policy-making process, rather than examining directly the nature of the process. Given the widespread perception of a cold-war environment (which most radicals say was contrived by the United States),[15] it should not be surprising that there was a great deal of unanimity within the United States regarding the nature of the threat and the character of the enemy. With large segments of the American population perceiving the existence of the Soviet Union and other communist states as having broad and largely singular implications for

---

[15] For example, see Joyce Kolko and Gabriel Kolko, *The Limits of Power* (New York: Harper & Row Publishers, 1972).

all of American society, the concept of bipartisanship or the submerging of different and parochial interests was undertaken for the sake of national unity against a common threat. Business, labor, and government all joined together to protect the American system from what was perceived to be both a political and economic threat. Thus, the radical view of business dominance is based upon an analysis of political and security issues on which there was wide agreement as to the nature of the situation and American objectives.

A Mutiplicity of Business Interests

By focusing on such political, security, and military issues to the exclusion of economic matters, the radical critics have not exposed themselves to a rich panoply of bureaucratic and political maneuvering that is found in the making of foreign economic policy. Here, the common perception of threat and the unified external posture (with many internal differences and disputes about tactics) dissolves into wrangling associated with the promotion of specific and contradictory objectives by many competing economic and business interests. Thus, the concept of a business interest dominating the foreign-policy-making process seems inappropriate for those foreign economic issues having particular relevance to domestic economic groups that are often at odds with one another. In short, because the radical view is founded primarily on analyses of overarching political, military, and security issues, some serious problems are created in the transferring of their conclusions to discussions of the formulation of foreign economic policy.

Because of this approach, the radical analysts have failed to define, much less operationalize, their notion of *the business interest*. Instead, they merely assert categorically the existence of a single unified business interest. Had they examined the policy-formulation process on trade or investment issues, though, they would have found something quite different. In the first place, different types of industries disagree greatly about the consequences of various foreign-economic-policy alternatives. For example, imposing tariffs or import quotas to protect the steel, textile, and shoe industries in the United States has been resisted by those industries who can successfully meet foreign competition and who themselves export to other countries. They fear that protectionist moves by the United States will be countered with similar actions by other countries, and that their export activities will thereby be harmed. To illustrate these differences, consider this partial list of industries and products that were the subject of congressional testimony by interested unions, trade associations, and companies on the Trade Reform Act of 1973–74:

Agriculture	Musical Instruments
Automobiles	Petroleum
Bicycles	Potash
Chemicals	Poultry
Clay	Shears
Dinnerware	Shoes
Eggs	Steel
Flowers	Textiles
Glue	Tools
Leather Goods	Vegetables
Marbles	Wine

These specific groups differed greatly on their positions regarding the desirability of raising or lowering tariffs. A precise and unanimous business interest cannot be observed among these industries, as a brief perusal of some of the conflicting testimony will indicate.

On certain issues, different firms within the same industry perceive different patterns of gains and losses to result from foreign economic policy. In the coffee industry, giant multinational corporations such as General Foods, Procter and Gamble, and Coca-Cola disagree over the nature of American policy towards the International Coffee Agreement. General Foods was quite concerned about the import of soluble coffee products from abroad, but the latter two companies, joined by other smaller firms, did not wish to stem the flow. Quite naturally, each side used political influence in an effort to insure that its position was advanced or protected by the policy that emerged.

An issue such as tariff reform may also highlight the very real areas of disagreement among different divisions of a multiproduct firm. In their careful study of the politics of tariff policy, Bauer, Pool, and Dexter point out that within the DuPont corporation the division manufacturing paint supported liberalization of trade whereas the rayon-yarn division tended to be protectionist. Other parts of the corporation were little interested in the issue.[16] Similar differences can be observed within other corporations that manufacture a variety of products.

In the area of foreign economic policy, at least, American business interests rarely support a single policy position solidly except on the broadest levels, such as enthusiasm for the concept of private enterprise. Instead, the various alternatives available have different implications for different industries, firms, and divisions within specific corporations. As a result, the process by which foreign economic policy is made seems to be subject to the same type of political struggles that radicals often reserve only for the domestic-policy-making process.

[16] Raymond A. Bauer, Ithiel de Sola Pool, and Lewis Anthony Dexter, *American Business and Public Policy* (New York: Atherton Press, 1963) , p. 270.

Foreign economic policy has important and varying implications for businesses. Thus, businesses and other economic interests—including unions and a potpourri of various social groups, each with their own conceptions of desirable goals—become actively involved in the domestic political process in order to influence the outcome of policy deliberations. As a result, the formulation of foreign economic policy provokes extensive and at times heated domestic political activity. For example, the hearings before the House Ways and Means Committee on the 1973 Trade Reform Act produced testimony by 96 industry associations and trade groups, 36 companies, 18 union organizations, 17 agricultural groups, 15 public interest groups, and 15 individuals. In addition, the Committee received written statements from 111 other such groups and individuals. An examination of the hearings emphasizes the lack of consensus among these groups or within each type of group. The positions advanced reflected very specific conceptions of self-interest—not some overall consensus position by business.

Business executives tend to become preoccupied with and most active in specific issues that have definite implications for their business. They are not usually trying to establish and promote a grand design regarding the foreign political and economic posture of the United States. For instance, there is some suggestion that business involvement in organizations such as the Council on Foreign Relations amounts to little more than political dilettantism. Even a leading radical analyst, Domhoff, quotes a study by Bernard C. Cohen that concludes that members of the Foreign Policy Association "seldom seriously discuss political policies at all, let alone alternative policies. They tend to keep discussions apolitical, emphasizing the social, economic, cultural, and historical aspects of foreign affairs."[17] Barnet claims that corporate executives "do not seem to know how to manipulate this great wealth to influence the great decisions of war and peace. Nor do they seem to be particularly interested in doing so."[18]

Differences Within Government

The political, military, and security perspective of the radical analysts has led them to understand the governmental process in a way that is not applicable to the formulation of American foreign economic policy.[19] Just as they assert *a* business interest, so also do they perceive *a*

[17] Domhoff, "Who Made American Foreign Policy 1945–1963?" p. 61.

[18] Barnet, *The Roots of War*, p. 186.

[19] This topic is discussed at greater length later in this chapter when we examine the pluralist view of the foreign-economic-policy-making process.

government view of United States foreign policy. Such an approach ignores the significance of the different perspectives and interests of various government agencies. Moreover, it neglects the specialized clientele and constituents of each department. Thus, the Departments of Labor, Commerce, and Agriculture have different interests and objectives regarding American foreign economic policy as a result of the different sets of pressures they are subjected to by labor, business, and farmers and as a result of different conceptions of the nature of their tasks. Furthermore, within each of these broad economic sectors and within each of these departments there are disagreements on the consequences of policy alternatives. Thus, it is an oversimplification even to view various departments as passive instruments of their constituencies (labor, business, farmers, and so on) in society, for these groups themselves are not united on all issues.

The Relationship Between Business and Government

Another critical assumption at the base of the radical view of the American foreign-policy-making process involves the nature of the relationship between business and government. As we discussed earlier, radicals feel that business interests dominate the government. However, there are numerous examples of United States policy that contradict this view. The Trading with the Enemy Act prohibits United States firms and their subsidiaries from trading with specified enemy countries in a number of defense-related products. Even in the mid 1970s this act inhibited some business interaction with Cuba, in spite of the requests of American firms to rescind its restrictive provisions. Antitrust concerns of the Department of Justice have also served to retard the growth and success of the foreign subsidiaries of American firms. Moreover, the years of cold war between the Soviet Union and the United States as well as the many years of American nonrecognition of China meant many missed opportunities for doing business with these countries. The inability of American business to change government policy on these matters long after allies and their corporate competitors had opened lucrative business and political contacts is another important instance in which the interests of many corporations were not served by government policy. Thus, one has to question the degree to which business in fact controls government policy.

Bauer, Pool, and Dexter suggest in a study that in many ways congressmen tend to use business lobbyists, rather than vice versa.[20] This

[20] Bauer, Pool, and Dexter, *American Business and Public Policy*, p. 488.

study, which examines business and government interactions on the question of tariff reform, indicates that lobbyists are most effective when they aid an already favorably disposed legislator in his attempts to convince his colleagues in the House or Senate of his position. Moreover, congressmen frequently utilize lobbyists to obtain information about an issue so that they can make up their minds on the issue. Although practices obviously vary widely, the basic conclusion of the authors is that congressmen are not captives of business lobbyists, or of any lobbyists for that matter.

However, radical analysts feel that the legislative branch is relatively impotent in the foreign-policy-making process. Thus, much of their argument is based on the extent of business control over the administrative branch. Basically, radical thinkers *infer* business control from the socioeconomic backgrounds of top-level officials recruited into executive agencies, without offering substantial evidence as to the precise nature of the linkage between background and decision making.

Radicals insist that former corporate employees carry their predispositions and parochial interests directly into their positions in government. Although there is substance to this argument, it is likely that the new experiences and role expectations accompanying their office expand the horizons of former corporate executives beyond their previous views. For example, in assessing the influence of foreign travel on business executives' conceptions of self-interest, Bauer, Pool, and Dexter found that it "made a man see the trade issue in national terms, rather than in the parochial terms of his own industry."[21] One cannot help but wonder whether journeys into government service do not have a similar effect.

The radicals insist that the legislative branch has little to do with the making of foreign policy on political and security issues. (This is the view of many nonradicals as well.) This is probably not the case in regard to international economic issues having important domestic implications. In these instances, different business interests and other economic interests actively seek to urge individual congressmen to represent their concerns in the legislative process. The administration's trade bill in 1973 and 1974 stimulated great pressure on Congress from numerous economic groups, and the passage of the bill was delayed by Congress until December, 1974. Similarly, political détente and expanded trade with the Soviet Union promised to benefit greatly a number of businesses, but Congress strenuously resisted granting "most-favored-nation" status to the Soviet Union until it altered its Jewish emigration policies. Congress does fulfill an active and important role in many issues involving foreign economic policy. Yet this role is disregarded by most radical

[21] Ibid., p. 168.

analysts because their frame of reference tends to be focused on military and security issues.

The radical conception of American foreign-policy-making implies or asserts that only high-level political appointees determine the content of foreign policy. Barnet suggests that these national security managers revel in their jobs because of "the sense of playing for high stakes."[22] These foreign policy officials are exhilarated and "intrigued by power, more than money and more than fame."[23] Even if we accept Barnet's characterization, it is hard to imagine these national security managers experiencing much thrill and excitement over attempts to get Japan to reduce exports to the United States or attempts to change the discriminatory trade policies of the European Common Market. Participation in many of these economic issues does not often yield fascinating memoirs testifying to one's diplomatic astuteness and importance. Many of these economic issues involve exceptionally technical details that are managed more competently by the technical experts in the civil service who inhabit the Departments of Treasury, Commerce, and Agriculture. Thus, the important role of the technostructure, on economic issues at least, should not be, but has been, ignored by radical critics, who perceive American foreign policy to be the preserve of a small number of political appointees in the State and Defense Departments. It is important to note that there is much more diversity in social backgrounds, educational experience, and career patterns among career civil servants than there is among the top political elites, upon whom the radicals focus.

The point is that business control of government, as proclaimed by radical analysts, is overstated. Radical thinkers fail to specify either what they define as control of foreign policy or the precise nature of the foreign policy decision-making process. They presume that broad conclusions about overall policy outcomes and the backgrounds of certain types of government officials are sufficient evidence to infer the control of business interests over the American foreign policy process. But radical analysts do not tell us what control is and how it can be observed. Their concept of the foreign policy decision-making process is developed from the presumption that a highly unified business interest dictates government policy. No inputs into the foreign policy process other than business interests are examined seriously. The role of Congress and the intense struggles among and within executive agencies, if they receive any attention at all, are considered inconsequential for American foreign economic policy.[24]

22 Barnet, *The Roots of War*, p. 98.

23 Ibid., p. 97.

24 This point is made by Gabriel Kolko, *The Roots of American Foreign Policy* (Boston: Beacon Press, 1969) , pp. 4–5.

THE PLURALIST PERSPECTIVE

An alternate view of American foreign economic policy and the process by which it is formulated is based on the concepts of pluralism and bureaucratic politics.[25] Rather than a dominant business interest, the pluralist approach perceives the existence and importance of a wide variety of internal interests and constraints that greatly complicate foreign economic policy making. Second, this view contends that American foreign policy in the economic arena is severely constrained by the economic objectives and actions of other states, whose own domestic groups have a vested interest in their government's actions. In short, the process by which United States foreign economic policy is formulated is subject domestically to widespread political bargaining and maneuvering and internationally to the actions and concerns of other states.

Domestic Constraints on Foreign Economic Policy

The extensive domestic political activity associated with American foreign economic policy occurs because some domestic interest groups stand to gain or lose as a result of the particular policy adopted. In order to achieve an outcome that is favorable to their particular set of interests, each of the affected groups mobilizes to protect and advance its concerns. For example, trade issues have both international and domestic implications; thus, labor, business, consumer, and other groups who feel that they may be affected by the United States policy will seek to influence it. A proposal to reduce tariffs in the 1973 Trade Reform Bill received the support of such diverse groups as the Aerospace Industries Association of America, the American Importers Association, the National Grain and Feed Association, the National Farmers Union, the League of Women Voters, and the United States Council of the International Chamber of Commerce. Those seeking to maintain the current tariff structure or to increase the duties included the Manufacturers of Small Tools and Metal Fasteners, the National Association of Marble Producers, the American Iron and Steel Institute, the United Rubber, Cork, Linoleum and Plastic Workers of America, the Nationwide Committee on Import-Export Policy, the AFL–CIO, and the Liberty Lobby.

25 Two books that represent this view are Bauer, Pool, and Dexter, *American Business and Public Policy;* and Morton H. Halperin, *Bureaucratic Politics and Foreign Policy* (Washington: The Brookings Institution, 1974) .

Investment issues provoke the same type of widespread and deeply committed interest-group activity and conflict. As we discussed in Chapter 4, the AFL–CIO and some of its affiliates were active promoters of the Burke-Hartke bill to restrict the ability of American corporations to invest abroad. This pressure was countered by the activities of numerous multinational corporations that were designed to protect their interests. Other American firms had little interest one way or the other in the proposed restrictions. Again, the determining factor of interest-group involvement is the perception that self-interest may be advanced or injured by the various policy options available. However, the critical point is that foreign economic issues directly affect various domestic interests in different ways, and these interests in turn seek to influence the substance of United States foreign economic policy by actively engaging in the policy-making process.

Regarding foreign economic matters, especially those involving trade issues, Congress is an important target of interest-group pressures and conflicts. The various interests affected by specific legislation and policy decisions present their concerns to individual congressmen, who represent a region according to how that region stands to gain or lose as a result of the policy adopted. For example, on trade issues labor and/or business interests are able to demonstrate precisely how an increase or decrease in tariffs will lead to more or less business and consequently to more or less employment in a specific geographical area. Since the policy has a direct impact on his constituents, the congressman at least takes notice. When he determines the overall impact on his district in light of his own interests in future elections, the representative may well actively seek to champion the interests of those groups with electoral power who will be significantly affected by governmental policy.

The nature of foreign economic issues is such that different regions of the country are affected differently by a policy. Thus, the textile interests in the South have obtained widespread support for their attempts to reduce foreign competition by enacting protectionist legislation. Similarly, Senator Edward Kennedy and other New England congressmen have advocated measures to protect the domestic shoe industry. And in steel-producing areas such as Pittsburgh, local members of Congress are leaders in protecting companies and unions who are disadvantaged by the imports of foreign steel. However, regional coalitions such as these face opposition from American farmers, who wish to reduce trade barriers, not increase them. Representatives from the Midwest advocate a free-trade position, especially with respect to EEC barriers, because it will aid their farming constituents. They are joined by other congressmen whose constituents would benefit from a reduction of trade obstacles.

It is important to note, though, that with respect to trade reform these coalitions of interests and congressmen from many parts of the country join together for the purpose of advancing common interests only at the most general level. These are coalitions of convenience and self-interest, not coalitions reflecting deep-seated consensus on the nature of American foreign economic policy. Large multinational firms may be concerned about how a policy under consideration affects their global operations. Executive-branch career civil servants and technocrats may have their eye on how certain policy proposals affect the fortunes of their department or office within the United States government apparatus. Congressmen, state and local officials, and most business and labor groups evaluate policy proposals in terms of the potential affect on production and employment in their particular geographic area or economic sector. The policy process in the United States must accommodate *all* these important economic and political forces. Because of this fact, foreign economic policy involves much more, and usually produces much less, than a coherent strategy that maximizes American power and advances American private interests around the world.

Many interest groups supplement their efforts to influence congressional deliberations with a strategy to gain access to decision makers in the executive branch. There are two basic objectives associated with such efforts: to influence the specific policy alternatives proposed and choices made as they emerge from the bureaucracy, and to influence the technocrats within the bureaucracy as they implement the policies established in the legislative or administrative sectors of government. In either case, interest-group involvement in the executive branch is frequent and widespread. Moreover, the congressional allies of interest groups also attempt to influence the appropriate parts of the bureaucracy through well-established patterns of communication and what amounts to congressional lobbying of the executive agencies. Thus, the pluralistic struggles of interest-group activity are carried directly into the bureaucracy.

According to the bureaucratic paradigm, the various agencies and departments within the bureaucracy engage in severe conflict among themselves. There are important differences among the perceptions, attitudes, goals, and operating procedures prevalent in different administrative units. Moreover, these units have different constituencies, whose views they are likely to adopt to at least some degree. Thus, in general, the Department of Agriculture represents the interests of farmers, the Department of Labor promotes the labor view, the Treasury Department looks after the concerns of banks and financial organizations, and the Department of Commerce tends to represent business. However, as we discussed earlier, it is inappropriate to speak of a single labor view or a single business view on specific issues, such as tariff reform. Various units or bureaus *within* the agencies have their own, more specialized constituencies, whose interests they often seek to represent and from whom they often receive support during budgetary allocations and other intradepartmental conflicts. It is also misleading to assume that the agencies are total captives of their natural constituency in society. A former official in the International Division of the Bureau of the Budget has noted, "Perhaps more than in any other area of policy, international trade pits agency against agency, advisor against advisor."[26]

These conflicts produce intra- and inter-agency struggles in which the many parties to these disputes utilize a host of political techniques to represent their concerns. In their relations with one another, they resort to the raw use of power, appeals to higher authority (the president), persuasion, manipulation, negotiation, and bargaining. The result is often a policy that is a mixture of the contending positions. Rarely does one set of interests succeed in obtaining all its objectives, for this essentially legislative process involves bargaining and compromise over different goals and strategies, and the eventual acceptance and incorporation of contradictory positions in the policy adopted. Thus, political conflict and political maneuvering is characteristic of the bureaucratic policy-making process regarding foreign economic issues. The differences within society are mirrored in and affect the nature of the decision-making process in the bureaucracy. The substance of foreign economic policy reflects the results of these intense battles in the policy-making process.

This tendency for a fragmented and political decision-making process to occur in regard to foreign economic policy is heightened by the fact that during most of the postwar period few high political officials have taken much interest in the specific issues raised. The president and his major advisors have not been much concerned with the rather mundane and often exceedingly complex and technical matters of international economics, as is illustrated by President Nixon's response to being told that the Chairman of the Federal Reserve, Arthur Burns, was concerned about the speculation against the Italian lira. His response, as captured on the White House tapes of June 23, 1972, was, "Well, I don't give a (expletive deleted) about the lira (Unintelligible)." Similar disinterest was expressed about the problems of the British currency.

Moreover, these issues, because of their domestic content and their repercussions in the many countries concerned, often involve long, drawn-out negotiations and trade-offs among technical specialists who are sub-

---

[26] Donald S. Green, "Government Organization for Policymaking and Execution in International Trade and Investment," in Commission on International Trade and Investment, *United States International Economic Policy in an Interdependent World*, Vol. II (Washington, D.C.: Government Printing Office, 1971), p. 420.

ject to severe domestic pressures and constraints. It is difficult to emerge from such a grueling process with an international reputation that will have much historical impact. In the absence of the direct and continuing interest and participation of top political officials, these difficult and technical matters have tended to be the concern of bureaucratic techno-crats. These specialists do not operate according to some grand design, but rather in a professional but limited way to advance their bureau-cratic and constituent interests. Thus, the political disputes are fre-quently carved out in a bureaucratic arena that is not at the top level of political officials. This lack of ongoing involvement by high-level political actors emphasizes the importance of interest groups promoting their objectives at the level of bureaucratic implementation, for sometimes the decisions of consequence are made during this implementation process.

This situation is beginning to change as international political relations increasingly involve questions of access to oil and raw materials, global inflation and recession, and other economic questions.[27] But the change is taking place slowly. For example, Henry Kissinger, as President Nixon's chief foreign policy advisor and later as Secretary of State, exer-cised tight control over foreign economic policy only sporadically during energy crises, such as the oil boycott by Arab oil-producing states. Be-cause of this situation, United States foreign economic policy has pro-ceeded in fits and starts and has continued by and large to be the preserve of technocrats while various high political officials have wrangled with one another over who would provide titular leadership of American foreign economic policy. Harald Malmgren, a Deputy Special Representative for Trade Negotiations, observed that for the most part the State Department has "consistently avoided taking the necessary steps to deal directly with domestic political and economic interests."[28] Instead of incorporating and organizing for these matters, the Depart-ment of State has been willing to allow other agencies to handle functionally or politically related matters. One result is that there are over sixty agencies, departments, or other institutions that "have direct interests and decision-making powers in international economic issues."[29] Consequently, there is extensive inter-agency bargaining and compro-mise on such matters but very little central planning and direction regarding United States foreign economic policy. The proliferation of multiagency coordinating committees in which some of this negotiation occurs is evidence of the fragmented nature of the process by which American policy and actions are developed. Indeed, Malmgren wishes

27 See Chapter 2 for a discussion of the political effects of some of these issues.

28 Harald B. Malmgren, "Managing Foreign Economic Policy," *Foreign Policy*, No. 6 (Spring, 1972) , p. 46.

29 Ibid., p. 43.

that American foreign economic policy exhibited the degree of coherence and consistency imputed to it by radical analysts.

Malmgren also notes that White House involvement in foreign economic policy often results from the implications of foreign economic issues for questions of domestic politics, and from the actions of contending domestic interest groups in regard to these issues. Thus, the White House is called upon to make decisions on international economic matters, but from the perspective of their effect on domestic politics. Consequently, the president and his advisors respond to specific issues and concerns without the benefit of an overall international economic policy, but instead in the context of furthering domestic political advantages. Examples from the Nixon administration serve to illustrate this point. Part of the Nixon reelection strategy in 1972 was to obtain the support of labor and the South. The former was partially accomplished by securing official AFL–CIO neutrality in the election in exchange for provisions in the administration's trade bill that would to some degree meet labor's concerns regarding foreign competition and United States multinational corporations. A cornerstone of the Southern strategy was the administration's willingness to heed the concerns of the Southern textile industry regarding the proposed trade bill and the government's textile negotiations with Japan. In both cases, United States foreign economic policy was perceived as a mechanism for obtaining domestic political support in the 1972 election. Further evidence of the general link between domestic politics and foreign economic policy can be found in the 1973–74 Trade Reform Act, which sought to make it necessary to secure congressional authorization in order to negotiate for higher as well as lower tariffs. A consistent and coherent United States policy on trade reform that was divorced from domestic interests and politics would have attempted to obtain permission either to raise tariffs or to lower them— not to do both depending upon the domestic and international circumstances.

External Constraints on Foreign Economic Policy

A pluralist approach also differs from the radical view with respect to the importance of external constraints on the policy-making process. A pluralist orientation recognizes that the objectives and desires of other states are difficult (though perhaps not impossible in every case) for the United States to disregard. In regard to economic issues, other countries have political and economic objectives that sometimes contradict the policies of the United States. During the early 1970s, France had views on tariff reform, monetary reform, and relations with petroleum-producing countries that were very different from those of the United States. In spite of the February, 1974 Washington conference of petroleum-consuming countries, which pledged to try to coordinate Western energy policies in response to the actions of OPEC, Japan and many of the European Common Market states proceeded to make separate arrangements with the Arab petroleum producers. In these cases, the ability of the United States to formulate and execute its policy effectively without considering the actions and reactions of other states was quite impossible. Clearly, it was beyond the capacity of the United States to control the actions of its allies.

As we pointed out earlier in our analyses of trade, monetary affairs, and investment issues, other states are subject to pressure by powerful domestic groups seeking to advance and protect their interests, as is true in the United States. These states are not able to disregard their domestic pressures in favor of faithfully following American directives. Through political activity the French farmers make it very difficult for the French government, even if it wishes to do so, to agree with the American position on reduction of trade barriers in the agricultural sphere. Negotiations on this and other issues are extremely difficult because each state's ability to compromise is restricted by the important positions held by various economic groups in domestic politics. Consequently, the link between domestic economics and politics and economic relations with other countries serves to reduce the decisional latitude of any single country, including the United States.

As we have seen throughout this study, the United States and other advanced states have a wide range of economic linkages with one another. Trade among advanced states accounts for the largest volume of international trade. A sizable majority of the funds invested by multinational corporations flow to facilities in other advanced economies. As a consequence of these factors and of a similar situation regarding other international transactions (such as tourism and shipping), the critical global economic issues for such states primarily involve their relations with one another. For advanced states, these linkages with one another are both numerous and intensive in terms of their impact on a variety of domestic interests. As a result, any advanced state—and the United States in particular, as the leader among the center states—is limited in its ability to formulate and implement a foreign economic policy without engaging in complex bilateral or multilateral negotiations to accommodate the interests of others.

Moreover, the United States is constrained by the fact that it is the most important economic and political power. Consequently, there have been some occasions where the necessity of being a reliable leader of the international political economy has forced it to forego policies of narrow self-interest. The underwriting of European economic recovery, maintaining the role of the dollar as the key international currency facilitating international transactions, accepting European and Japanese protectionist policies in order to facilitate their economic revival, providing military security for both Europe and Japan, thereby relieving them of huge expenses—all are examples of American actions designed to aid allies in spite of some costs to the United States. This does not mean that the United States did not also reap benefits from these actions, but international obligations muted American opposition to some of its allies' policies.

In brief, the effect of many of the external constraints identified above can be summed up by the concept of interdependence.[30] Because of the interdependent nature of the global economic system, the United States does not have the requisite degree of autonomy to implement successfully whatever policies it would like. Indeed, there is a similarity between a situation of dependence and interdependence. Both imply that there are severe constraints on the ability of a state to control effectively its own relations with the global economic system and other states. In the dominant/subordinate situation that the radical analysts visualize in the global political economy, the dependent state alone is constrained. In an interdependent economic system *all* parties have lost some degree of autonomy, though some may be more constrained than others.

It is appropriate to recognize the limiting effect of other countries and their domestic economic and political systems. The view that the United States can, and does, do whatever it desires seems to be a relic of the days of American leadership of a devastated Western world confronted with a unified communist camp during the height of the cold war. Moreover, this perception is based largely on observations of international political issues during these relatively few years and not on international economic matters over a longer span of time. It is possible that on any single issue the United States can call upon its reserves of political and economic influence to obtain its own objectives at the expense of other advanced industrial states. In the long run, though, such a policy is likely to be self-defeating, since many other states are gaining economic strength relative to the United States; too much American pressure now will probably heighten their resistance to accommodate the United States on other issues.

---

[30] The concept of interdependence was discussed in Chapter 3, p. 54.

A CRITIQUE OF THE PLURALIST VIEW

The pluralist view of foreign economic policy making requires criticism, just as the radical view did. The image of extensive conflict among interested economic groups, among various agencies in a fractionalized executive bureaucracy, and between Congress and the White House suggests a degree of anarchy and overall purposelessness that is hard to accept. On specific issues various groups in society and the government do differ and clash over objectives and strategies, but, more generally, there also seems to be a consistent thrust to the foreign economic policies of the United States. Chaos and competition have not become so pervasive as to produce a system incapable of identifying or furthering economic and political goals that are widely held among important and interested segments in society. Moreover, although various government agencies may seek to advance their particular interests, and those of their constituents, it is inappropriate to assume that foreign economic policy is totally uncoordinated. High political leadership and coordination may be missing, but among bureaucrats and technocrats below the highest levels of government there are numerous inter-agency coordinating groups that do seek to achieve a degree of consistency and coherence in policy. The output of such groups may be a series of compromises and agreements to disagree on certain specific issues, but to describe this system as one of unfettered conflict and confusion is just not accurate.

Continuity and direction in the general area of American foreign economic policy is fostered further by the widespread acceptance of capitalism and the American business ethic. Radical thinkers have quite correctly pointed out that leading corporate and political officials tend to come from similar backgrounds and, thus, tend to have common interests, values, and perceptions—even if the radicals may have overstated the consequences of these tendencies for policy. Perhaps even more important is the fact that a great majority of congressmen, government bureaucrats, and members and leaders of economic interest groups have been raised in a culture that approves of the American brand of capitalism. Consequently, many responsible individuals in government and society act in ways that are consistent with a positive view of American business. This does not mean that there will be no conflicts over specific issues; it does mean that most actions and proposals will not fundamentally contradict the milieu provided by American history and society. The importance of these general predispositions towards American business and private enterprise is illustrated by a State Department paper drafted in 1972 to consider alternative postures towards American direct foreign investment.

This position paper outlined three possible approaches. The negative alternative examined ways in which the government could actively seek to inhibit the activities of American-based multinational corporations. The positive position suggested ways of promoting American investment in other countries. The third view—in the paper's terms, a "neutral" approach—was to maintain the existing policy of neither promoting nor hindering multinational enterprises. This "neutral" view failed to recognize the supportive character of the important set of incentives that is offered by the United States government for foreign investment. Tax credits, tax deferrals, a host of preinvestment services, and many other policies cannot be termed a neutral approach to American investment abroad. Neutrality, like beauty, is in the eyes of the beholder, and the neutral view of the State Department and American society is based on an acceptance and approval of American business and private enterprise.

The process by which foreign economic policy is formulated does entail conflict over specific issues, as the pluralist orientation suggests, but the conflict takes place within a capitalist system. Consequently, there is and has been an overall thrust towards liberal economic solutions in America's approach to international economic relations. This prevailing theme evolves from the nature of the contemporary American system as well as from its history. There is nothing surprising about this, as the radicals sometimes suggest; nor should it be ignored, as it has been in most pluralist and bureaucratic analyses of American foreign economic policy.

Moreover, while recognizing the external constraints on American foreign economic policy, it is important not to overlook the political and economic strength that the United States does bring to any controversy. If events of the 1960s and 1970s have shown that Europe, Japan, and the oil-producing countries can themselves wield significant amounts of political and economic influence, events have also shown that none of them have the combination of size, unity, industrial and technological capability, and natural resource and food reserves that the United States possesses. These strengths, combined with the military might and the wide-ranging political and economic activity of the United States, insures it of a critical and powerful position in conflicts with other countries. The United States cannot often dictate international economic policy in its relations with other advanced states. It is quite a bit less than dominant, but it is also something more than the equal of any of its major economic partners.

Methodologically, the pluralist thinkers exhibit some of the same failings as the radical critics. Their reliance upon pluralist and bureaucratic models of the policy formulation process largely determines the nature of what they analyze and therefore conclude. Pluralists study interest-group and bureaucratic conflicts and quite naturally ascribe great importance to them. Their presumption of conflict among disparate interest groups and agencies of government tends to prevent their consideration of larger forces that unite officials representing conflicting interests and that confine conflicts within rather narrow bounds. Pluralist and bureaucratic analysts discussing foreign economic policy tend to ignore the fact that some interests generally prevail over others, even if they document the existence of conflict surrounding all questions of American foreign economic policy. Pluralists as well as radicals provide useful insights about United States foreign policy, but both fail for the most part to establish empirical links between the nature of the policy-making process and the actual policy outcome. Consequently, our understanding of the formulation of American foreign economic policy is underdeveloped conceptually and empirically.

These inadequacies are unfortunate, for if the United States is to improve its capabilities of dealing with the conflicts posed by the international political economy, it needs to improve its policy formulation processes. The United States needs to accommodate its many competing domestic interests while evolving an international posture that recognizes American interdependence with the global political economy. The development of domestic policies that strengthen the ability of the United States to compete in and adapt to new realities of the global political economy seems to be indicated. A more global orientation needs to be supplemented by a willingness to commit resources to ease the transition of groups who are adversely affected in the process. This, of course, involves the necessity of making some very hard political choices about which domestic economic groups will be able to thrive under the new conditions and which will need assistance to adjust to a changed environment. A more thoughtful and comprehensive domestic policy of this sort ought to be based upon a concerted and creative effort by American policy makers to participate with other states in the construction of an international order capable of managing more equitably the economic relations among states. Such an approach is being forced upon the United States by changing global economic and political relations. It is important that in this effort the United States and other center states recognize the legitimate concerns of the less-developed countries. Poor states feel that in present international economic and political relations their interests are being ignored. A stable world order cannot be maintained as long as this is the case.

9

International Political Economy: Current Problems and Future Needs

Writing a conclusion for this book is a difficult task, for its intent is to introduce the subject, to identify and describe relationships, to expose political and economic dilemmas, to demonstrate policy prescriptions based on alternative theoretical orientations, and hopefully to stimulate further analysis and research. Consequently, a conclusion seems to be inappropriate for what we consider to be a beginning, if not for others, at least for ourselves. Instead of seeking to gather together and integrate the most important points examined in earlier chapters, we will discuss several fundamental characteristics of the field of international political economy that have crucial implications for scholarly analysis and policy making. These characteristics apply to all the substantive areas examined in this study.

As an academic discipline and as an area for policy analysis, the politics of global economic relations have been undernourished, if not ignored. Some of the reasons for this neglect were examined in Chapter 1, but there are two conceptual aspects of the problem upon which we would like to elaborate. In the first place, the study of the international political economy, and thus policy making, is complicated by the existence of multiple sets of substantive interconnections that refuse to fit comfortably into well-established and traditional academic or bureaucratic departments. As a result—and this is the critical second point—there are few useful conceptual frameworks or theories that are comprehensive or sensitive enough to incorporate and build upon these interconnections. Since the subject is rarely approached as a substantive and conceptual whole, the related disciplines of economics and political science, as well as their bureaucratic counterparts, have generally been content to focus only on that part of the interconnection that is familiar and comfortable. Economists focus almost exclusively on the economic dimensions of these issues, either ignoring the political aspects or merely "playing" with the political angle without the benefit of any systematic theory. Political scientists, on the other hand, tend to ignore the economic sphere in terms of its relevance for politics, other than including it as an element of national power in world politics, or as a factor important to developing countries. The lack of useful theory that accommodates these interconnections has presented severe obstacles to policy makers. Policy prescriptions generated within government, or by academics and others, are based primarily upon different sets of values and assumptions rather than on a full appreciation of the variety of political and economic interrelations that only a comprehensive theory of political economy can provide. An adequate comprehensive theory of international political economy does not exist presently. We would not pretend that one has been developed in this study; indeed, we have merely demonstrated in numerous substantive contexts the need for such a theory.

RECOGNIZING CRUCIAL INTERRELATIONSHIPS

A complete understanding of the international political economy (and an adequate comprehensive theory of it) requires, at the minimum, a systematic examination of several sets of interrelationships. These are the interrelationships among various substantive issues, between political and economic matters, between the domestic and international arenas, and among governmental and nongovernmental actors at all levels of domestic and international society. It is important to appreciate the fact that these various sets of interrelationships are themselves linked to one another. The inordinately complex nature of the global political economy behooves us to think more in terms of identifying empirical interdependencies and their effects on various actors than in simple cause-and-effect terms. The latter can occur only after the former has been accomplished.

All analysts embrace the notion that there are many interconnections among the various substantive issues regarding the international political economy. But there is repeated evidence of a lack of comprehension of precisely how these issues are related to one another. The significance and character of the interconnections become evident only after events occur that wreak havoc on national and international economies and polities.

The oil embargo and price increases imposed by oil-producing states during 1973 and 1974 are a dramatic example of how interconnections between substantive economic issues transmit shocks throughout the global political economy. The actions produced an energy shortage and staggering import bills that curtailed general economic production in rich and poor states. They also produced simultaneously a fertilizer shortage that aggravated an already precarious global food situation; huge balance-of-payments deficits in virtually all rich states; increased needs for foreign exchange by poor states in amounts that exceeded their total foreign aid receipts in 1973; a revolutionary alteration of the distribution of monetary reserves within the global economy; and a dramatic boost to an already unprecedented level of inflation plaguing the global economy, along with a rapidly spreading economic downturn in many countries. This is not to mention the effects of the actions by oil-producing states on international and domestic political coalitions. Although everyone agrees that there are important interconnections between oil supplies and other aspects of international economic political relations, no one, before the fact, clearly recognized the scope of these first-order and other consequences of the use of oil as a political weapon by Arab states and the control of oil prices by a cartel of oil-producing states.

The existence of interconnections among various forms of transnational economic relations not only transmits shocks throughout the world, it also poses great problems for a state attempting to protect itself from certain aspects of international economic relations. Unless the nature of these interconnections are fully understood—and they usually are not—the cure chosen by a state may be worse than the disease. For example, in the early 1900s Canada was greatly concerned about its high degree of dependence upon products imported from the United States and the stiff competition Canadian firms faced from their American counterparts. As a consequence, it enacted tariff barriers to keep out American goods, only to find that American firms secured and expanded their Canadian markets by drastically expanding investment in Canada. Now, over 60 percent of Canadian manufacturing is owned by American investors. These and other instances of interconnections among various forms of international economic relations are appreciated but not fully comprehended by analysts and/or policy makers.

There are also interconnections among what have traditionally been identified and dealt with as economic *or* political issues. This was clearly demonstrated in the examination in Chapter 3 of alternative means by which the United States might reduce its balance-of-payments deficit. What at first appears to be a series of economic decisions becomes transformed into a series of political decisions about America's power profile in the world and about which elements of American society will

bear the brunt of the adjustment process—will it be multinational businesses, tourists, laborers in noncompetitive American production, all of
us as consumers? Similarly, manifestly political issues, such as whether the
United States should interrupt all relations with regimes such as those in
China, South Africa, or previously, Portuguese Angola, have substantial
economic implications for special interests within the United States and
for their competitors abroad. In all societies, economic interests are
expressed through political as well as economic activity. Political and
economic analysts tend to consider only the dimensions of these challenges and processes with which they are most comfortable, in spite of the
fact that few important issues are either purely economic or purely
political in their implications.

Interconnections between domestic concerns and processes and
international relations are particularly evident in analyses of international political economy. Analysts of world politics have always noted the
existence of these interconnections, but they frequently leave the systematic examination of domestic political processes to their colleagues in
American or comparative politics. Neither government officials nor students of international political economy can afford the luxury of such a
fine division of labor. For example, it is simply impossible to comprehend
the agricultural trade dilemma facing the United States and Europe
without directly examining the domestic as well as international linkages
that define the dimensions of the problem. Demands by European
farmers, particularly those in France, for artificially high government
supports for the prices of their products have resulted in the establishment of trade barriers that reduce the ability of American farm products
to compete in the large EEC market. Consequently, responding to the
pressures of American farming interests, the United States has sought to
reduce the barriers established by the Common Market. These linkages
are diagramed in Figure 9-1.

While recognizing the integral relationship of behavior in both the
domestic and international arenas, it is increasingly important to examine nongovernmental as well as governmental actors in analyses of international political economy. It seems likely that the role of nongovernmental organizations will continue to increase as international economic
interdependence becomes more pervasive. This is bound to stimulate
greater activity by nongovernmental interests seeking to secure advantage
from direct participation in transnational economic relations.

Specifically, the multinational corporation is one of the major
vehicles by which the economies of states are linked. Consequently, both
analysts and policy makers need to account for the behavior and interactions of these nongovernmental actors in their assessments and predictions regarding the international political economy. In addition to

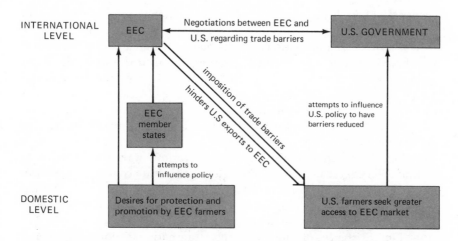

INTERNATIONAL
LEVEL

EEC

Negotiations between EEC and
U.S. regarding trade barriers

U.S. GOVERNMENT

EEC
member
states

imposition of trade barriers

hinders U.S exports to EEC

attempts to influence
U.S. policy to have
barriers reduced

attempts to
influence policy

DOMESTIC
LEVEL

Desires for protection and
promotion by EEC farmers

U.S. farmers seek greater
access to EEC market

FIGURE 9-1. The Domestic and International Interconnection: Trade Policy and EEC Agriculture

multinational corporations, many other important nongovernmental actors—such as international banks, international trade union secretariats, domestic pressure groups, international money speculators, and a host of other organized interests—are concerned about various aspects of the international political economy. Some of these nongovernmental organizations can be found active in any of the issues discussed in this book; some restrict their direct activities, though not all their consequences, to the domestic level; others focus on international activities; and still others are active both within states and between states. Similarly, some of these actors are most concerned with political issues, others are most concerned with economic issues, and some fail to see the distinction and act accordingly. The interconnections among states do not bother truly transnational nongovernmental actors, for they develop attitudes among their personnel, processes, and institutions that are designed to be responsive to and effective in the global economic system.

The influence of these nongovernmental actors is exerted in several different ways. Some of these groups, domestic interest groups particularly, attempt to advance their objectives by pressuring their local and national governments to act in ways favorable to their specific interests. The normal techniques of interest-group representation that are characteristic of a particular political system are pursued in the attempt to influence government policy at all levels of domestic society.

Other nongovernmental actors, such as multinational corporations and regional and international trade union organizations, seek to advance their particular interests by participating directly in the global economy. These institutions are truly transnational actors: even though they may have national components, the scope, nature, and target of their activities are international in character. Of course, some also engage in subnational and state-oriented activities, and in this respect they differ little from the actors in the previous category. However, their uniqueness and importance in the study of international political economy is that they themselves have become international in orientation because of the necessity of representing their interests and pursuing their activities on an international basis.

Figure 9-2 attempts to illustrate the various ways that nongovernmental actors exert influence on the global political economy. As you can see, not only do nongovernmental actors affect national and international or regional actors, some of them also act on the international level without the need for governmental intermediaries.

The existence of domestic and transnational nongovernmental actors reduces the decisional latitude of national governments, to the extent that they must be responsive to the demands of these groups. Since developments in the global economic system have widespread consequences for domestic interests within states, the governments are likely to be subject to extensive and conflicting pressures regarding appropriate policy postures. This type of interest-group activity is likely to delay the development of policy, hinder the establishment of clear and bold directions in policy, confuse the implementation of policy, and generally complicate the policy-making process.

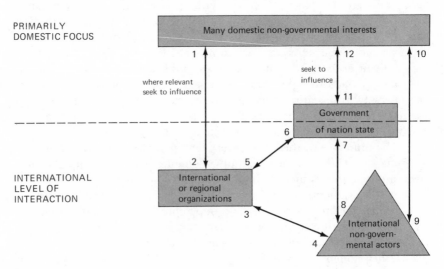

FIGURE 9-2. Nongovernmental Actors in the Global Economic System

Specific examples of relations identified
in Figure 9-2:

1. The International Labor Organization sets labor standards strengthening the bargaining position of domestic labor unions with management.
2. National trade unions in Europe seek to influence EEC company law regarding worker participation in management.
3. Council of the Americas tries to modify provisions of the investment code of the Andean Common Market.
4. United Nations attempts to draw up a code of conduct regulating activities of multinational corporations.
5. Belgium attempts to change EEC ruling on the inappropriateness of its investment incentives.
6. The EEC seeks to legitimize and also limit the emergency measures of Italy to overcome balance-of-payments problems in 1974.
7. The International Metalworkers' Federation works against the anti–trade union policies of Spain.
8. South Korea establishes policies designed to attract multinational corporations.
9. Unions from Germany and the Netherlands apply pressure to a European multinational chemical firm.
10. Henry Ford visits the United Kingdom and urges the British people to adopt measures to improve the chaotic labor relations climate in the United Kingdom.
11. The AFL–CIO lobbies for a bill to restrict the ability of American firms to invest abroad.
12. The French government assures its farmers that in return for their support of the EEC, policies will be adopted to inhibit competition from American agricultural imports.

The existence and increasing activity of international nongovernmental actors means that some developments in the international political economy are beyond the control of individual states and also international governmental organizations. Thus, a state's monetary, trade, or pollution policy may be thwarted by nongovernmental actors that know how to operate effectively in the international system in their own behalf to bypass government constraints. We discussed in Chapter 4 how nations are concerned about the ability of multinational corporations to circumvent or ignore national policy. The problem is compounded by the fact that governments have not been able to develop effective multinational intergovernmental institutions to try to control or counterbalance the effective maneuvers of such organizations. The point is that both analysts and policy makers must take into account the actions of such organizations, their ability to impede governmental policies, and their role in structuring the substance and process of the global economic system.

These various interconnections complicate the tasks of critical analysis and policy prescription by requiring a more comprehensive and systematic view of the relationships and problems involved in international political economic relations. Any approach employed by decision makers or academics that focuses on only one aspect of the field, to the exclusion of other relevant linkages, will be incomplete, simplistic, and very likely misguided. Similarly, each set of interconnections is interrelated with the others, thereby demanding analysis and policy making that take into account second- and third-order consequences and linkages of major importance. In sum, this is an exceptionally complex set of policy concerns, which must now be dealt with in the absence of a well-developed conceptual or empirical understanding of the precise character of these crucial interrelationships.

THE LINKAGE BETWEEN VALUES, THEORY, AND POLICY PRESCRIPTION

The field of international political economy is itself intricate. However, adding to the difficulty of making policy or conducting useful analysis is the fact that the issues of importance generate extensive disagreement over what is a desirable state of affairs, the causes of various problems, useful remedies, and the consequences of various policies. More fundamentally, policy makers and scholars in rich states and poor states, as well as within any specific state, often have sharply divergent sets of values regarding the international political economy and its consequences for states and the global system. These conflicting sets of values often produce contradictory perceptions of the problems, their causes, and their solutions. Even where there is agreement on values and objectives, there may be substantial differences of opinion regarding the best strategy with which to seek common goals.

In this study, the beliefs and analyses of the radical view have been juxtaposed with those of the classical liberal perspective on a variety of substantive problems in international economic and political relations. However, disputes over desirable objectives and appropriate strategies do not exist solely between the radicals and the classical liberals. Indeed, as we mentioned often in earlier chapters, there is no single radical view, nor is there a universally embraced traditional liberal perspective. Instead, there are many shades and nuances within each viewpoint. What policy makers and analysts share in each perspective are a set of basic values and assumptions that essentially predetermine their explanations of international political economy. Students, analysts, and policy makers must strive to understand the value positions and primary assumptions of a particular analyst in order to evaluate his or her assessments of the nature of the problem, desired goals, or reasonable solutions. This is important not only for constructive criticism of others' perspectives, but also for achieving a genuine dialogue among analysts and policy makers of different analytical persuasions who now usually talk past each other.

THE CONCERNS OF RICH AND POOR STATES

Throughout this study we have examined the major challenges to both advanced industrial states and less-developed countries as they relate to the global political economy. Advanced industrial states are preoccupied with the conflicts and problems that affect them the most. Generally, the critical issues faced by advanced states involve difficulties that stem from interdependent public and private relationships with other industrialized countries. These problems tend to be particularly conflictive and intense since most advanced industrial states have highly developed pluralist political systems with numerous domestic groups seeking to influence state policy in support of their interests. Because of internal pressures and the nature of the external problems, advanced state policy makers concentrate on ways to adjust and enhance economic transactions among themselves. For example, industrial states' proposals for structural reform in the trade or monetary system naturally tend to focus on how changes would facilitate economic relations among the advanced countries.

This orientation of advanced industrial states is understandable since a significant majority of their trade, monetary, and investment transactions are among one another. However, this concentration on advanced state concerns has contributed to a virtual neglect of the different but severe set of problems faced by the developing countries, whose international economic interactions are primarily with advanced states, not with other less-developed countries. This neglect can also be found at the levels of the major international economic organizations, for, historically, their focus on advanced states' issues has reflected the dominance of these states in these organizations.

Recent events such as the oil embargo and the rising prices of petroleum, shortages of other natural resources, food shortages, and in general the use of economic clout by poor states over rich states have forced the latter to become cognizant of the developing countries. However, the reaction of the advanced states has primarily been one of trying to protect themselves against this newly found and exercised power enjoyed by some of the developing countries. Rather than dealing creatively with the concerns of the poor states, the industrialized countries seek to circumvent this economic pressure by finding and developing new supplies of scarce commodities, by instituting programs of conservation and recycling, and by unleashing research and development funds to find substitutes for the critical resources. In short, advanced states seem to be concerned about developing countries' problems only to the extent of trying to avoid economic pressure of this sort in the future. They exhibit much less interest in attempting to develop mechanisms that integrate the poor states more closely and equitably into the global economic system so that their critical problems become of paramount concern to the entire system.

For example, as the largest parent state of direct foreign investment, the United States has consistently touted the economic and political benefits of private investment for host states. Now, as Europe, Japan, and oil-producing states seek to invest within the American economy on a large scale, concern is being expressed about foreign control over American industry and jobs. The United States is beginning to appreciate the sense of political and economic vulnerability long felt by states that are host to American capital. So far, few stringent controls on foreign capital have been implemented by the United States. But particularly in the face of massive capital flows from oil-producing states, elements of society, with the cooperation of some congressmen, have sought measures to insulate the United States from the global economy. These elements seek to avoid further integration of the American and the global economies, which would necessitate a greater appreciation of the concerns of poor states.

In summary, the previous discussion implies that the development of a community of interest regarding the international political economy between rich states and poor states, and within each of these two types of countries, will be hindered by the fact that each perceives a different set of problems to be the most critical. Advanced states seek to facilitate the extensive international economic interactions they enjoy with one another. Developing countries would like the system to be more responsive to the needs of development. Perceiving different problems, having different priorities and domestic pressures, enjoying vastly different influence capabilities, it is not surprising that there is little agreement between advanced states and developing countries on the appropriate nature of the international political economy or on suggestions for its reform.

CONCLUSION

Policy Recommendations

The complexity of global economic relations has several important implications for policy prescription. In the first place, it argues strongly for a global, multilateral approach to the many critical issues of the global political economy. Even problems that used to be perceived as domestic, such as inflation, are now global; thus, they must be resolved at the international level. As we have indicated with respect to trade, monetary, investment, ecological, and developmental issues, unilateral measures by a single state generally have the effect of imposing costs and creating problems for other states. As a result, the affected countries often retaliate in a fashion that imposes new problems and costs on the initiating state. The basic point is that problems involving global interaction cannot be resolved by the actions of individual states; multilateral approaches are required.

However, we are well aware of the difficulty in organizing and achieving satisfactory multilateral approaches. There are well-developed institutions, such as the IMF and GATT, in the monetary and trade areas, but these have no counterparts in the investment or technology transfer areas. Moreover, neither the IMF nor GATT as they currently exist are confronting effectively the full range of problems in their respective areas. In addition, of course, the problems we have discussed rarely fit neatly into the jurisdiction of one international institution without having widespread effects on the others.

Probably an even greater hindrance to the development of global approaches to global problems is the fact that within each state, politically powerful domestic groups concerned about their immediate interests and problems exert great pressure on their governments to advance their particular values. To such groups in advanced states and developing states, counter arguments pointing out the aggregate or long-run benefits of a different policy will not be accepted. Thus, governmental officials are faced constantly by the dilemma of promoting national or global economic welfare in the long run at the expense of well-organized special interests. These officials are very likely to suffer domestic political retaliation if they ignore special interests. On the other hand, they advance the demands of special interests at the risk of disrupting relations with other states and with nongovernmental actors. Those states and nongovernmental actors hurt by the disruptions are likely to retaliate in a manner that ultimately prevents the achievement of the domestic goals being pursued and imposes unpopular domestic costs on the originating state.

This basic conflict cannot be ignored, nor is it easily resolvable. Granting the difficulty of the problem, our very general recommendations for policy prescription constitute a two-pronged strategy. First, we clearly recognize the need for global approaches to international problems. Consequently, states as well as international institutions need to develop the basic orientation that multilateral action is required for the establishment and maintenance of an international political economy that facilitates economic interactions and yet is responsive to the less fortunate states. The problems confronting advanced states and developing countries are resolvable only by international action. This international strategy needs to be based upon courageous and creative leadership by national officials. It also demands a more conscious and comprehensive attempt to develop workable and broadly responsive international institutions. These organizations not only need to attack their particular problems more vigorously; they must also interact with one another more constructively to develop an approach that is effective across the broad spectrum of international economic issues. Nations and international organizations have much room for improvement in these directions.

The second part of our recommendations concerns the development of domestic policies that are designed to ease the disruptions and dislocations caused by the increased interdependence of states. Actions at the international level must be combined with attitudes and programs that consciously reduce the costs of a closer integration between particular states and the international economic order. For example, during the first eight years of its existence, the United States adjustment assistance program to aid workers and companies put out of business by foreign competition was not once declared to be applicable. This reflects a lack of commitment to efforts necessary to confront the domestic problems created by international economic transactions.

In sum, we are calling for a national and international approach to the evolving global economic system. Neither strategy can work effectively without the other. Moreover, given the nature of the international political economy, no other set of strategies will work either. However, having indulged in a bit of preaching about appropriate policy directions, we are well aware of the immense operational difficulties implied by these recommendations, in addition to the obvious political problems at both the national and international level. Indeed, we are recommending the conscious creation of a system that increases interdependency among states and thus reduces the individual state's autonomy. The political implications and obstacles to such an approach are enormous. Frankly, we doubt very much the existence of a necessary degree of commitment by rich and poor states, as well as by various domestic groups. Moreover, we are concerned that the requisite political and economic skills have yet to be developed and refined. Yet we see no other reasonable course likely to produce acceptable results.

A Plea for Theory Building and Research

One of the major reasons for our pessimism regarding the development and implementation of effective policy in this area is that academic analysts have been of little help to policy makers in the construction of frameworks and theories, much less research, that contribute to an understanding of the international political economy. Throughout this study we have seen how the assumptions, values, and theories of liberal economists, radical analysts, and others have determined their suggestions regarding policy. Unfortunately, these assumptions and values are rarely questioned rigorously, and they seem to be based on categorical assertions rather than well-designed and carefully executed research. Moreover, the more dispassionate analysis of these issues and linkages has just not been undertaken by either political scientists or economists. Consequently, their policy prescriptions (as well as ours) are very general and not well grounded in either theory or research.

As a result, in the light of the critical nature of the political and economic issues emerging from the international political economy, it is appropriate, indeed mandatory, to develop theory that promotes understanding of these issues. Specialists in international politics need to alter their traditional theories of world politics to accommodate and account for the economic considerations explored in this book. In addition, the complex linkages with domestic economics and politics, as well as the important role of nongovernmental actors, ought to be incorporated in their full richness into theories of world politics. Theories of international politics that focus almost exclusively on the military, security, and status concerns of national actors cannot serve effectively to guide policy recommendations that confront the major international economic issues of today.

Political science is not alone in neglecting, from a theoretical and research perspective, these important issues and linkages. To the extent that they take account of political realities, most economists have been far too willing to ignore their rigorous economics training when they examine the political aspects of international economic relations. Often, the strictly economic aspects of these issues are approached in a systematic and sophisticated fashion, but the political implications either are swept under the *et ceteris paribus* (all other things being equal) rug or are examined in a superficial, journalistic way—the implication being that these political questions need not be examined with the same degree of analytical, theoretical, and logical rigor as the economic dimension of a problem.

Both economists and political scientists have essentially ignored the crucial issues of the international political economy. As we have suggested throughout this study, these issues may well be supplanting the military and security issues of the postwar period as the most crucial questions faced by the world. The greater interdependency of the advanced industrial states, along with the plight of the developing countries, seems to insure the centrality of the issues discussed in this book. Our objective has been to examine some of the important problems and linkages and to emphasize how closely their political and economic dimensions are intertwined. We have also sought to show the direct relationship among assumptions, values, theories, and policy prescription, whether we are examining radical thought, liberal economic ideas, or the behavior and recommendations of government officials. The intrinsic importance of these substantive problems and the inadequate understanding we have of them makes it incumbent upon scholars of international politics and economics to generate conceptual refinements and new empirical findings. Both must be of much greater sensitivity if they are to be of use to the decision makers who must forge policy—with or without adequate understanding of the overall effects of their choices.

Index